EX AUDITU

An International Journal for the Theological Interpretation of Scripture

VOL. 33   **2017**

Ex Auditu is published annually by Pickwick Publications, an imprint of
Wipf and Stock Publishers, 199 West 8th Avenue, Suite 3, Eugene, Oregon 97401, USA

SUBSCRIPTIONS

Individuals:
U.S.A. and all other countries (in U.S. funds): $20.00
Students: $12.00

Institutions:
U.S.A. and all other countries (in U.S. funds): $30.00

This periodical is indexed in the ATLA Religion Database, published by the American
Theological Library Association, 300 S. Wacker Dr., Suite 2100, Chicago, IL 60606, Email:
atla@atla.com, www: http://www.atla.com/; *Internationale Zeitschriftenshau für Bibelwissen-schaft; Religious and Theological Abstracts; and Old Testament Abstracts.*

Please address all subscription correspondence
and change of address information to Wipf and Stock Publishers.

©2018 by Wipf and Stock Publishers
ISSN: 0883-0053
PAPERBACK ISBN: 978-1-5326-4620-1
HARDBACK ISBN: 978-1-5326-4621-8

EX AUDITU

An International Journal for the Theological Interpretation of Scripture

Stephen J. Chester, Editor
D. Christopher Spinks, Associate Editor
Klyne R. Snodgrass, Editor Emeritus

North Park Theological Seminary
3225 West Foster Avenue
Chicago, Illinois 60625–4987
USA

Tel: (773) 244–6238
email: schester@northpark.edu
Web site: http://wipfandstock.com/catalog/
journal/view/id/12/

EDITORIAL BOARD

Terence E. Fretheim, Luther Seminary,
St. Paul, MN
Richard B. Hays, The Divinity School,
Duke University, Durham, NC
Jon R. Stock, Wipf & Stock Publishers,
Eugene, OR
Miroslav Volf, Yale Divinity School,
New Haven, CT
John Wipf, Wipf & Stock Publishers,
Eugene, OR

VOL. 33   EX AUDITU   2017

CONTENTS

Contents

ANNOUNCEMENT OF THE 2018 SYMPOSIUM

North Park Theological Seminary in Chicago, Illinois, is pleased to announce that the thirty-third Symposium on the Theological Interpretation of Scripture will take place September 27–29, 2018. The Symposium will start at 6:00 p.m. on Thursday September 27 in Nyvall Hall with a worship service and will extend through to Saturday afternoon on September 29. The theme in 2018 will be Human Violence. The following persons have agreed to make presentations:

Nancy deClaissé-Walford, Old Testament, McAfee School of Theology
D. Darrell Griffin, preaching, Oakdale Evangelical Covenant Church
Drew Hart, Theology, Messiah College
Kyle Gingerich Hiebert, Theology, Toronto Mennonite Theological Centre
Seyoon Kim, Emeritus New Testament, Fuller Theological Seminary
Xi Lian, Church History, Duke Divinity School
Jesse Nickel, New Testament, Columbia Bible College
Elizabeth Pierre, Pastoral Care, North Park Theological Seminary
Ruben Rosario-Rodriguez, Theology, St. Louis University

Those interested in attending sessions should go to https://www.northpark.edu/seminary/calendar-and-events/symposium-on-the-theological-interpretation-of-scripture/ and follow the link provided to the registration page. Any queries should be addressed to the Symposium administrator, Luke Palmerlee (lrpalmerlee@northpark.edu) at North Park Theological Seminary, 3225 W. Foster Avenue, Chicago, Illinois, 60625. Meals may be taken at North Park and assistance can be provided in finding nearby lodging.

ABBREVIATIONS

Unless listed here, all abbreviations are as specified in *The SBL Handbook of Style: For Biblical Studies and Related Disciplines*, 2nd edition (Atlanta: Society of Biblical Literature, 2014).

CO	John Calvin, *Ioannis Calvini Opera Quae Supersunt Omnia*, edited by Wilhelm Baum, Edward Cunitz, and Edward Reuss, 59 vols.Vols.29–87 of the *Corpus Reformatorum* (Brunswick: C.A. Schwetschke and Sons, 1863–1900).
ECT	Martin Chemnitz, *Examination of the Council of Trent*, translated by Fred Kramer, 2 vols. (St. Louis: Concordia, 1971).
Institutes	John Calvin. *Institutes of the Christian Religion*, 1559 edition, translated by Ford L. Battles and edited by John T. McNeill, 2 vols. (Philadelphia: Westminster, 1960).
LM	Gregory of Nyssa, *The Life of Moses*, edited by Abraham J. Malherbe and Everett Ferguson, CWS (New York: Paulist, 1978).
LT	Martin Chemnitz, *Loci Theologici*, translated by J.A.O. Preus (Saint Louis: Concordia, 1989).
LW	Martin Luther, *Luther's Works*, American Edition. 55 vols. original series; 9 vols. new series (St. Louis: Concordia, 1955–1986, 2010-).
PdÄ	Probleme der Ägyptologie Series (Leiden; Boston: Brill)
SBTS	Sources for Biblical and Theological Study Series (Winona Lake, IN: Eisenbrauns)
ST	Thomas Aquinas, *Summa Theologiae*, Latin Text and English translation, introduction, notes, appendices, and glossaries, 60 vols. (London: Eyre and Spottiswoode, 1962–1980).
TNC	Martin Chemnitz, *The Two Natures in Christ*, translated by J.A.O. Preus (St. Louis: Concordia, 1971).
WA	Martin Luther, *D. Martin Luthers Werke. Kritische Gesamtausgabe. Schriften* (73 vols. Weimar: H. Böhlau, 1883–2009).

INTRODUCTION

It is a great privilege to write this introduction to the 2017 (volume 33) issue of *Ex Auditu*, which is my first as editor. I must begin by paying tribute to the work of my predecessor, Klyne Snodgrass. By my reckoning Klyne was involved in organizing every symposium from the first to be held at North Park in the fall of 1990 until the most recent symposium in the fall of 2017, a total of 28 events. He also edited every edition of the journal from 1992 (volume 8) until 2016 (volume 32), a total of 25 issues. Whichever way you look at it, a very large number of symposium presenters, respondents, and preachers have interacted with Klyne as he has sought to further the agenda of theological interpretation for the church.

Klyne's gifts were not only those of a shrewd matchmaker, skillfully joining together the right scholars with topics and themes where they had something important to say, nor only those of a skillful and careful editor. Both of these gifts were very important but, above all, Klyne blessed the symposium and the journal with his gift for friendship. What I have heard those participating in the symposium say again and again is that they experience it as an arena in which there is serious critical discussion of scholarly work but in a context of fellowship and of shared commitment to the ministry and mission of the church. It is Klyne who created and sustained this environment and who also ensured that the dialog stimulated by the papers presented was not simply one between scholars, but also included pastors, students, and interested lay people. Everyone knew that Klyne was genuinely and generously interested in them and their work. I also have benefitted from Klyne's friendship in too many ways to number here, but I am deeply grateful. As the new editor of the journal and principal organizer of the symposium I have a wonderful example to follow and I will do my very best to continue the legacy that Klyne has left.

It is very fitting that the theme of the final symposium organized by Klyne was "Participation in and with Christ." In recent years this biblical vocabulary of being in Christ, and of being united with Christ, has been a focus of Klyne's personal research, culminating in the publication of his recent book, *Who God Says You Are: A Christian Understanding of Identity* (Grand Rapids: Eerdmans, 2018). Here he writes that "'Participation' is the language the church should be—*must be*—using to describe the gospel and conversion. The gospel is a gospel of participation. Faith in Christ is participation in Christ, and participation with Christ will change your identity" (99). This edition of the journal thus takes us to the heart of what Klyne understands to be the gospel that the church is called to proclaim. Yet, as a category of theological and biblical thought, participation is also peculiarly difficult to capture in terms that communicate clearly in the contemporary world. We can articulate the gospel in terms of a new relationship with Jesus since we know day by day what it means to enter into relationships of many various kinds with other human beings. However, as Klyne observes, "we do not speak of being *in* any other person" (96). There is something about participation in and with Christ that evades our cognitive grasp and defies intellectual analysis. If participation is the language in which the gospel must be expressed, how are we to come to terms with our inability to explain exactly what participation is?

Yet, while the gospel does have to be proclaimed intelligibly, perhaps we should hesitate before we mourn the fact that participation cannot easily be explained in ways that make immediate sense in twenty-first century western cultures. Perhaps the very resistance of participation to easy explanation, its stubborn refusal to be translated from the biblical and the theological into other categories of thought, is a cause for celebration rather than vexation. If the gospel truly re-makes personal identity in the way that Scripture claims, at once cutting across and yet fulfilling all other merely human dimensions of who we are, then it is fitting that the very vocabulary that describes these divine actions is itself incommensurable with the other ways in which we speak about our identity. It exceeds our grasp because God exceeds our grasp, and that of which the vocabulary of participation speaks is the gift of our true selves that comes from beyond our selves. If we truly participate in Christ, then as the people of God we make as much sense in any normal categories as do bushes that burn but are not consumed. On such holy ground we are to remove our sandals and be ready to receive God's revelation of who God is.

Our authors and respondents in this volume of *Ex Auditu* help readers to do just this, exploring what it means for the people of God to participate in Christ. As Martin Luther once wrote, "Christ says, 'I am the way, the truth, and the life;' he does not say I give you the way, truth, and life, as if Christ stood outside of me and worked such things in me. He ought to be, dwell, live, speak in me, not through me or into me . . . so that we would be the righteousness of God in him . . ."[1] In the pages that follow, as we read and ponder the mystery of this participation in and with Christ, may we be led to live faithfully in him.

Stephen Chester
Professor of New Testament
North Park Theological Seminary

---

1. WA BR6: no.1818, 98–101. The translation is that of Timothy Wengert, "Melanchthon and Luther / Luther and Melanchthon" in *Philip Melanchthon, Speaker of the Reformation: Wittenberg's Other Reformer* (Burlington, VT: Ashgate Variorum, 2010) 69.

YOU BECOME WHAT YOU WORSHIP: THEOSIS AND THE STORY OF THE BIBLE

Ben C. Blackwell

Introduction: Irenaeus and the Unity of the Bible

Writing near the end of the second century, Irenaeus (ca. AD 130–200) provides an early witness to Christian theologies of human participation in God. With depth and nuance Irenaeus explores how the God–man Jesus Christ unites believers to God through the Spirit in central passages like *Adversus haereses* ("Against Heresies") 3.16–19.[1] Against those who would emphasize separation—between God and humanity, the creator and creature, the spiritual and physical, creation and salvation—Irenaeus highlights the possibility of unity while not collapsing these items into a monism. There is one area, however, where unity-in-distinction does not hold in his theology: the creator God of the OT is one and the same as the saving God of the NT, and he is directly revealed by his Son and the Spirit. Though Irenaeus shows the unity in the overall story and doctrine of the Bible,[2] he does not merely paint a picture of harmony. For example, much of *Haer.* 4 deals with the disunity between the Mosaic and gospel economies. In *Haer.* 4.20, another central passage like *Haer.* 3.16–19, Irenaeus accounts for what is later called "progressive revelation" and explains the balance between old and new by arguing that new revelation does not discount the reality of previous revelation. The Son and the Spirit are not in opposition to the creator Father, but actually further reveal him, uniting the end to the beginning, eschatology to protology.

Within this larger argument about the coherence of progressive revelation, Irenaeus uses participatory themes to capture a summary of the biblical narrative: "the

---

1. See Ben C. Blackwell, "Two Early Perspectives on Participation in Paul: Irenaeus and Clement of Alexandria" in *'In Christ' in Paul: Explorations in Paul's Theological Vision of Union and Participation*, edited by Kevin J. Vanhoozer, Constantine R. Campbell, and Michael J. Thate (WUNT II/384; Tübingen: Mohr Siebeck, 2015) 331–55.

2. I am using "Bible" here anachronistically for Irenaeus. While the OT was established for Irenaeus (through the LXX traditions), the NT canon was not fully settled in his time. However, he uses the majority of texts that came to shape the NT so there is little difference between what we might consider as the "Bible" and his authoritative "Scriptures."

1

glory of God is a living human, and the life of humans consists in seeing God" (*Haer.* 4.20.7).[3] This is a problem because in the OT the text states that no one will see God and live (Exod 33:20) and yet the opposite, Irenaeus says, is the goal of the biblical narrative—to see God and live. He argues that believers truly see God and become like him in Christ and through the Spirit because believers truly share in divine glory and live: "Therefore humans will see God in order to live, becoming immortal by the vision and attaining to God" (*Haer.* 4.20.6).[4] According to Irenaeus in *Haer.* 4.20, the encounter with God as vision ("seeing") is at the heart of the unity of the Bible. What the prophets in the OT foresaw is what NT believers truly "see" when they experience God directly in the Son and Spirit. His primary examples to ground this narrative unity are what we would describe as *worship experiences* and this raises a question: To what extent does worship ground the unity of the biblical narrative? That question is a bit too large for one essay to answer, but given our interest in participation we can begin to address how the biblical narrative presents the relationship between worship and participation in God's glory. That is, how well does Irenaeus' statement—"the glory of God is a living human, and the life of humans consists in seeing God" (*Haer.* 4.20.7)—capture a central biblical theme? To delimit our study we will focus on key worship passages in the Bible that address glory. I will argue that Irenaeus' claim about participation in God's glory captures a key motif that helps unite the story of the Bible: you become what you worship. Those who worship the living God of glory share in his glory and become fully alive, whereas those who worship idols become deadened in their senses and in their bodies. While there is much diversity between the OT and NT economies, this theme—worship leading to the transformation of the worshiper into divine likeness—is a key point of unity in the Bible. As we turn now to the body of this essay, I will focus on worship and the transformation of worshipers in the OT and NT.

3. This is taken from the translation by Robert M. Grant, *Irenaeus of Lyons* (New York: Routledge, 2007), which only includes translations of selected passages. The full translation *Adversus hareses* ("Against Heresies") is still only to be found in volume 1 of the *Ante-Nicene Fathers*, edited by Alexander Roberts and James Donaldson, 1885–1887, 10 vols. (Repr., Peabody, MA: Hendrickson, 1994); however, a complete and updated translation of books 1–3 has been published in the Ancient Christian Writers series (New York: Newman Press, 1992–2012) vols. 55, 64–65.

4. This transformation is as much noetic as it is somatic, for seeing is an experience of revelation, as believers are transformed into immortal glory. Though there is not a direct intertextual connection between these writings, this noetic and somatic combination is central to Athanasius' *On the Incarnation*. The noetic is sometimes undervalued in Irenaeus: see William P. Loewe, "Irenaeus' Soteriology: *Christus Victor* Revisited," *AThR* 67 (1985) 1–15.

The Story of the Bible: Worship and Worshipers

From the beginning of the Bible with the sacrifices of Cain and Abel in Genesis to the end with God's direct presence with his people in Revelation, God's people are a worshiping people, and they experience his presence in worship. Since the expressions of worship described in the Bible are so diverse, I will mostly limit our discussion to the theme that Irenaeus pointed us to—humans worshipping the God of "glory"—so we will focus specifically on passages where glory is mentioned. Even with this delimitation, our treatment can only be selective. I have, however, attempted to focus on narratives and discussions that inform wider biblical developments.[5] We begin with the OT.

Worship in Old Testament

Worship, while at times framed as an individual encounter, is most often communal, and we repeatedly see how the Israelite communal relationship with God is shaped by worship. OT texts are concerned with both the proper object of worship and the modes of worship, so the OT regularly addresses issues of idolatry and cultic issues (not least among these being location). As noted above, our selective discussion of worship in the OT will focus on some of the passages that speak of divine glory (and of becoming like the object of worship). We will first address the Pentateuch and then later passages that advance these earlier ideas.

Exodus and Leviticus

Several key worship experiences frame Genesis, but in Exodus and Leviticus we see worship in the context of God's glory, so this is where we will direct our attention. Several passages from these books—especially that of the golden calf and Moses's experience of glory (Exod 32–34)—serve as fodder for Christian discussions of glory in the NT, so they will be important for understanding the narrative unity of the Bible.

In light of the deliverance narrative in Exodus, worship is not always the first thing we think of when speaking of Exodus, but over half of the book addresses worship, namely through the tabernacle instructions. Canonically, Lev 1:1 reads as a

---

5. The topic of worship in the Bible has been treated in depth and with skill by others, so I will only highlight the fruit of their work here. See especially, Daniel I. Block, *For the Glory of God: Recovering a Biblical Theology of Worship* (Grand Rapids: Baker, 2014); Gregory K. Beale, *The Temple and the Church's Mission: A Biblical Theology of the Dwelling Place of God* (Downers Grove: IVP, 2004); Gregory K. Beale, *We Become What We Worship: A Biblical Theology of Idolatry* (Downers Grove: IVP, 2008).

direct continuation from the discussion of God's presence at the tabernacle in Exod 40:34–38. Yet, with the break between Exodus and Leviticus, we sometimes miss the progression of the cultic themes that link the two books. Notwithstanding the discussions about the sources and composition of the Pentateuch, the coherence of the final form is helpfully addressed by John Sailhamer, when he shows how the narrative portions of Exodus and Leviticus are interwoven with the covenantal and legal material.[6] He argues that the legal sections are specifically set within the narrative structure in order to show the relevance of worship as an interaction with a *holy* God. As the community fails at its calling to worship God and serve as a kingdom of priests and a holy nation (Exod 19:4–6) God offers more specific instructions on how to engage with him.

According to Sailhamer, there are two primary cycles or groupings. In the first cycle, we see three parts: the covenant (Exod 19), the stipulations with a focus on tabernacle worship (Exod 20–31), and then failure with the golden calf (Exod 32). The second cycle also has three parts: the covenant renewal (Exod 32–34), a more detailed list of stipulations marking out tabernacle worship (Exod 35–Lev 16), and another failure, this time with the goat idols (Lev 17). In response to this last failure a further exploration of the Holiness Code is given for the people (Lev 17–26). The first failure was that of the priests, Sailhamer argues, so the further stipulations in the second cycle were focused on the priests, whereas the second failure was of the people, so the holiness code was more generalized, including the people and priests.[7] Whether or not Sailhamer is fully correct,[8] he rightly shows the thematic continuity of Exodus and Leviticus: the people are to worship a holy God in a holy manner.

If holiness is so important to the structure, what about the focus of our study: the topic of glory? In the same way that holiness is foremost a divine characteristic that humans share in, so is glory. For example, God's defining act of deliverance in Exodus is viewed through the lens of his glory. God declares that he will receive "glory" (Exod 14:4, 17–18) and Moses recognizes God's glory in his praises for their deliverance: "Who among the gods is like you, Lord? Who is like you—majestic in holiness, awesome in glory, working wonders?" (Exod 15:11).[9] This is not just an honorific glory, the narrative is shaped by God's glory being manifest among the people. They see God's glory from afar (Exod 16:7, 10) and later Moses directly encounters God's glory on Sinai (Exod 24:16–17). After the golden calf incident, Moses

6. John H. Sailhamer, *The Pentateuch as Narrative: A Biblical-Theological Narrative* (Grand Rapids: Zondervan, 1992) 44–51.

7. Ibid., 50.

8. The reference to goat idolatry in Lev 17 is oblique and not a central narrative transition, so this limits the strength of this aspect of his proposal.

9. All biblical quotations are from the NIV, unless noted otherwise.

again experiences God directly after he asks to see God's glory (Exod 33:18–34:9) and God reveals himself to Moses.[10] Thus, glory is one of the primary ways the text refers to God's immanent presence.

This experience of God's glory is set in the context of worship. Just as Moses worships God (Exod 34:8), the people and priests are instructed in the practice of worshiping God in the latter half of Exodus. The covenantal stipulations (which focus mostly on covenantal worship—Exod 20–31) begin with the Ten Commandments. The first two speak to God's unique identity and how his people should relate to him uniquely in worship (Exod 20.3–6). To be God's covenant people is to be a worshiping people.[11] The people's worship of the true God will allow them a unique access to God's presence, by which they are transformed. When speaking of the altar in the tabernacle, this transforming presence is evident in the correlation between God's glory and his holiness (see Exod 15:11):

> There [the altar] I will meet you and speak to you; there also I will meet with the Israelites, and the place will be consecrated by my glory. So I will consecrate the tent of meeting and the altar and will consecrate Aaron and his sons to serve me as priests. Then I will dwell among the Israelites and be their God. They will know that I am the Lord their God, who brought them out of Egypt so that I might dwell among them. I am the Lord their God (Exod 29:42B–46).

The people do not simply make themselves holy; rather, God's glorious presence is the basis of their sanctification: "the place will be consecrated by my glory." This correlation between God's presence and holiness grounds the later Holiness Code in Lev 17–26, and its fundamental pronouncement: "Be holy because I, the Lord your God, am holy" (Lev 19:2). The command to be like God—"be holy because I am holy"—is predicated upon God's identity—"for I am the Lord your God." His identity and presence as the God of glory and holiness, which the people experienced in worship, was therefore the foundation for their own experience of glory and holiness. They become like the one they worship.

This ideal of worship and consecration, however, is interrupted in the narrative, as incidents of the golden calf (Exod 32) and the unauthorized fire (Lev 10) show. As the people gain greater access to God's holy presence, the consequences are more stark and immediate when false worship occurs. In Exod 32 the people turn away from the Lord God to false gods, and God calls them a "stiff-necked people" (Exod 32:9), a description that is repeated several times in the OT. In his study on idolatry,

---

10. Indeed, through that revelation we learn of one of the most fundamental affirmations of God's grace and discipline in Exod 34:6–7.

11. While God is unique and worship is to be aniconic (i.e., without idols) we cannot miss the strong visual elements present in the tabernacle instructions with angels, trees, etc. in the prescribed art work.

Beale argues that this term "stiff-necked" is used as a metaphor, identifying the cow-worshiping people with a cow that will not follow its master.[12] Rather than becoming like the true God, they now become like their false idol. As a result, the people were almost sent away permanently from God's presence, though God relents through Moses's intercession.

In the post-rescue Exodus accounts the people (and animals) were segregated from God's presence, but now with the tabernacle God is graciously granting greater access. This is both a great opportunity and potentially a great danger because un-holy things cannot withstand God's holy presence, as we see with the unauthorized fire offered by Nadab and Abihu (Lev 10). Their fire is in contrast to the fire of God, his glory, that appeared before the people (Lev 9:6, 23–24).[13] In response to their false worship, God declares: "Among those who approach me I will be proved holy; in the sight of all the people I will be glorified" (Lev 10:3, NIV modified). Rather than worshiping God falsely, the priests were supposed to "distinguish between the holy and the common, between the unclean and the clean" (Lev 10:10). A common contemporary refrain is that "God cannot be in the presence of sin." Yet this gets the idea backwards. The better description is that "sin cannot be in the presence of God" without lethal consequences (see Exod 19:12–13; 2 Sam 6:6–11).

In the Exodus and Leviticus accounts, we see that God is making his holy and glorious presence available to his covenant people through their worship, and they too can share in his holiness through his consecrating presence. At key turns in the narrative, the people, however, become stiff-necked like their object of false worship or experience death. In these positive and negative examples of worship, they become like the one they worship, and these examples serve as paradigms for the rest of the OT, as our discussion of selected texts and themes below will show.

Old Testament Idol Polemic

Positive discussions of worship show up throughout the OT, though the vast majority of encounters—the monthly and annual festivals—go unrecorded. Many of the Psalms point directly to the regular cultic practice associated with this Temple worship. As more unique experiences, there are specific encounters with God's glory narrated by prophets (e.g., Isa 6; Ezek 1). Rather than these positive encounters, the OT text tends to focus on aberrations and events that shift the direction of the people, and the more consistent refrain is negative as a challenge to idolatry. Important

---

12. Beale, *We Become What We Worship*, 82–83.

13. God's glorious presence is also likened to a consuming fire in Exod 24:16–17.

for our consideration of worship and participation, this language also fits directly in the wider biblical theme—you become what you worship.[14]

The OT idol polemic reflects themes we first saw in the Torah. The prohibition in the Ten Commandments is based on the unique nature of God's identity as well as his actions to deliver his people (Exod 19:1–6). In contrast, false gods are unable to save because they are incapable of action. They are inanimate: they cannot see, hear, eat, or smell (see Deut 4:27–28; Hab 2:18–20). The critique of idols and idol worship also goes further by proclaiming that those who worship inanimate idols become like them. Ps 115 provides a clear example of this type of assessment:

> But their idols are silver and gold,
> made by human hands.
> They have mouths, but cannot speak,
> eyes, but cannot see.
> They have ears, but cannot hear,
> noses, but cannot smell.
> They have hands, but cannot feel,
> feet, but cannot walk,
> nor can they utter a sound with their throats.
> Those who make them will be like them,
> and so will all who trust in them (Ps 115:4–8 [see Ps 135:15–18]).

As in other OT texts, the idols are said to be inanimate; they do not have life. Taking the argument further, those who make and worship them "will be like them." Rather than giving glory to the false idols, this glory should be given to God alone "because of [his] love and faithfulness" (Ps 115:1).

Besides discussions of idolatry in general, a common polemic against idols relates to the two aberrant worship sites set up by Jereboam in Bethel and Dan using golden calves (1 Kgs 12:25–33), an episode which directly echoes the golden calf incident in Exod 32. This false worship is the recipient of constant critique, and the discussion of the last king of Israel in 2 Kings identifies the consistent influence of idolatry on the northern tribes. The text argues that God gave repeated calls to obedience and warnings to the people through the prophets,

> But they would not listen and were as stiff-necked as their ancestors, who did not trust in the Lord their God. They rejected his decrees and the covenant he had made with their ancestors and the statutes he had warned them to keep. They followed worthless idols and themselves became worthless (2 Kgs 17:14–15).

---

14. Beale's study of idolatry in *We Become What We Worship* strongly shapes the discussion of this section.

They, like those in Exodus, are "stiff-necked," and we see how they become like the idols they worship: "They followed worthless idols and themselves became worthless" (see Jer 2:5). Not only are the idol worshipers inanimate, but the context points out that they become immoral, "sell[ing] themselves to do evil in the eyes of the Lord" (2 Kgs 17:17).

The paradigmatic nature of the golden calf episode in Exodus also shows up in descriptions of how idol worshipers "exchange the glory of God" for their idols. For example, in Ps 106, the psalmist notes how "we have sinned, even as our ancestors [in the Exodus] did" (Ps 106:6). After listing a number of his ancestors' sins, he adds: "They made a calf at Horeb and worshiped a cast image. They exchanged the glory of God for the image of an ox that eats grass" (Ps 106:19–20 NRSV). Other texts like Jer 2 pick up this same charge of exchanging the glory of God for "worthless" idols like those in Exodus (Jer 2:11),[15] and like in 2 Kgs 17 the people become like their idols: "They followed worthless idols and themselves became worthless" (Jer 2:5).[16] Those who worship idols follow in the same pattern as the first idolatry of the people of Israel: they exchange the glory of God and they become worthless and inanimate like them.

OT Conclusion

While forming a brief and selective survey, these various passages, from the Pentateuch through the prophets, identify (proper) worship as a fundamental orientation of the covenant people to God as a community. They are consecrated by his glory, and thus they become like the one they worship. Likewise, false worship orients humans to inanimate gods. Rather than becoming like the animate and active God full of life and holiness, those who are idolaters become inanimate and worthless like their worthless gods. They too become like the ones they worship. We explored the presence of God's glory in the tabernacle, but key texts like 2 Chron 7:1–3 locate God's glory in the Jerusalem Temple. The idolatry of the people ultimately leads to their exile and God's glory departing the Temple (Ezek 10), yet the eschatological hope of restoration for Israel includes the return of God's glory (Ezek 43). These themes and texts are taken up by the NT, and we will turn there now.

---

15. See also Hos 4:7.

16. Beale, *We Become What We Worship*, 102–17.

Worship in New Testament

Our topic of discussion is how participation in God's glory in worship helps establish the unity of the biblical narrative, so as we move into the NT we will continue to focus on passages that highlight the theme of God's glory and that of transformation. Any discussion of God's presence in the NT must start with Jesus. He, of course, transforms the nature of how we engage God, not least by his association with the name "Emmanuel" ("God with us," Matt 1:23) and by naming his own body as the temple (see John 2:19–22). Alongside his embodiment of God's presence is his healing ability and contagious holiness that overcomes (contagious) impurity. Also, the transfiguration is a central glimpse of Christ's embodiment of God's glory (Mark 9:2–8 and parr.). While several important perspectives on worship come from the Gospels and from the important worship scenes in Revelation, the more direct connection between worship and glory is found in the epistolary material so we will focus our attention there. Though we are not limiting our discussion to passages that make use of the OT accounts we have explored earlier, the intertextual connections are informative, showing that the NT writers also support the idea that you become what you worship. We begin with 2 Cor 3.

New Covenant Glory: 2 Corinthians 3

In 2 Cor 3 we see both unity in the biblical story and a progression as new elements are incorporated and emphasized, not unlike with Irenaeus in *Haer.* 4.20.[17] The unity is evident through the intertextual connections to both Exodus and the prophets, and these OT frameworks allow Paul to ground the new life available in Christ and through the Spirit as a defense of his ministry. His main point is that his is a new covenant ministry built on the Spirit: "for the letter kills, but the Spirit gives life" (2 Cor 3:6). Since the Corinthians have experienced the life of the Spirit, they should concede that Paul's ministry was valid. The use of the phrase "new covenant" comes from prophetic literature, and Paul interweaves themes from Jer 31 with Ezek 36–37. He contrasts this new covenant with the "old covenant," but he also compares the new experience of glory positively with Moses's on Sinai (in the context of the golden calf episode) especially from Exod 32–34.

As 2 Cor 3 progresses, Paul interweaves the topics of "life" and "glory." In contrast to the ministry of Moses that brought death, the ministry of the Spirit brings

---

17. This chapter in Paul's letter has received much attention. For further details on the exegetical issues, see Ben C. Blackwell, *Christosis: Engaging Paul's Soteriology with His Patristic Interpreters* (Grand Rapids: Eerdmans, 2016) 174–96. Also, see Jeffrey W. Aernie, *Is Paul also among the Prophets?: An Examination of the Relationship between Paul and the Old Testament Prophetic Tradition in 2 Corinthians* (LNTS; London: Bloomsbury, 2012).

life. Moses experienced and reflected a real glory but it is fading, whereas the ministry of the new covenant brings an enduring glory that is more substantial.[18] The climax of the chapter is 2 Cor 3:18 where Paul describes how all Christians "reflecting the glory of the Lord as in a mirror are transformed into the same image, from glory to glory."[19] This is not explicitly framed as "worship," but Paul is describing a direct encounter with God, which was framed as worship in his primary intertext—Exod 34:8. Paul introduces the term "image" (*eikōn*) without previously designating who or what the image is, but, based on his ascription of this image to Christ in 2 Cor 4:4, most commentators agree that this process of transformation means that believers are transformed into the image of Christ, sharing in his divine glory through the Holy Spirit.

Paul frames this reflection of Christ in an eschatological manner. The thrust of his argument in chapter 3 is that believers share in new covenant life and glory presently through the Spirit, but in chapter 4 he balances this with the very real experience of suffering that believers encounter as they await the final restoration. Thus, the experience of believers reflects Christ's suffering as well as his life (2 Cor 4:10–12). Ultimately, this current and momentary suffering produces an eternal weight of glory (2 Cor 4:17). The climax of chapter 3 (3:18) and the climax of chapter 4 (4:17) both speak about glory, one present and one future. Both are conceived in terms of sharing in the life of Christ through the new covenant renewal of the Spirit, but in the present believers equally share in Christ's death. As "we are being transformed into the same image," we will embody his death and his life. A similar, but more developed account occurs in Romans.

The Story of Glory: Romans

In Romans, glory serves as a *leitmotif* throughout the letter, though at times underappreciated in light of attention to other themes like justification.[20] What is interesting is how this theme of glory harkens back to the OT worship commands and prohibitions. After the introductory material that highlights the centrality of the

18. The discussions of 2 Cor 3 by Hays and Watson are especially enlightening: Richard Hays, *Echoes of Scripture in the Letters of Paul* (New Haven: Yale University Press, 1993) ch. 4; Francis Watson, *Paul and the Hermeneutics of Faith*, 2nd ed. (London: Bloomsbury, 2016) ch. 6.

19. Many translations render the participle as "contemplating" or "viewing" the glory of the Lord as in a mirror, instead of as "reflecting." This does not make much sense of the surpassing direct experience Christians have in contrast to Moses. Based on the reflection idea communicated by this participle, I also understand "from glory to glory" as "from God's/Christ's glory to the glory of believers." More simply, believers reflect the glory of God. For a defense of my translation, see Blackwell, *Christosis*, 183–93.

20. See Ben C. Blackwell, "Immortal Glory and the Problem of Death in Romans 3:23," *JSNT* 32 (2010) 285–308. Also, James D.G. Dunn, *Romans 9–16* (WBC; Dallas: Word, 1988) 533–34.

death and resurrection of Christ as the revelation of God's saving righteousness for all (Rom 1:1–17), the body of the letter begins with the problem of idolatry using OT language (Rom 1:18–32). The wrath of God is poured out due to human wickedness, which is idolatry:

> For although they knew God, they neither glorified him as God nor gave thanks to him, but their thinking became futile and their foolish hearts were darkened. Although they claimed to be wise, they became fools and exchanged the glory of the immortal God for images made to look like a mortal human being and birds and animals and reptiles (Rom 1:21–23).

With the language of "exchanged the glory of God," Paul has given a modified quotation of Ps 106:20 and is engaging in a traditional idol polemic related to the golden calf episode.[21] As in the OT idol polemic, the worshipers become inanimate like the idols. The idolaters become senseless and ultimately experience mortality like the *mortal* images (see Rom 1:32) since they have given up the glory of the *immortal* God.

When transitioning to the next major section of Romans in 3:21, Paul briefly summarizes a key element of Rom 1–3 using glory: "There is no difference between Jew and Gentile, for all have sinned and lack the glory of God" (Rom 3:22–23). This statement of the human problem both points back to Paul's previous discussion of glory in Rom 1 as well as pointing forward to his discussion of the effects of Adam's sin in Rom 5:12–21. The latter gains more attention from commentators due to Second Temple Jewish discussions of Adam's experience and loss of glory in the garden, as we see for example in *The Greek Life of Adam and Eve*.[22] However, when we consider this in light of Rom 1, the loss of glory is a common human predicament because humans have turned from proper worship of the God of glory. Rather than sharing in the divine glory of the immortal God, they become mortal (i.e., experience death) like the mortal images they worship. This association of glory with immortality is repeated throughout the letter, so that we should understand the experience of glory in Romans as primarily an experience of immortality (as well as social honor).[23]

---

21. This section of Romans is generally seen as a condemnation of *Gentile* idolatry, with a discussion of *Jewish* disobedience more the focus in chs. 2–3. For our purposes, we do not need to decide whether this is Gentile or Jewish idolatry because it speaks to the broader problem of idolatry to which each could be liable.

22. M. D. Johnson "Life of Adam and Eve: A New Translation and Introduction," in *The Old Testament Pseudepigrapha*, edited by James H. Charlesworth (New Haven: Yale University Press, 1985) 2.249–94.

23. For a close reading of key texts in Romans in support of this argument, see Blackwell, "Immortal Glory and the Problem of Death."

The remainder of chapters 3–8 explores how God restores humans from the problem of sin and mortality. In Rom 4 Paul describes this salvation-historical narrative as beginning with Abraham: He "did not waiver in unbelief regarding the promise of God, but was strengthened in faith and gave glory to God" (Rom 4:20). In contrast to the idolatry of others, Abraham returned glory to God, and those who have faith like Abraham not only experience righteousness by faith (Rom 5:1), but also the hope of the glory of God (Rom 5:2), which is the resurrection hope of Rom 4:16–25. Later Paul attributes renewed moral agency to those walking in new life as Christ was raised in glory (Rom 6:4). This restored experience of glory ultimately stands as the climax of the whole soteriological discussion in chapter 8.[24] Those in Christ and the Spirit are liberated from condemnation and death as they experience the life of God (8:1–11). Believers are adopted into God's family, receiving the Spirit of adoption as co-heirs with Christ (8:14–17). This experience of life, much like in 2 Cor 3, is then described as an experience of glory which is nonetheless marked by sharing in Christ's suffering (8:16–30). The chapter climaxes with this summary:

> For those God foreknew he also predestined to be conformed to the image of his Son, that he might be the firstborn among many brothers and sisters. And those he predestined, he also called; those he called, he also justified; those he justified, he also glorified (Rom 8:29–30).

As a description of the goal of salvation, Paul states that they are "predestined to be conformed to the image of his Son" and this ultimately results in their sharing in his glory, just as they share in his righteousness.

Much has been written on the importance of participation in God's immortal glory (i.e., sharing in the resurrection life of Christ) in this passage, but we should not miss the wider motif of worship that helps frame this experience of glory in Romans. Of course, this worship is not a one-time conversion experience or a future experience at the resurrection. Indeed, we see that Paul grounds his whole discussion of obedience to God in Rom 12–15 as an act of worship in Rom 12:1–2. As a result, we see in Romans a deep unity between the present life of obedience and the future life of resurrection, much like in 2 Cor 3–4.

In this letter Paul tells a story. In direct contrast to those who exchanged the glory of the immortal God for mortal images and experience death as in the golden calf episode, those who follow in the path of Abraham's faith in, and glorification of, God are properly oriented to God and therefore experience his glory. They become what they worship: they share in the life of God in Christ and through the Spirit. In

---

24. For further discussion about the various aspects of this wonderfully deep chapter of Paul's letter, see Blackwell, *Christosis*, 117–73.

terms of Rom 8:29–30, they are "conformed to the image of the Son,…[being] glorified." One other passage that addresses glory and being conformed to the Son is that of Heb 2–3, so we will now turn there.[25]

The Son Brings Many Sons and Daughters to Glory: Hebrews 2–3

With the significant quantity of intertextual references, Hebrews clearly places its discussion within a wider biblical narrative, particularly that of the Mosaic economy. In Heb 3 the author warns his readers not to follow the disobedience of the Israelites. Unlike 2 Corinthians and Romans where the disobedience of the golden calf incident was in focus, here it is the general Israelite disobedience over the course of 40 years in the wilderness (Heb 3:7–11), so the direct concern with worship may not seem as central. Indeed, the focus is mostly on Jesus' identity as the Son of God, but as the discussion progresses, the cultic frame is evident because of Jesus' role as "high priest" (Heb 2:17) who we later learn "is holy, blameless, pure, set apart from sinners, exalted above the heavens" (Heb 7:26). With an emphasis on Jesus' incarnation and death,[26] the Son is "crowned with glory and honor because he suffered death" (Heb 2:9; see Ps 8:4–6) but he also brings "many sons and daughters to glory" (Heb 2:10). The Son through his sacrifice enables others to become sons and daughters of God, and they share in his glory when they experience the "salvation" offered in Christ (Heb 2:3; 10) and freedom from death (Heb 2:15). Not unlike Paul, the author of Hebrews correlates sharing in the sonship of Christ and the experience of glory with and through Christ.

How might worship relate to this? Finding Christ as the speaker in the Psalms, the author quotes a psalm that includes the idea of worship, "I will declare your name to my brothers and sisters; in the assembly I will sing your praises" (Heb 2:12; see Ps 22:22). Rather than focusing on their common faith in Christ as a basis for their unity like Paul does, here they worship together. Taking the discussion further, the author draws this conclusion for this worshipping family: "Therefore, holy brothers and sisters, who share in the heavenly calling, fix your thoughts on Jesus, whom we confess as our apostle and high priest" (Heb 3:1).[27] Most of Hebrews focuses on worship via the new covenant, the true high priest, the perfect sacrifice, and

---

25. I am grateful to my colleague Jason Maston for pointing out the relevance of this passage.

26. Christ's resurrection also shapes the wider frame of Hebrews. See David M. Moffitt, "Blood, Life, and Atonement: Reassessing Hebrews' Christological Appropriation of Yom Kippur" in *The Day of Atonement: Its Early Interpretations in Early Jewish and Christian Traditions*, edited by Thomas Hieke and Tobias Niklas (Leiden: Brill, 2012) 211–24.

27. This is similar to a visually-focused charge in Heb 12:2 to "fix our eyes on Jesus the pioneer and perfecter of our faith."

the heavenly temple.[28] Jesus is the holy and blameless high priest and sacrifice who makes "the people holy through his own blood" who are thus called to "offer to God the sacrifice of praise continually" (see Heb 13.12–15). While addressing the topic from a different angle than Paul, the ultimate focus is the same. Worship of God leads believers to become like Jesus—they become sons and daughters, and they share in his glory and in his holiness.

The Story of the Bible: Genesis to Revelation

This whistle stop tour through the Bible was necessarily selective, but these various passages have given us an important window on how worship shapes participation within the biblical narrative. Though we followed Irenaeus' lead and focused primarily on passages where glory played a prominent role, it turns out that these passages represent some of the most central biblical passages on worship and participation. Throughout the Bible worshipers become what they worship through this participation, whether positive or negative. Those who worship God experience his glory and holiness, whereas those who worship false and inanimate gods become inanimate themselves. In the NT the focus becomes more sharply focused on participation in Christ through the Spirit. As believers are transformed into the christological image through the Spirit, they share in his death and life now while waiting for the fullness of the glorious life that will be received later. The central recalibration in the wider biblical narrative in the NT is the inclusion of Jesus and the expanded role of the Spirit. Thus, whereas worshipers in the OT become like YHWH (LXX: *kyrios*) worshipers in the NT become like *kyrios* (YHWH) now more fully known as Father, Son, and Spirit.[29]

Though our focus on worship has been selective, the pervasive role of worship in the biblical narrative is undisputed. One aspect that is at times underestimated is that of the temple in biblical theology.[30] This has not been our focus here, but I think it is important for helping frame the study. In the last few decades the temple has become much more of a focus in biblical studies.[31] As a *leitmotif* of the Bible,

28. The author does not condemn the old covenant as empty ritual and ceremony, as if ritual and ceremony is by nature empty. Rather the old was merely temporary in contrast to the eternal. Jesus participated in this eternal and heavenly ritual and ceremony (Heb 9–10).

29. See C. Kavin Rowe, "Biblical Pressure and Trinitarian Hermeneutics," *ProEccl* 11 (2002) 295–312.

30. Even in my previous work on "glory" in Romans, I underestimated it. See Blackwell, "Immortal Glory and the Problem of Death," which focuses more on the Rom 5 parallels to Rom 3:23 rather than on the Rom 1 context.

31. See, for example, *Heaven on Earth: The Temple in Biblical Theology*, edited by T. Desmond Alexander and Simon Gathercole (Carlisle: Paternoster, 2004); Nicholas Perrin, *Jesus the Temple*, (Grand

discussions of the theme of temple help shape the focus on the worship of, and engagement with, a holy God. There is much that might be addressed, but I will only note the bookends of the Bible: Genesis and Revelation. We might think that notions of temple and tabernacle first arise in Exodus, but many scholars see Eden itself as a reflection of the temple (and the temple as a reflection of Eden). This reinforces the idea that worship is fundamental to the human identity and vocation. In fulfillment of this creational orientation, in the final re-orientation of creation described in Rev 20–22 the themes of Eden and of the temple are again intertwined. Thus, the vocation and fulfillment of human identity is oriented to temple worship.[32]

Set within this wider frame, worship does help give a unity to diverse voices found in the Bible, and yet, as the focus on glory helps draw out, this worship is participatory.[33] While one might not immediately be drawn to the term "participation" in a more philosophical sense to describe this worship encounter, we often describe worship as an act of participation. The community of faith participates in worshiping God, but the biblical material also points to the theological and transformative aspects of participation, as Irenaeus described. In the encounter with God, his covenant people are transformed into his glory. Irenaeus, thus, does capture this when he argues in *Adversus haereses* ("Against Heresies") that "the glory of God is a living human; and the life of humans consists in seeing God" (*Haer.* 4.20.7).

The Church's Worship, Theosis, and the Secular Age

When we seek to allow reflection upon Scripture and patristic sources like Irenaeus to benefit contemporary pastoral theology, what can help us to deepen our understanding of participation and what issues present road blocks to such deeper understanding? In relation to a biblical theology of worship, I submit that an ancient and a modern context can, respectively, help and hinder our reading of these texts. In the ancient context I have found the doctrine of theosis to be a helpful lens on participation and the narrative unity of God's work in creation and salvation, whereas in the modern context cultural and philosophical shifts marginalize participation as a category for understanding reality, so we can struggle in the church to communicate this biblical paradigm. Accordingly, as we explore these two interpretive contexts, I hope they will prove fruitful for our discussion and exploration of participation.

Rapids: Baker, 2010).

32. See Margaret Barker, *Temple Themes in Christian Worship* (London: T. & T. Clark, 2007).

33. Many other texts that relate to participation and worship, namely, those related to the Lord's Supper, would be highly relevant, but they fell outside our criteria for study here.

Theosis and the Unity of the Bible

Theosis and deification are not terms commonly taught in Protestant seminaries, and they are virtually absent from contemporary preaching. However, the ideas behind these terms can be helpful for understanding the scope of biblical soteriology and would benefit the practices and preaching of the church. The terms are Greek and Latin equivalents that speak of believers "becoming gods" as the heart of soteriology. This sounds blasphemous, but all the patristic theologians that helped define our central perspective on God as Trinity—Athanasius, Cyril of Alexandria, and Augustine, just to name a few—use this language to describe salvation. How could they get God so right and yet get salvation so wrong? Or did they? The idea of becoming gods spoke differently to the Greek and Roman cultures than it does to ours, but a fundamental premise shapes their use of this language: God the Creator is infinitely greater than his finite creation, so if believers are called "gods," this is only an analogy.[34] That is, believers do not become gods by nature, but by adoption, by grace. Believers, no matter how much they progress towards God, never become God, the eternal Trinity. Yet, the patristic theologians are willing to use language that is potentially confusing because it speaks to the heart of the message of the Bible: to become like God is the goal of humanity, and believers will continue in the process of becoming like God for eternity, for it is an infinite goal that we as finite beings can never exhaustively attain.

When we see biblical texts repeatedly ground the idea that you become what you worship, this points directly to the patristic notion of theosis. The focus of theosis is participating in divine attributes, or becoming like God, which is at the heart of our study here. In fact, one of the most common ways to describe theosis is "participation (or sharing) in the life of God."[35] This is captured through exposition of key texts like Lev 19:2; Ps 82:6–7; and 2 Pet 1:4, but patristic theologians grounded the theology in key texts related to adoption, resurrection, and the presence of the Spirit.[36] The most popular image to describe this participatory transformation is an iron sword put in a fire that remains a sword but takes on the attributes of light and heat like the fire.

34. I discuss patristic notions of theosis in Blackwell, *Christosis*, esp. 99–110. I make the distinction between "essential deification" in which believers actually become gods, and the patristic notion of "attributive deification" in which believers take on divine attributes but always remain distinct from God.

35. See, for example, Norman Russell, *Fellow Workers with God: Orthodox Thinking on Theosis* (Crestwood: St Vladimir's Seminary Press, 2009) 127–41.

36. Two accessible discussions about the biblical and theological issues related to theosis are Russell, *Fellow Workers with God*; and Daniel A. Keating, *Deification and Grace* (Naples, FL: Sapientia, 2007).

Although we may have to define the term initially with an expansive discussion, the term theosis gave patristic writers a quick way to point to the nature and destiny of humanity in terms of being conformed to Jesus, participation in the Spirit, and union with the Father. It not only captures the central notion of human transformation, it places that transformation in a theocentric and salvation-historical framework. The patristics scholar Andrew Louth, in his description of theosis, contrasts this to what might be perceived as a traditional Protestant perspective that unfortunately shapes popular views, if not always scholarly views.[37] He mentions how Protestants often focus on the narrative arch from the Edenic fall as the problem to the solution of Christ on the cross. Humans become guilty before God, and the cross is God's gracious response that brings resolution to that guilt, an idea captured with the doctrine of justification. The Orthodox, following patristic theologians, orient their theology to a wider arch, that of creation to re-creation, or creation to resurrection. This outer arch only makes sense in light of the inner arch, but the focus of salvation is not only sharing in the benefits of Christ's death but also his resurrection. And salvation is not abstracted from the original intention of creation, but is a restoration and fulfillment of creation. God created humanity in the image and likeness of God, and through Christ, the true image, and by the Spirit, believers are transformed into divine likeness—they share in the life of God.[38] Accordingly, theosis speaks to the unity of protology and eschatology as much as it speaks about the unity of the divine and human in Christ.

When speaking of participation and the unity of the biblical narrative, theosis is a natural term to capture God's personal and salvation-historical work. It is no wonder then that Irenaeus, the theologian of unity, found deification and related themes to be essential in his exposition of Christian theology that sees a fundamental coherence between creation and new-creation.[39] I commend those interested in participation to explore this theme more deeply, not least for its integrative nature, particularly with regard to sacramental theology and worship.[40]

---

37. Andrew Louth, "The Place of Theosis in Orthodox Theology," in *Partakers of the Divine Nature: The History and Development of Deification in the Christian Traditions*, edited by Michael J. Christiansen and Jeffrey A. Wittung (Grand Rapids: Baker, 2008) 32–44, at 35.

38. The image to which believers are conformed is that of Christ, and it is for this reason that I at times describe the process of theosis as *christosis*, without seeing a contrast between the two.

39. See Blackwell, *Christosis*, 35–70.

40. See, for example, Daniela C. Augustine, "Liturgy, Theosis, and the Renewal of the World," in *Toward a Pentecostal Theology of Worship*, edited by Lee Roy Martin (Cleveland: CPT Press, 2016) 165–85; more generally see Andrew B. McGowan, *Ancient Christian Worship: Early Church Practices in Social, Historical, and Theological Perspective* (Grand Rapids: Baker, 2014).

Participation in a Secular Age

As we shift from an ancient context that gives us terms and concepts to help us understand participation to the modern context, we begin to lose cultural resources to aid our discussion of participation. With limited space here I will focus primarily on the work of Charles Taylor and Hans Boersma, who both narrate the shift from the premodern to modern setting.[41] They comment on how the de-sacramentalization of worship in the Protestant tradition, whether the sacraments themselves or "sacramentals" (holy objects, icons, etc.), reveals the marginalization of participation within modern theology.

While I might quibble with aspects of Taylor's discussion of how we got here, Taylor and Boersma point to a common problem with our contemporary epistemology: we think of the world in flat terms. All matter is the same; we are just one point on a limitless universe. Accordingly, our social imaginary (or worldview) is dominated by (if not limited only to) the immanent frame, the natural world. Ancient Christians, however, thought of the world as a cosmos, an ordered hierarchy of reality. Accordingly, they understood the immanent in light of the transcendent, with sacraments and other sacramentals linking the immanent world with the transcendent.[42] (When I speak of the "transcendent" here, I am using it as a shorthand for all that is supernatural.[43] I do not mean it in some generic, pantheistic sense but rather for reference to the personal triune God and the created reality that exists beyond the immanent.) As we communicate Christianity to the world, and even more, Christianity to Christians, Taylor and Boersma point to the need to help people to see the reality of the transcendent as informing and shaping the immanent.

41. Charles Taylor, *A Secular Age* (Cambridge: Belknap, 2007); Charles Taylor, *Sources of the Self: The Making of the Modern Identity* (Cambridge: Harvard University, 1989); Hans Boersma, *Heavenly Participation: The Weaving of a Sacramental Tapestry* (Grand Rapids: Eerdmans, 2011). While there are many influences towards secularity, Taylor highlights Protestant theology, particularly in the Reformed tradition, as a major stimulus towards de-sacramentalization. While the Protestant focus on individual readings of the Bible and questioning of tradition did contribute to these wider shifts, movements centuries prior to the Reformation already set European Christianity down this path. The critiques offered by the Catholic *Nouvelle Theologie* highlight these issues, and this is well documented by Boersma.

42. Along with a rejection of a hierarchical cosmos for the flat universe, modern (Protestant) Christians generally reject other hierarchies, such as ones related to holiness. The affirmation that all sins are equal, for example, is distinct from patristic and medieval conceptions about the varying severity of sin and therefore of punishments (see Luke 10:12–14; 12:47–48; John 19:11–12).

43. The terms natural and supernatural have heuristic value, but they also speak to a division reinforced by the Enlightenment that patristic theologians would not hold. Supernatural action as a "miracle" is not a breaking of natural laws (an Enlightenment explanation) but God acting to make nature run as it is supposed to (a patristic explanation).

Indeed, to even speak of "participation" entails some intersection of the transcendent and immanent. However, if we, according to a modern social imaginary (even those prevalent in the church) perceive our reality according to the immanent frame, how can we truly understand participation? Rather than viewing the supernatural and natural as overlapping and interlocking spheres, we tend to think in terms of the immanent frame and of God as disengaged in the world. Taylor argues that we need things that provide an "epiphanic" experience of the transcendent,[44] which helps us not only verbally affirm the transcendent but also to live according to a robustly enchanted social imaginary. Worship, the sacraments, and liturgy are avenues for this epiphanic experience. We should rightly be concerned with the social, ethnic, and gender hierarchies that pervaded ancient cosmologies, but by giving up the accompanying sacramental hierarchies and the notion of the sacred, we almost do not have the categories even to comprehend participation anymore.

I would submit that the doctrine of theosis as a participation in the life of God is exactly a doctrine that helps us frame our social imaginary according to the transcendent.[45] The conjunction of theosis and worship thus fits well together. For worship is at its basic level taking us beyond the immanent frame. But even more worship itself is formative and transformative, as we have seen in our discussion of the biblical narrative. James Smith, among others, has explored the formative nature of liturgy recently. We are constantly performing liturgies, both secular and sacred, such as that of the modern shopping mall as well as at church.[46] He is rightly calling the church back to a more robust understanding of liturgy, ritual, and ceremony as necessary for a proper spiritual formation. Liturgy helps provide spiritual muscle memory so that Christians not only engage God but have a social imaginary shaped by God's engagement in the world.

If this is the case, what in our liturgy points to the transcendent and goes beyond creating a personal feeling? Our prayers and singing to God are the common features in our liturgies. Yet are these sufficient? Do these sufficiently guard against a sentimentality, a feeling or experience, that can sometimes be a substitute for substantive encounter? For instance, does our prayer and singing include lament as well

---

44. Taylor, *Sources of Self*, 512.

45. Taylor, *Secular Age*, 640–44 also sets down the criterion of the "maximal demand." That is, a robust theology of human identity needs to point humans beyond themselves without destroying humanity. It must point to a fulfilled humanity rather than one that transcends humanity so much that one becomes un-human. Theosis fits this maximal demand quite well, as patristic discussion of soteriology in light of the hypostatic union in Christ shows. See Ben C. Blackwell and Kris Miller, "Theosis and Theological Anthropology," in *Ashgate Research Companion to Theological Anthropology*, edited by Joshua R. Farris and Charles Taliaferro (Burlington, VT: Ashgate, 2015) 303–17.

46. James K.A. Smith, *Desiring the Kingdom: Worship, Worldview, and Cultural Formation* (Grand Rapids: Baker, 2009).

as praise to help people follow biblical patters of relating to God and help them to participate liturgically in the death as well as the life of Christ? Taking the question a step further, what in our liturgy not only points to God but engages people in the transcendent? Protestant worship is often focused on only one of the five senses—hearing—whereas Orthodox and Catholic worship engages all five, not unlike that of temple worship described in Exodus and the rest of the biblical narrative. Ironically, a reduced use of created things in worship (sights, smells, tastes, etc.) to point to the transcendent is correlated with the rise of social imaginaries that cannot see beyond created things. Biblical worship does not ignore created realities because of the intimate connection between encountering God and embodied transformation. The patristic church thought much about liturgy and the use of sacraments and sacramentals. While we may not accept the fullness of their theology,[47] giving consideration to their practice and doctrine will surely enrich our worship.

Conclusion

Among their well-known videos, the Bible Project has one on "Heaven and Earth" where they correctly state that "the union of heaven and earth is what the story of the Bible is all about."[48] In that video they speak of the temple, fulfilled through Jesus, as the mediating place that allows heaven and earth to reunite, as it was in Eden. This is not far from what patristic theologians talked about with the doctrine of theosis. Through Christ and the Spirit, believers are united with God because God is generous and shares his life with those united with him. In the words of Irenaeus, "the glory of God is a living human; and the life of humans consists in seeing God" (*Haer.* 4.20.7). This life is both present and future, both sanctification and resurrection, and is a participation in the life of God, a gift shared from God himself. As the community partakes in worship together, we have the sure hope that we will encounter God and become like him since as the biblical text consistently affirms, you become what you worship.

---

47. Indeed, we cannot fully accept their theology without accepting a very different social imaginary informed by cosmic hierarchies, including for instance gender hierarchies. A redemptive hermeneutic will be necessary for patristic texts as well as biblical ones that speak of socio-economic hierarchies like that of slavery.

48. https://thebibleproject.com/videos/heaven-and-earth/, accessed August 10, 2017.

RESPONSE TO BLACKWELL

Cynthia Peters Anderson

Let me begin by thanking Ben Blackwell for his work in this paper. I am not someone who has to be convinced of the orthodoxy of theosis. As I was reading the paper, I remembered, first in seminary and later in my PhD studies, encountering Scripture through the eyes of Ireneaus, Athanasius, and Cyril of Alexandria. I was so struck by how beautiful and life-giving and exciting this story is of a God who became human so that we might participate in the fullness of God's life, so that we might become fully human—and holy in that full humanness. As a pastor who leads worship every Sunday, I especially appreciate the way this paper calls our attention to the connection between theosis and the formational power of worship. Blackwell reminds us that we need to be clear about who is at the center of our worship and raises intriguing points about the ways in which our patterns of worship help to shape us into the pattern of God's life.

While there is much to explore in the paper, this response focuses on some observations offered in the hope of deepening and extending the underlying theme of the paper itself, and then in drawing out what we might learn from Blackwell's work as we consider how our worship helps us live more fully as participants in the life of God.

First, some overall observations. The sections in the latter portions of the paper focusing on worship, theosis, and the secular age through to the end seemed underdeveloped in comparison with the paper's earlier discussion of the unifying theme of worship in Scripture. It would be helpful to see the argument expanded, particularly in the section on theosis and the church's worship, and the section on liturgy. The connections between these sections could be strengthened by a fuller attention to the ways in which conceptions of theosis can illumine and vivify worship practices and their formative role in the lives of God's people.

Now for some specific observations. In the discussion of the Old Testament, the reminder that stiff-necked people are reflective of the stiff-necked idols they worship can be a helpful and challenging question to consider when reflecting on our current patterns of worship. We have difficulty seeing our idols precisely because they have such an insidious hold on us. However, perhaps we might more easily be able to see them by the shadows they cast and the symptoms they manifest in our lives, in our world, and in our worship. One of the fruits of this paper is its potential to more clearly illuminate the idols that have us in their grip by raising for us the question: what symptoms do we see that indicate something is amiss in our worship, and what might those symptoms tell us about our idols? What idols do we most worship? Perhaps, specifically what idols do we most worship in the church? In all of our conversation about the decline of the church in North America, what might we learn about what has led us to appear dead and inanimate in the eyes of so many?

Turning to the latter sections of the paper, in the discussion of the relationship between glory and immortality in Romans 3, Blackwell notes that "the loss of glory is a common human predicament because humans have turned from proper worship of the God of glory. Rather than sharing in divine glory of the immortal God, they become mortal (i.e., experience death) like the mortal images they worship. This association of glory with immortality is repeated throughout the letter, so that we should understand the experience of glory in Romans as primarily an experience of immortality (as well as social honor)." There is room here for a fuller explication of what it means to say the experience of glory is the experience of immortality and the implications that has for our forms of worship. Towards the conclusion of the section on Romans, Blackwell notes that this worship is "not a one-time conversion or a future experience in the resurrection" and talks about the role of obedience as an act of worship. The implications are that when God is at the center of our worship, we encounter God's presence and share in God's glory, and that glory gives us a share in immorality through the resurrection. This glory, this share in immortality is not simply a one-time conversion, nor is it merely eschatological, but is rather ongoing and grounds our current obedience. It would be helpful to say more about how the theme of participation relates to Paul's thought here—particularly in terms of the relationship between the divine and human relationship and how our proper worship leads to obedience. For instance, Cyril of Alexandria's conception that participation leads to both an inward transformation of who we are and an outward expression of that change through obedience in moral living could be a helpful framework. How might we see Paul as being in dialogue with the early church's conception of theosis in these terms of glory and obedience?

Turning to the section entitled "Theosis and the Unity of the Bible," there is reference to the "wider arch" of the patristic understanding of the biblical story and its helpfulness in understanding the relationship between God and humans in salvation and worship—and in counteracting modernity's flattening of the world into immanence. In the discussion of Louth's argument that traditional Protestant perspectives have a narrower arc, Blackwell seems to be suggesting that the wider arc of participation could be a helpful corrective. To deepen the argument, I suggest this captivity to immanence is related to our ongoing struggle to see an analogical, grace-initiated, grace-filled conception of the relationship between God and creation, between transcendence and immanence that's so important to conceptions of participation. I'm drawing on the insights of deLubac and particularly Balthasar here in arguing that we must see the relationship between God and creaturely reality through an incarnational lens—which means that created things have a divinely gifted integrity through which the divine goodness, truth, and beauty are revealed and encountered. How can our worship, in all of its elements—liturgy, sacraments, music, preaching—help us heal a modern rupture between the transcendent and the immanent and expand our ability to see the transcendent in and through the immanent in ways that enlarge our imaginations? A fuller exploration of these connections between participation and the practices of worship would strengthen the paper and provide fruitful insights.

In the discussion about the flattening of the world into immanence, the paper notes the rise of social imaginaries that cannot see beyond created things, and points toward liturgy specifically as the practice that can point us toward the transcendent in ways that reform or transform our imaginations. Considering the role of liturgy as it relates to an ability to point toward the transcendent, there may be a related question that needs to be addressed in this argument: what is the relationship between subjective and objective elements of worship within the framework of becoming what we worship? That is—what is a proper relationship between subjective "experience" in worship and the more "objective" elements of liturgy? In the church worship wars, we often thinking we are fighting about music and liturgy, but we are really disagreeing about the interplay and varying emphases of expression and formation. When people object to or resist liturgy, it's often because we've not helped them see liturgy as iconic—as a practice that helps us see God's presence—or as formative—that is as an act that actually forms our faith and practice through language and movement. There is always the danger that we begin to think of liturgy—just as we can think of the worship band, or the preacher—as the key element that can control or make God "appear"—that can "manufacture" an encounter with a transcendent God. Some fuller discussion about the markers of worship that point us toward an encounter with the living presence of God—that transform us into greater holiness—would enrich the paper. Specifically, what role might beauty have in drawing people toward transcendence? How is worship—particularly liturgy—iconic? How would liturgy be helpful in teaching us to better worship God and to become fully living human beings?

The paper opens up a potentially fruitful discussion of the relationship between our worship practices and our formation into the people of God. It sets the stage for a fuller conversation about theosis, or participation, as a framework that can help us understand and practice worship in ways that open us to the gift of God's presence, point us toward transcendence, and transform our imaginations in worship.

THE OLD TESTAMENT AND PARTICIPATION IN GOD (AND/IN CHRIST?): (RE-)READING THE LIFE OF MOSES WITH SOME HELP FROM GREGORY OF NYSSA[1]

Brent A. Strawn

Introduction

"Participation with Christ" is not the most obvious topic for an Old Testament professor to address—not, at least, for the past few centuries of biblical scholarship. Some, maybe even most, scholars presently active in the guild would deem the topic completely out of bounds since Christ as such does not appear in the Old Testament, the Greek translation of "Messiah" as *Christos* in the Septuagint[2] and/or other so-called "messianic prophecies" notwithstanding.[3] To be sure, if the Old Testament professor at hand is a Christian, especially one open to the kind of figural interpretation that marked Jewish and Christian exegesis before the modern era (and still does, to no small degree, at least homiletically), the theme of participation with Christ in the Old Testament may not be impossible to imagine. The rock that accompanied the people of Israel, after all, was Christ according to Paul (1 Cor 10:4)—let

---

1. I am thankful to the conveners of the North Park symposium for their kind invitation to participate in the 2017 colloquium. I also thank my respondent, J. Nathan Clayton, for his gracious response. I also wish to thank Mark McInroy for helpful discussions on participation and for many bibliographical suggestions prior to my writing as well as for commenting on an initial draft. I am also thankful to Collin Cornell and Anthony Briggman for giving me feedback on the piece. Early in my thinking Klyne Snodgrass was gracious enough to share a copy of his own paper on participation, which is now published as "The Gospel of Participation," in *Earliest Christianity within the Boundaries of Judaism: Essays in Honor of Bruce Chilton,* edited by Alan J. Avery-Peck, Craig A. Evans, and Jacob Neusner, BRLA 49 (Leiden: Brill, 2016) 413–30.

2. See, e.g., Lev 4:5, 16: 6:15; 1 Sam 12:5; 16:6; 24:7, 11; Isa 45:1; Hab 3:13; Amos 4:13; Lam 4:20; Dan 9:26; etc.

3. Some such prophecies are applied to Christ already within the New Testament itself. See, for example, Donald Juel, *Messianic Exegesis: Christological Interpretation of the Old Testament in Early Christianity* (Philadelphia: Fortress, 1987). Of course, messianic prophecies from the Old Testament need not apply directly or only to Jesus of Nazareth, as evidenced, inter alia, by non-Christian Jewish messianic expectation at Qumran and elsewhere. See, generally, *The Messiah: Developments in Earliest Judaism and Christianity,* edited by James H. Charlesworth et al. (Minneapolis: Fortress, 1992) esp. the essay by J. J. M. Roberts, "The Old Testament's Contribution to Messianic Expectations" (39–51).

the reader understand (Matt 24:15 // Mark 13:14)! Or, in a different vein, the biblical texts were written also for us and for our sake (1 Cor 9:10) if only one has ears to hear (Mark 4:9 // Luke 8:8; Mark 4:23; Luke 14:35).[4]

The shadow of historical criticism—or at least its thin veneer of historicism—still looms large in the guild of biblical scholarship, however, and is usually accompanied by a strong distaste of so-called "pre-modern" interpretations of the Bible, even among Christian exegetes, and so a figural approach, while viable and in many ways resurgent in certain circles,[5] will probably make a number of people uncomfortable, whether they are religious adherents or not: such is the power and the rootedness of historical criticism in the study of Holy Scripture. Stepping back somewhat, then, but in some ways depending on a deeper foundation (or assumption) one might appeal to orthodox Trinitarianism such that any instance of "participation with God" (however that phase is defined—and it isn't yet here)[6] would be equally an instance of participation with the Son, though of course also with the Spirit who ought not be neglected. I myself have advocated such an approach for reading the Old Testament in a way that *permits* but *does not require* christological connections.[7] But, insofar as a Trinitarian approach is decidedly *post*-textual (insofar as the full-blown doctrine of the Trinity is the distinguished achievement of later Christian centuries)

4. Immediacy in terms of applicability is a widely shared assumption by those interested in and practicing the reading of the Bible for the life of faith. In my judgment, this assumption depends on a prior disposition—namely, to hear Scripture as a word of address. For some general reflections on this matter, especially in the light of Christian preaching of the Old Testament, see Ellen F. Davis, *Wondrous Depth: Preaching the Old Testament* (Louisville: Westminster John Knox, 2005).

5. See, for example, David C. Steinmetz, "The Superiority of Pre-Critical Exegesis," *ThTo* 37 (1980) 27–38; and John David Dawson, *Christian Figural Reading and the Fashioning of Identity* (Berkeley: University of California, 2002); more recently, consult Ephraim Radner, *Time and the Word: Figural Reading of the Christian Scriptures* (Grand Rapids: Eerdmans, 2016); and see also John L. Thompson, *Reading the Bible with the Dead: What You Can Learn from the History of Exegesis that You Can't Learn from Exegesis Alone* (Grand Rapids: Eerdmans, 2007).

6. This is at least partly by design and for at least two reasons: the first is that Gregory's own work depends on various philosophical positions that are not operative, at least to the same degree, in the biblical texts, and I do not want to force Gregory's categories on the Old Testament's unduly. The second is that, precisely given the difference delineated in the first reason, I think it would be most helpful to treat the general idea of participation inductively, touching on the various themes and texts which seem most pertinent to the notion. I fully concur with Gary A. Anderson, when he writes (of purgatory) that "a proper grasp of what the doctrine intends to teach is crucial for determining whether it has a biblical basis" (*Christian Doctrine and the Old Testament: Theology in the Service of Biblical Exegesis* [Grand Rapids: Baker Academic, 2017], 185). Even so, the present essay proceeds intentionally with a somewhat underdefined or undertheorized notion of participation so as to not constrain the biblical text unduly and to let Scripture say things back to the idea that might otherwise be ignored (see at n45 below).

7. See Brent A. Strawn, "And These Three Are One: A Trinitarian Critique of Christological Approaches to the Old Testament," *PRSt* 31 (2004) 191–210. The only thing that might be forbidden in a Trinitarian approach is an overly-wrought Christocentrism; all varieties of Christomonism would definitely be out of order.

or, probably better, *pre*-textual (insofar as it operates with some form of pre-understanding that informs and guides the interpretation of the text), and insofar as this a priori situation may be quite totalizing but at the same time rather non-specific (i.e., every place where one member is operative/present all members are operative/present...but what does that mean, specifically, for text *x*, *y*, or *z*?), it, too, may not be particularly helpful in specific cases beyond reiterating the general principle that, wherever one might participate in God in the Old Testament, one must also understand such participation as being "in Christ" (and the Spirit!). So what, then, can we say about the subject at hand—"participation with Christ"—from the perspective of the Old Testament?

I shall return to a Trinitarian (pre)understanding at the end of this essay, but, thus far in the secondary literature—or so it seems to me—the place of the Old Testament's contribution to the notion of divine participation has been somewhat staid or lackluster, limited largely to the question of "background." Any decent and thorough investigation of the idea of participation will include at least some summary treatment of its antecedents. There are actually a large number of antecedents for the idea of participation, and one of them, to be sure (and also to say the very least) is the Old Testament. So it is that scholars appeal to various notions in the Old Testament as precursors or anticipations of the idea.[8] Studies disagree, of course, on

---

8. See, for example, Norman Russell, *The Doctrine of Deification in the Greek Patristic Tradition* (Oxford: Oxford University Press, 2004) 53–55 (on ancient Israel, just one of five parts of what he calls "the Jewish paradigm," and which focuses almost exclusively on Enoch and Elijah, both of which are deemed to be "comparatively late accounts of extraordinary events which did not in any way affect the expectations of the ordinary Israelite" [55]); Gregory Glazov, "Theōsis, Judaism, and Old Testament Anthropology," in *Theōsis: Deification in Christian Theology*, edited by Stephen Finlan and Vladimir Kharlamov, PTMS 52 (Eugene, OR: Pickwick, 2006) 16–31 (who, of "Israelite royal-sonship ideology" says only that it "could have contributed to the later emergence of Christology and theōsis" [25] and that "biblical anthropological models taken from covenant salvation history and wisdom narratives provide many bases for a biblical theōsis theology" [29]); and Jules Gross, *The Divinization of the Christian according to the Greek Fathers* (Anaheim, CA: A & C Press, 2002) translated by Paul A. Onica [French original 1938], 61–69 (who speaks of "the seeds of a doctrine of deification contained in the oldest books of the Old Testament" which were fertilized by the author of Wisdom to "prepare the way for the Christian revelation" [69]). There is wide agreement that Ps 82:6 was an important text for the doctrine, esp. as read through John 10:34–38. See esp. Carl Mosser, "The Earliest Patristic Interpretations of Psalm 82, Jewish Antecedents, and the Origin of Christian Deification," *JTS* 56 (2005) 30–74. Prior still to the Old Testament, see the comment by Thorkild Jacobsen about ancient Mesopotamian religion: "As it was thought possible for a man to achieve partial identity with various gods, so could one god enjoy partial identity with other gods and thus share in their natures and abilities" ("Mesopotamia," in H. and H. A. Frankfort, John A. Wilson, Thorkild Jacbosen, and William A. Irwin, *The Intellectual Adventure of Ancient Man: An Essay on Speculative Thought in the Ancient Near East* [Chicago: University of Chicago, 1977] 133). Erik Hornung, *Conceptions of God in Ancient Egypt: The One and the Many*, translated by John Baines (Ithaca: Cornell, 1982) does not think Egyptians had a similar notion. An intriguing ritual that highlights the complexity of divine and human inter-workings is the Mesopotamian *mīs pî* ceremony; a similar ritual is attested in Egypt. See *Born in Heaven, Made on Earth: The Making of the Cult Image in the Ancient Near East*, edited by Michael B.

just *how* important the Old Testament is to this "background" especially vis-à-vis other possible datasets. In some instances, that is, the Old Testament is deemed to be only one of several helpful resources; in others, it might be considerably less than that.[9] So, even if it is a source or fount, the Old Testament is just one such and maybe not the most important; that takes the wind out of the sails a bit, to say the least.

Whatever the case, the present study will not rehearse this kind of approach once more, though it is tempting to do so to see if it makes any difference if the writer in question is first and foremost an Old Testament professor rather than, as is so often the case, a New Testament or patristic one. Instead, I propose to look at one specific but extended instance of divine-human participation in the Old Testament—namely, the life of Moses, especially as found in the book of Exodus. Justification of this choice, as opposed to some other, will be mostly implicit in what follows insofar as the material proves useful to the subject.[10] Even so, an appeal to Moses as a test/text-case may need no more (explicit) justification than the well-known fact that Gregory of Nyssa's classic treatise on the spiritual life, too, takes as its paradigm Moses's life. It is equally well known that Gregory depends heavily on Philo of Alexandria's prior treatment (*De Vita Mosis* I-II) which is to say that understanding Moses as exemplar in the life of faith and in the life with (and in) God has both Jewish and Christian precedent.[11]

Dick (Winona Lake: Eisenbrauns, 1999).

9. See the previous note. Note also that many studies omit explicit and extended treatment of the Old Testament: for example, Michael J. Christensen and Jeffery A. Wittung, eds., *Partakers of the Divine Nature: The History and Development of Deification in the Christian Traditions* (Grand Rapids; Baker Academic, 2007); and Pedro Urbano López de Meneses, *Theosis: La Doctrina de la Divinización en las Tradiciones Cristianas: Fundamentos para una Teología Ecuménica de la Gracia* (Pamplona: Ediciones Universidad de Navarra, 2001); though studies like these often do have Scripture indexes demonstrating at least some engagement with Old Testament texts here and there.

10. For other possibilities, one may perhaps compare the notion of seeing God. See, for example, Mark S. Smith, "'Seeing God' in the Psalms: The Background to the Beatific Vision in the Hebrew Bible," *CBQ* 50 (1988) 171–83; and Brent A. Strawn, "To See/Not See God: A Biblical-Theological Cutting on the Knowability of God," *Koinonia* 7 (1995) 157–80. Another kind of approach to participation—one via literature and literary effect focused on the *piyyutim*—can be found in Laura S. Lieber, "The Rhetoric of Participation: Experiential Elements of Early Hebrew Liturgical Poetry," *JR* 90 (2010) 119–47. Note also, most recently, Tim Meadowcroft, "'One Like a Son of Man' in the Court of the Foreign King: Daniel 7 as Pointer to Wise Participation in the Divine Life," *JTI* 10 (2016) 245–63; and also, Tim Meadowcroft "Daniel's Visionary Participation in the Divine Life: Dynamics of Participation in Daniel 8–12," *JTI* 11 (2017) 217–37. On this latter option, see further below.

11. Perhaps one should consider 2 Cor 3:7—4:6 at this point, though what I (and Gregory!) say about certain details of Moses's life below offer at least a slightly different take than some of this text's more dismissive and supercessionist aspects. In any event, due to time and space constraints, as well as the focus of the North Park symposium on Christian notions of participation, I leave aside discussion of Philo. The notes in *Gregory of Nyssa: The Life of Moses*, edited by Abraham J. Malherbe and Everett Ferguson, CWS (New York: Paulist, 1978) are good on connecting the *LM* and Philo (and many other antecedent and contemporary works). Hereinafter the text is cited as *LM* followed by book and

In what follows, I begin with a brief overview of Moses's life via Gregory's filtering of that story (or sequence) and its contemplation as instruction for the progress of the soul.[12] Next, I revisit several key moments in Exodus that seem particularly important for an understanding of participation with God and assess them once more in that light. In these instances, I do not intend to try and go one better than the great Cappadocian Father, but seek, instead, to (re)assess these texts once more from the perspective of contemporary (i.e., *non*-pre-modern) study of the Old Testament, on the one hand, and with an eye on some of the more recent developments and controversies in the study of participation, on the other. I conclude the study by returning to the question of how a Trinitarian pre-understanding proves useful, and in the most foundational of ways, for a biblical approach to the issue of participation.

Gregory on the Life of Moses *in Nuce*

Gregory of Nyssa (ca. 335–395 CE) probably wrote the *Life of Moses* sometime in the early 390s.[13] It has two unequal parts (books), the first, shorter book taking up the challenge of presenting its reader with "some counsel concerning the perfect life" (*LM* I, 2),[14] especially the question of perfection in virtue,[15] which is discussed more generally before mention is finally made of Moses as "our example for life in our treatise" (*LM* I, 15).[16] Once Moses has been selected, Gregory proposes to "go through in outline his life as we have learned it from the divine Scriptures" (*LM* I, 15). This "history" (*historia*) comprises the balance of Book I (*LM* I, 16–77). After this "outline," Gregory indicates that "we shall seek out the spiritual understanding which corresponds to the history in order to obtain suggestions of virtue" (*LM* I, 15). This understanding (*dianoia*) or contemplation (*theōria*) is what is found in Book II

---

section number according to this edition. For Philo's treatment, see conveniently *The Works of Philo: New Updated Edition*, translated by C. D. Yonge (repr., Peabody, MA: Hendrickson, 1993) 459–517.

12. For Gregory's use of "sequence," see, for example, *LM* II, 39, 49–50, 136, 148, 150, 188; also Malherbe and Ferguson, *Gregory of Nyssa*, 13 (see also 164 n59) who think it "should not be pressed in an absolute sense. Moses's life is not made to fit a schematized progression of spiritual experience." For the use of *historia* and *theōria* in Gregory, see ibid., 7.

13. See Malherbe and Ferguson, *Gregory of Nyssa*, 1–2.

14. The reader is identified by name as a certain "Caesarius": see *LM* II, 319; Malherbe and Ferguson, *Gregory of Nyssa*, 2–3 and 143n13; and *Gregorii Nysseni: De Vita Moysis*, edited by Herbert Musurillo (Gregorii Nysseni Opera 7.1; edited by Werner Jaeger and Hermann, Langerbeck; Leiden: Brill, 1964) 1, 143, for other possibilities represented in the manuscript tradition.

15. "Concerning Perfection in Virtue" is, in fact, the treatise's alternative (or complete) title. See Malherbe and Ferguson, *Gregory of Nyssa*, 3; Musurillo, *De Vita Moysis*, 1.

16. In his *On Perfection (De perfectione)* Gregory instead proposes Paul as the example. See Malherbe and Ferguson, *Gregory of Nyssa*, 149 n4. For other passages that refer to Moses in Gregory's corpus, see ibid., 20–22 and 148 nn82–85.

(*LM* II, 1–318). "Through such understanding," Gregory concludes, "we may come to know the perfect life" for humankind (*LM* I, 15).

Gregory's treatment is rich and detailed, as is the history of scholarship surrounding it; this is not yet to mention its status as a classic of spirituality. For present purposes, then, the following three key points should be underscored.

1. First, the pursuit of true virtue is defined early on in the *LM* in terms of *participation*—and one that is ongoing, indeed never-ending:

> Certainly whoever pursues true virtue participates in nothing other than God, because he is himself absolute virtue. Since, then, those who know what is good by nature desire participation in it, and since this good has no limit, the participant's desire itself necessarily has no stopping place but stretches out with the limitless. (*LM* I, 7)

Perfection, therefore, is a matter of participation and is one that is ultimately processural or progressive: constantly able to be perfected further or susceptible to further growth in grace.[17] "For," Gregory writes, "the perfection of human nature consists perhaps in its very growth in goodness" (*LM* I, 10).[18]

2. In response to the problems that face humans seeking perfection in virtue, Gregory suggests turning to "Scripture as a counselor in this matter" (*LM* I, 11), particularly the memories of those distinguished individuals who might serve as beacon lights: "It may be for this very reason that the daily life of those sublime individuals is recorded in detail, that by imitating those earlier examples of right action those who follow them may conduct their lives to the good" (*LM* I, 13). *Imitation*, generally, and *imitation of Scriptural examples*, specifically, is the way forward, therefore, though Gregory immediately admits of a problem someone might raise—a problem that is largely due to a flat-footed (and overly literal?)[19] understanding of such imitation:

---

17. Phil 3:13 is in many ways the key text for the treatise. See *LM* I, 5; II, 239; also Malherbe and Ferguson, *Gregory of Nyssa*, 12–13, 146 n61, 149 n11, 186 n322. Note also *LM* II, 224–27, on how it is the nature of the soul to move "upward, soaring from below up to the heights" (*LM* II, 224); and *LM* II, 191 on how the blue color of the priestly vestments may signify the sky and air, so that "we should be close to what rises upwards and is light and airy, in order that when we hear the last trumpet we may be found weightless and light in responding to the voice of the One who calls." See also Malherbe and Ferguson, *Gregory of Nyssa*, 16: "Bodies, once having received an initial thrust downward, continue in that direction, whereas the soul, incorporeal and airy, unless hindered rises upward toward God."

18. This makes perfection profoundly paradoxical: "undoubtedly impossible to attain…since… perfection is not marked off by limits" and yet commanded by the Lord (Gregory cites Matt 5:48) so that "we should show great diligence not to fall away from the perfection which is attainable, but to acquire as much as is possible" (*LM* I, 8–10).

19. In the contemporary setting discussed in passing above, it seems better to deem this a kind of "historicizing" position. Insofar as such an approach reads the text wrongly (misinterpreting, say, a poetic figure for an historical report) it is "literal(izing)" in the worst sense of the term, for which see

> Some one will say, "How shall I imitate them, since I am not a Chaldaean as I remember Abraham was, nor was I nourished by the daughter of the Egyptian as Scripture teaches about Moses, and in general I do not have in these matters anything in my life corresponding to anyone of the ancients? How shall I place myself in the same rank with one of them, when I do not know how to imitate anyone so far removed from me by the circumstances of his life?" (*LM* I, 14)

Gregory responds by pointing out that not everything in Scripture is to be imitated, especially in so wooden a fashion:

> To him we reply that we do not consider being a Chaldean a virtue or a vice, nor is anyone exiled from the life of virtue by living in Egypt or spending his life in Babylon, nor again has God been known to the esteemed individuals in Judaea only, nor is Zion, as people commonly think, the divine habitation. We need some subtlety of understanding and keenness of vision to discern from the history how, by removing ourselves from such Chaldaeans and Egyptians and by escaping from such a Babylonian captivity, we shall embark on the blessed life. (*LM* I, 14)

This strategy of "subtlety of understanding" and "keenness of vision" is then immediately put to work by lifting up Moses as "our example for life" (*LM* I, 15).

3. To participate in God and make progress in perfection, therefore, one must imitate Scriptural examples and, in this treatise, the example par excellence is Moses. The final point that should be made before moving on is that Gregory's reading of Moses's life with reference to virtue, participation in God, progress in perfection, and so forth takes place on at least two levels:

- The first level is represented by *the numerous comments found throughout the work that relate specific details from Moses's life to the life of faith*. There are too many of these to list here, but, regardless, as the second point above indicates, the whole idea of using Moses as an exemplar is precisely to identify imitable elements for those who would also choose to progress in virtue as he did. This first level is thus quite obvious and explicit.

Brent A. Strawn, "Focus on Jonah: Jonah and Genre," Oxford Biblical Studies Online (https://global. oup.com/obso/focus/focus_on_jonah/; accessed 9/12/17) and the various uses in the *Oxford English Dictionary* cited there, especially the adjective "literal-minded": "having a literal mind; characteristic of one who takes a matter-of-fact or unimaginative view of things. Hence *literal-mindedness*." For Gregory the kind of "literal(izing)" reading that is best avoided would seem to pertain not only to specific textual details (for example, being a Chaldean) but to the entirety of Scripture and its macrogenre. How does one read it rightly? The answer is in no small measure to read it as a collection of models to imitate in the spiritual life toward perfection in virtue—a far cry indeed from excessively historicizing/literalizing approaches. Note also Anthony Briggman, "Literary and Rhetorical Theory in Irenaeus, Part 2," *VC* 70 (2016) 31–50, esp. 33–39, for the interest among early church writers for type and antitype to correspond to each other in reasonable fashion.

- The second level is more implicit but equally as obvious given the nature, purpose, and execution of the work—it is simply this: that Gregory's recommendation to imitate Moses's life depends on *the prior participation of his reader(s) with the story of that life*. It is, indeed, this foundational participation with the Scriptural text that facilitates an imitation of Moses, which, in turn, permits participation with God. The participation with Scripture is also what supercharges the biblical text with meaning such that its many details—virtually its every detail—has meaning *beyond* what Gregory calls "the bare history of the man." In point of fact, the bare history of Moses is not worth dwelling on extensively (*LM* I, 21).[20]

Gregory's words from the conclusion of his work (*LM* II, 319–321) nicely capture the three points highlighted above:

> These things concerning the perfection of the virtuous life . . . we have briefly written . . . tracing in outline like a pattern of beauty the life of the great Moses so that each one of us might copy the image of the beauty which has been shown to us by imitating his way of life . . . Since the goal of the virtuous way of life was the very thing we have been seeking, and this goal has been found in what we have said, it is time for you, noble friend, to look to that example and, by transferring to your own life what is contemplated through spiritual interpretation of the things spoken literally, to be known by God and to become his friend. This is true perfection . . . This, as I have said, is the perfection of life. (*LM* II, 319–320)

The Life of Moses: Revisiting Moments in (Non-)Participation

With this brief overview of Gregory's *Life of Moses* in place, and with the Cappadocian Father as inspiration at least, if not guide (at points), we may now re-examine a few of the most salient moments in the life of Moses for an understanding of participation with God therein. Following Gregory's focus on the primary human protagonist in the Pentateuch,[21] we may begin with Moses's formal introduction to God in the call narrative of Exodus 3, but, before doing so, two points should be made. First, Moses is introduced in the Torah, and in significant ways, *before* Exodus 3. It is possible in hindsight to "find" or somehow retroject Moses's post-call life into

20. Dwelling on it at least in part, however, is the work of Book I. Here is not the place to comment on exactly how closely Book I and Book II are correlated. It is obvious that Book II goes into far greater detail than Book I, though Book I, too, is not entirely without comments that that could fit the contemplation found in Book II (see, e.g., *LM* I, 46–47). Gregory admits, at the conclusion of Book I, that he has "of necessity...amplified the account as to bring out its intention" (*LM* I, 77).

21. For an excellent overview of the importance of Moses in the Torah, but especially in Deuteronomy, see Patrick D. Miller, "'Moses My Servant': The Deuteronomic Portrait of Moses," in *A Song of Power and the Power of Song: Essays on the Book of Deuteronomy*, edited by Duane L. Christensen, SBTS 3 (Winona Lake: Eisenbrauns, 1993 [orig. 1987]) 301–12.

his pre-call life such that the latter is seen as providentially guided and protected, even vocationally anticipated, and in various ways—though such anticipations are probably best seen as by definition incomplete and premature.[22] Second, and moving beyond Moses himself, the narrative of Exodus prior to chapter 3 suggests a good bit of *non*-participation with God. God may very well be lurking behind the prosperity of Israel in the opening verses of Exodus 1, especially given the obvious connections of these verses with the opening of Genesis,[23] but God is mostly absent during the struggles of Exodus 1–2 (with the notable exception of 1:21) and, indeed, according to the internal biblical chronology, God is largely out of touch for 430 years (12:40). God's first major appearance is found in 2:23–25, where God, as it were, "wakes up" to the people's plight (see Pss 35:23; 44:23; 59:4; 80:2). The newly awakened divine attention is motivated by two things: (i) Israel's suffering and (ii) God's remembrance of the covenant with Israel's ancestors.[24] The attention God pays in this passage is extensive and intimate, with the verbs for God corresponding (four-to-four) to the words used to describe Israel's pain (*šm□ zkr, r□h, yd□,* and *□nh, z□q, šw□h, n□qh,* respectively). Significantly, what transpires in 2:23–25 leads directly into the next chapter and what takes place there in what appears to be a close, even causal relationship (note especially the repetitions between 2:23–25 and 3:7–9). Before 2:23–25 (and what follows thereafter) however, one may worry about a noticeable *lack* of participation and that at least some of that absence is on the part of the divine (again excepting 1:21). Perhaps this second point suggests that participation can be frustrated or complicated by the divine side of the equation as much as by the human side: failure to participate in God, in other words, isn't solely a problem with human will or desire; it would seem that such failure can originate from the divine (non-)participant as well.[25] That is a sobering observation, chastening any overly

22. See, for example, Dennis T. Olson, "Violence for the Sake of Social Justice? Narrative, Ethics and Indeterminacy in Moses's Slaying of the Egyptian (Exodus 2:11–15)," in *The Meanings We Chose: Hermeneutical Ethics, Indeterminacy and the Conflict of Interpretations*, edited by Charles H. Cosgrove, JSOTSup 511 (London: T. & T. Clark, 2004) 138–48.

23. Particularly the use of the verbs "to be fruitful" (*prh*), "to be prolific" (*šrṣ*), and "to multiply" (*□bm*) with the result being that "the land was filled" (*ml□ + □ereṣ*) with the Israelites in Exod 1:7. Note the presence of these key terms also in Gen 1:22, 28; 9:1, 7.

24. Note the debate on this point between John J. Collins, "The Exodus and Biblical Theology," *BTB* 25 (1995) 152–60; and Jon D. Levenson, "The Exodus and Biblical Theology: A Rejoinder to John J. Collins," *BTB* 26 (1996) 4–10.

25. Note, mostly by way of contrast, Gregory's treatment of the hardening of Pharaoh's heart in *LM* II, 73–88, where he goes to great lengths to see that situation as the result of free will, which "through its inclination to evil does not receive the word which softens resistance" (*LM* II, 76). For more on "the place of the freedom of human choice in Gregory's thought," which "is fundamental to the *Life of Moses*," see Malherbe and Ferguson, *Gregory of Nyssa*, 16–17. It should be observed in this general connection that, according to Gregory, there are also *poor* examples to be found in Scripture that one might imitate to their detriment, the Egyptians being one such instance (*LM* II, 83).

confident or triumphalistic understanding of divine participation—namely, that it is always available to the human participant or always desired by God.[26] But, be that as it may, it must also be quickly asserted that all that follows 2:23–25 is predicated on God's extensive and intense participation with Israel's pain (šmᵡ, rᵡh, ydᵡ) and with Israel's ancestors (captured via the weighty syntagm *wayyizkōr . . . běrîtô*, "he remembered his covenant") precisely in the experience of Israel's grief and suffering.

The Call of Moses

The call of Moses in Exodus 3:1–4:17 is remarkable for many reasons, but of necessity our discussion should focus on what is most pertinent to the notion of participation (for this unit, see *LM* II, 19–41). The repetition of key verbs of 2:23–25 in 3:7–9 has already been noted above (viz., šmᵡ, rᵡh, and ydᵡ). Indeed, there is so much repetition that readers may be forgiven if they occasionally miss three significant differences that are present in 3:1–12 vis-à-vis 2:23–25. The first is that 2:23–25 was third person narration *about God*, but in 3:7–9, *God speaks directly* in first person discourse. The narrator is validated, therefore, regarding what was said in 2:23–25, and so the narrator may be trusted: God does indeed do the things the narrator had previously claimed about God.[27] The second difference is that beyond *the verbs of attention* found in 2:23–25, which are repeated in 3:7–9, God now adds *a decisive (compound) verb of action*:

> I have seen . . . heard . . . know (3:7; cf. 2:23–25) → I have come down to deliver. (3:8a)

This verbal act of deliverance is instantly glossed by another: "to bring them up," which is immediately described as an action that leads "out of Egypt" and "into a good and spacious land" (3:8b). *To come down* in order *to deliver* and *to bring up from* and/in order *(to bring) into* appears to comprise yet another set of four key terms like the twinned set found earlier in 2:23–25:

> To groan—to cry out—cry for help—moan (ᵡnḥ, zᵡq, šwᵡh, nᵡqh)
>
> To listen—to remember—to see—to know (šmᵡ, zkr, rᵡh, ydᵡ)

---

26. See Gregory's sober reflections in *LM* II, 279, where he notes that sometimes "individuals punish the passion of desire by living a disciplined life," but then "thrust themselves into the priesthood, and with human zeal and selfish ambition…arrogate to themselves God's ministry."

27. Of course, it goes without saying that the narrator is also responsible for the discourse in chapter 3. For reliable narrators, see, inter alia, Wayne C. Booth, *The Rhetoric of Fiction*, 2nd ed. (Chicago: University of Chicago Press, 1983) esp. 211–40. Note also Paul J. Kissling, *Reliable Characters in the Primary History: Profiles of Moses, Joshua, Elijah, and Elisha*, JSOTSup 224 (Sheffield: Sheffield Academic, 1996).

To come down—to deliver—to bring up from—(to bring) into (*yrd, nṣl, ⊠h mn*, [⊠*h*] ⊠)

though the most recent quartet advances the action considerably, providing us with information that the narrator either did not know in chapter 2 or just did not report.[28]

The third and most important difference is that *God's* verbal actions that were noted in 2:23–25 and then repeated and advanced in 3:7–9 are now intimately and immediately conjoined with another subject, *Moses*: "So, therefore, go: I will send *you . . .*" (v. 10).

The sequencing of chapter 2, especially 2:23–25, with chapter 3—at a larger level—and the sequencing of 3:7–8 and 3:10[29]—at the more immediate level—suggests that God has heard Israel's "prayer"[30] (reinforced by the repetition in 3:9 of "seen" and "heard") and is now answering that prayer *by, through, and with Moses*. This is remarkable and mustn't be passed over too quickly without considerable reflection: God answers Israel's prayer by sending, not a divine messenger (at least not a super-natural one) but a human being to Pharaoh. A divine-human synergy is initiated here in a way unlike anything that has come before in the Old Testament. To be sure, Moses's call sets a pattern for other call narratives,[31] but the synergistic relationship manifested in the call of Moses is stunning, not only because it is first, but because it is so massive in scale: it flies in the face of the greatest entities in the narrative world (Pharaoh, Israel, Egypt) and the most profound of human issues (suffering, oppression, slavery). Perhaps only the call of Mary in Luke 1 can be compared in terms of sheer scale and import.[32]

Nothing short of divine participation is found in Moses's call, therefore: participation in God—participation in God's own verbs of attention and action, and thus participation in the very mission of God in the world, which is, via those selfsame

28. See previous note.

29. See n12 above on Gregory's use of the (literary) sequence.

30. Israel's articulation in 2:23–24 is not explicitly directed at God but it need not be so to nevertheless qualify as prayer, especially since God eventually attends to it (cf. Gen 4:10). Furthermore, at least one of the key terms used there, z⊠q (and its by-form ṣ⊠q) is frequently used in prayer. See Patrick D. Miller, *They Cried to the Lord: The Form and Theology of Biblical Prayer* (Minneapolis: Fortress, 1994) 44–46.

31. The classic study remains that of Habel, "The Form and Significance of the Call Narratives," *ZAW* 77 (1965) 297–323.

32. See Brent A. Strawn, "Luke 1:26–38," in *The Lectionary Commentary: Theological Exegesis for Sunday's Texts, The Third Readings: The Gospels*, edited by Roger E. Van Harn (Grand Rapids: Eerdmans, 2001) 286–90. To be sure, Jeremiah's call to be a prophet to the nations is also quite expansive in scope (Jer 1:4–10). Beyond the texts that are formally related to Moses's call narrative, the figures of Abraham and Paul would also loom large in considering divine-human synergy in the Bible.

verbs, traced to God's own being.[33] This participation is not beatific, however, but instead profoundly perilous, a fact that is clearly not lost on Moses, who immediately protests that he is not up to the job (v. 11).

Moses's concerns vis-à-vis his calling drive the rest of the account, but it is v. 10's call to participate in God's missional activity that should most arrest our attention and summon our deepest reflection. I know of no better formulation of what is at stake here than that of Walter Brueggemann:

> Verse 10 makes a radical and decisive break, which must have stunned Moses when he heard it, and must have stunned Israel each time it was reiterated. What had been all pious promise now becomes rigorous demand: "Come." *In one brief utterance, the grand intention of God has become a specific human responsibility, human obligation, and human vocation.*[34]

Not only is this so, *no other missional strategy is considered or deemed plausible*—not, at least, from what is given to us in the text of Exodus. *This* way, and *only* this way—through divine-human participation or synergy—is how God's most foundational salvific act in the Old Testament, if not the entire Christian Bible, will, and indeed *must*, take place.[35]

Now perhaps the human participant need not have been Moses. Despite his pre-call "credentials," and even if we speculate that Moses might have somehow escaped his task, the textual logic implies that someone else would have had to be found to replace him. Indeed, the closest we get to proving this hypothesis true is when, as a last ditch effort, Moses begs God, "O my Lord, please send someone else" (4:13; NRSV). Note: *someone else*; not: "Do it *yourself*, Lord!"[36] Furthermore, God's (angry)

---

33. Perhaps Gross would deem this kind of connection "external" (*Divinization of the Christian*, 66) and, in Glazov's terms, it seems to relate to what he calls the divine "energies" and thus not divine essence or being ("Theōsis, Judaism, and Old Testament Anthropology," 16–31) but I am not sure the biblical texts, at least the Old Testament ones, will always permit a hard and fast division between divine ontology and economy. For the place of participation in creating missional individuals, see Jacobus (Kobus) Kok and John Anthony Dunne, "Participation in Christ and Missional Dynamics in Galatians," in *Participation, Justification, and Conversion: Eastern Orthodox Interpretation of Paul and the Debate between "Old and New Perspectives on Paul,"* edited by Athanasios Despotis, WUNT 2.442 (Tübingen: Mohr Siebeck, 2017) 59–85.

34. Walter Brueggemann, "The Book of Exodus: Introduction, Commentary, and Reflections," in *NIB* 1:677–981, here 713 (emphasis added). Brueggemann's use of "come" reflects the NRSV. The translation offered earlier, "So, therefore, go: I will send you" is my own. The key verb is *lĕkāh* (an imperative of *hlk*) and either translation, "come" or "go," works in English translation, though "go" may underscore the missional aspect more: Moses is not to come to or toward God but rather to go to Pharaoh. See the CEB: "So get going. I'm sending you to Pharaoh . . ."

35. For the exodus as the fundamental salvific act in Scripture, see, inter alia, Brent A. Strawn, "Exodus," in *The New Interpreter's Bible One Volume Commentary*, edited by Beverly Roberts Gaventa and David L. Petersen et al. (Nashville: Abingdon, 2010) 33–34.

36. The Hebrew construction is admittedly somewhat vague here and perhaps not as clear with

response to this final request from Moses is to provide Moses with a companion, Aaron. Aaron is added to the leadership team—Moses is no longer alone (3:12a notwithstanding!)—but the addition is precisely of "an Aaron": another person, that is, not a divine or semi-divine partner (contrast, for example, the angel's role in the story of Balaam in Numbers 22). Now to be sure, the Exodus narrative will go on to speak of additional entities that play key roles in what happens. Several are already mentioned in Exod 3:1–4:17: an angelic messenger (3:2) and various divine signs (3:12b, 4:5, 8, 9), especially those done with "the staff of God" (4:2–6, 20). Others that will come into the narrative include another (?) angel or angels (14:19; 23:20, 23; 32:34; 33:2; see 3:2; Ps 78:49) and the pillar(s) of fire and cloud (Exod 13:21–22; 14:19, 24; 33:9–10).[37] But it does not seem to be going too far to say that these other things are, at best, bit players serving specific and limited roles. So much of what happens next, therefore, is specifically Moses's (and Aaron's) "work."[38] This leads directly into the next section on agency in Exodus writ large, but before moving to that material four important points from Exod 3:1–4:17 should be underscored:

1. The first, and most obvious, is that the divine-human participation that is at work in the life of Moses, which begins at the burning bush, comes *at the initiative of God*. This may be the narrative counterpart to the non-participation of God in Exodus 1–2 noted earlier. That is, just as God can *prohibit, frustrate, or be absent from* participation, God is also the one who *inaugurates, permits, and facilitates* participation.

2. The second point concerns the divine name that is given to Moses in 3:14: "I am who I am" (NRSV). Much has been written about the origin and significance of this name that needn't be rehearsed here. For present purposes, the most important observation is that God's "I am" in 3:14 echoes God's "I am" in 3:12. There, in 3:12, in response to Moses's first objection that he was not up to the job for which God had commissioned him (but who is?)—"Who am I that I should go to Pharaoh . . . ?"

---

regard to the "someone else" as the NRSV would make it seem. See William H. C. Propp, *Exodus 1–18: A New Translation with Introduction and Commentary*, AB 2 (New York: Doubleday, 1999) 212–13 for discussion. Indeed, it is perhaps possible that *šĕlaḥ-nā⊠bĕyad-tišlāḥ* ("send by the hand you will send") might be construed as something close to "doing it yourself," though one could imagine clearer constructions. Whatever the case, the next verse makes it unmistakable that, whatever the precise sense of Moses's statement, it was a cause of anger to God who does not, in fact, "do it himself" but simply adds another human to the mix.

37. These have their own complexities regarding symbiosis and/or synergy, as reflected in 14:19 (angel) and 14:24; 33:9 (YHWH). See more generally on the issue Benjamin D. Sommer, *The Bodies of God and the World of Ancient Israel* (Cambridge: Cambridge University Press, 2009).

38. See Brueggemann, "The Book of Exodus," 713: "It is Moses (not God) who will 'bring out' (*yāṣā⊠*) 'my people.' It is Moses who acts in God's place to save God's people." But see further below on the thoroughly intermixed nature of divine-human synergy in Exodus. Brueggemann's formulation may favor Moses overmuch.

(3:11)—YHWH speaks not to *who Moses is*, but addresses *Who is with Moses*. "I will be with you" (*ehyeh ʿimmāk*; 3:12a) is the divine reply. Now, in response to a second objection from Moses (potential Israelite disbelief over who sent him) God's name is given in this enigmatic, elusive, and rather unclear form: "I am who I am" (*ehyeh ʾišer ʾehyeh*; 3:14). God's name, it seems, is given and yet not given, offered and yet held back by means of this odd verbal construction—the precise meaning and nuance of which is ambiguous, perhaps by design. And yet, whatever confusions may remain, one thing is quite clear about this God "who is": precisely because of the earlier text in 3:12, this God is a God who is "with Moses." This is to say that God may be *ehyeh ʾišer ʾehyeh*, "I am who I am" or "I will be who I will be" (inter alia) but one of those things God is or will be is precisely *ehyeh ʿimmāk*, "I am with you." God will not (cannot?) answer Israel's prayer without Moses, but neither must Moses answer that prayer alone. Instead, divine-human synergy is the order of the day and in equal part(icipation)s, or so it would seem.

3. Third, it must be observed that God's call for participation in the divine mission can be resisted, though perhaps not ultimately: Moses's string of objections proves unsuccessful and the same can be said for other call narratives in Scripture. That would be the fourth point developed further below: that God can, and frequently does, overcome human resistance to the invitation to participation.[39] But this third point is simply to underscore what seems implicit in the English word "participation"—namely, that participation is not a given but volitional.[40] One cannot be forced to participate but, rather is invited to do so, and that invitation can be rejected, or at least delayed. This is to say that the invitation to participate is *limitable*.[41] Further invitations may be necessary; additional motivations and reasons might need to be

39. God can also overcome *divine* resistance to participation, as is evidenced in 2:23–25 and its relationship to 3:1–12. The sequencing of these two units, as well as the specific content, however, suggests that such overcoming is in no small way the result or work of human beings: their grief, suffering, and cries for help, as well as their history of faithful forebears. This is just another instance of divine-human synergy (or perhaps symbiosis in this case) and it anticipates not only the point made here but also the key moments of Mosaic intercession in the Pentateuch (especially surrounding the golden calf debacle).

40. Despite the formulation above which stresses the *will*, I think the point actually negotiates the dichotomy found in more recent debates on divine-human participation in Martin Luther, which has set ontology against volition. It may be that volitional obedience need not be entirely contrasted with ontological participation. See Carl E. Braaten and Robert W. Jenson's remarks in *Union with Christ: The New Finnish Interpretation of Luther*, edited by Carl E. Braaten and Robert W. Jenson (Grand Rapids: Eerdmans, 1998) viii–ix. See n25 above for the importance of free will in Gregory's *Life of Moses*.

41. See Everett Ferguson, "God's Infinity and Man's Mutability: Perpetual Progress according to Gregory of Nyssa," *Greek Orthodox Theological Review* 18 (1973) 59–78 (68): One "receives a knowledge of God and participates in his goodness 'according to his capacity.' [Humans'] knowledge of God is limited by [their] capacity, not by the transcendent object."

provided. Participation, according to Exod 3:1–4:17, is thus quite interactive if not downright dialogical. If, per Gregory, participation is a matter of following God's leading (which is what he thinks it means "to see God's back"; *LM* II, 252) it is also, contra Gregory, the case that God apparently turns around, at least on occasion, to participate in dialogue and discussion—even face to face (see Exod 33:11; contrast *LM* II, 253). Still further, taking the life of Moses as a paradigmatic pattern for the human soul and its progress (or lack thereof), perhaps it is not going too far to say that the default position—our first response as humans—is to *resist* God's call to participate in the divine mission which is rooted in the very life of God.

4. The fourth point, already indicated above, is that Moses's resistance is overcome in Exod 3:1—4:17. In the end, if he does not happily assent, he at least succumbs to God's call to be a participatory agent in the *missio Dei*. Other individuals who are called in the pattern of Moses do the same, though some texts in Jeremiah and Ezekiel, especially, suggest that this kind of assenting or succumbing is not always smooth, nor does it signal an end of the dialogue or an absence of problems for the divine-human synergy moving forward.[42] Perhaps those texts should make us re-read Moses's participation similarly: that it was not all smooth-sailing, after all;[43] if so, it would be true, not only that participation can be *resisted*, but that it can be *varied* in its experience and "success" (efficacy) as well. Even so, the life of Moses writ large, now in the canon and read in Gregory's way suggests that even resistance is brought into the life of faith and obedience via the dialogics of call and response.[44] It is worth noting, however, that for his part Gregory does not mention Moses's resistance or objections to God's call. Does he deem such negativity outside the pale of participation altogether; only a hindrance to the soul's perfection in virtue—a regression as it were?[45]

---

42. I am thinking especially of Jeremiah's "confessions," which reveal a tumultuous relationship between the prophet and God (see, for example, Jer 15:15–18). Similarly, Ezek 3:14b may suggest that the prophet was bitter and angry about having to perform the prophetic task that lay ahead of him.

43. See Propp, *Exodus 1–18*, 213, for the possibility that Moses's response in 4:13 "arguably betrays sullenness."

44. Perhaps the same should be said of Moses's "radical and dangerous" prayers/protests (see Walter Brueggemann, *Old Testament Theology: Essays in Structure, Theme, and Text*, edited by Patrick D. Miller [Minneapolis: Fortress, 1992], 30): these, too, are part of his life and his example for other souls on the journey.

45. See *LM* I, 21, which is where Moses's objections would fit in the *historia* account, but which is exactly where Gregory encourages the reader to "not dwell extensively on the bare history of the man" (cited more fully above). Similarly, the contemplation section in Book II also passes over the objections without comment (*LM* II, 19–41). Gregory only treats the book of Numbers briefly and so does not discuss the crucial (but highly ambiguous) moment of Mosaic disobedience in Num 20.

Agency in Exodus: Thoroughly (Inter-)Mixed

The fact that God's deliverance of Israel from Egypt necessarily involves Moses (and Aaron) in what is a profound instance of divine-human synergy leads one to consider agency in Exodus more generally. This is a large topic and so it suffices to depend on a recent essay on the matter by Terence Fretheim.[46]

"A close study of the book of Exodus," begins Fretheim, "generates complex theological reflections regarding issues of agency."[47] His own analysis leads him to claim that "God works in both history and creation in and through agents. God does work directly, but *always* through means/agents, ranging from human words and deeds (both within and without Israel) to nonhuman activities such as natural events."[48] Indeed, at one point in his essay, Fretheim goes so far as to state: "One might ask whether God *ever* acts . . . unilaterally."[49] In his opinion, divine action via human agents—what I have referred to as divine-human synergy above—is the order of the day. Questions remain, however. So, while "one must not diminish the distinction between God and God's agents, discount the real power of the agent (a divine gift) or claim that God acted alone," it is equally the case that "just how God is involved in this activity cannot be fully factored out."[50]

The first part of that statement leads Fretheim to distinguish his reading from others that differ from his own—to greater or lesser degrees.[51] He ultimately commends the "major emphases in Brueggemann's interpretation," and proceeds to "move through key texts that both support and expand upon such an understanding of [divine-human synergistic] agency in Exodus."[52] He specifically discusses Exodus 1–2; 3:1–7:7; 7:8–12:51; 13:1–15:21; 15:22–18:27; and 32:1–34:35,[53] before concluding his study by stating that "God *always* uses agents in God's working in Israel and the larger world."[54] He adds that "God does not perfect human beings (or other creatures) with all their foibles and flaws, before deciding to work in and through

46. Terence E. Fretheim, "Issues of Agency in Exodus," in *The Book of Exodus: Composition, Reception, and Interpretation*, edited by Thomas B. Dozeman, Craig A. Evans, and Joel N Lohr, VTSup 164 (Leiden: Brill, 2014) 591–609.

47. Ibid., 591.

48. Ibid.

49. Ibid., 599n33.

50. Ibid., 592.

51. See ibid., 592–95.

52. Ibid., 595 (my addition). These emphases in Brueggemann's work are very much like the ones cited above; indeed, Fretheim quotes the same passage from Brueggemann on Exod 3:10 that I provided earlier (see at n34 above; Fretheim, "Issues of Agency in Exodus," 597–98n28).

53. One has to look to Fretheim's earlier commentary for treatment of Exodus 19–31, 35–40. See Terence E. Fretheim, *Exodus,* Interpretation (Louisville: John Knox, 1991).

54. Fretheim, "Issues of Agency in Exodus," 606.

them . . . Hence, such work by the agents will always have mixed results, and will be less positive than what would have happened had God chosen to act alone."[55]

Fretheim is obviously concerned with matters other than the ones relating to participation that are the focus of the present essay, but his analysis is useful nevertheless. It affirms, first, that the kind of synergy identified earlier is not an idiosyncratic interpretation but one also noticed by other interpreters and, more importantly, an extensive and repeated motif in Exodus. And not only there. Inspired by Gregory who does not stop at the book of Exodus but continues on into Numbers to discuss a few key points in the narrative there (particularly the spy story and the account of Balaam; see Numbers 13–14, 22–24; cf. *LM* II, 264–68, 291–304), I would note that the "confusion of properties" that is at work in YHWH and YHWH's messenger seems to also be at work at certain moments with Moses. One particularly curious instance of this in Exodus is considered in the next section. But, beyond Exodus, one might note other examples like the ambiguity in the Hebrew text of Deut 1:4 which states "this was after he had defeated [*hakkōtô*] King Sihon . . . and King Og." Syntactically, the subject of this verb could be either YHWH or Moses. The nearest antecedent is Moses but the last mentioned verbal subject is God: so who, exactly, did the smiting? Perhaps Deut 2:24, 31; 3:2–3; and especially 31:4 would clinch the matter for God, not Moses (cf. also Pss 135:11; 136:19–20) and if *only one* agent can take the credit, it is likely that the deity is the one in view. But Fretheim's work would query any hard and fast division in this regard: "God *always* uses agents. . . ," he would assert. And, in this vein, it is worth noting that Moses claims the victory for the Israelites (see 3:3–4; 29:7) or with them (4:46) in a few passages in Deuteronomy. All of this is to say that Deut 1:4, also, may showcase the divine-human synergy between Moses and God, and perhaps still more: that their work can be "interconfused." The very last chapter of the last book in the Torah contains a passage that is very much apropos on this point:

> No prophet like Moses has yet emerged
> —the LORD knew him face to face!—
> with regard to all the signs and wonders that the LORD sent Moses to do in the land of Egypt
> —to Pharaoh, to all his servants, and to his entire land—
> and with regard to all the great power and all the awesome deeds that Moses did before the eyes of all Israel. (Deut 34:10–12; my translation)

Here too the syntax is somewhat complicated, with the lineated version offered here clarifying that with only partial success. The most important point, regardless,

---

55. Ibid.

is that language that is usually used elsewhere of God (e.g., "great power," "awesome deeds," and actions performed "before the eyes" of others) is here attributed, not to YHWH first and foremost, but to the agency of Moses. One might counter that Moses's actions here are dependent on God's primary verb of sending (*šlḥ*) but that does not refute the fact that the passage ascribes to Moses language that is typically reserved for God. If both the beginning and ending of Deuteronomy "ambiguate" the work of God and Moses—what belongs to whom?[56]—this is just further proof of Fretheim's point about agency in Exodus. But it is also, for our purposes, additional evidence that speaks to the question of participation in the divine—one that extends so far that the two subjects are intertwined, intermixed, at times even confused.[57]

Moses's Face and Two Bodies

A text like Deut 34 can be confusing, syntactically no less than theologically, but the kind of synergism, replete with a good bit of unresolved if not unresolvable ambiguity, that is especially pronounced at the beginning and end of Deuteronomy is also traceable in Exodus. An example might be the event at the Re(e)d Sea in Exod 14–15, where we encounter different perspectives on what, exactly, took place there. It has been the special burden of historical critics to worry about the "exactly" part, with much of the results unfortunately and finally atomizing—succeeding by attributing this perspective to one tradition/source, and that perspective to another tradition/source, mostly due to a priori assumptions that traditions/sources within themselves must somehow be logical or consistent, or, even better (!) logically consistent. In my judgment, such filleting never satisfactorily answers the problem of the current, overfull text as it now stands. Exodus as it now stands, furthermore—however multilayered it may be, and no doubt is—does not require or even invite such textual dissection. Instead, Exod 14–15, no less than Deut 1 or 34, stubbornly presents a full-orbed if confusing synergistic picture in which God and Moses, Moses with God, God through Moses, and perhaps still other iterations are responsible for the miracle at the sea.

---

56. See Fretheim, "Issues of Agency in Exodus," 607–8: "Both God and agents have crucial roles to play, and their spheres of activity are interrelated in terms of function and effect. God is not only independent and the agents involved only dependent." Instead, Fretheim argues for a profound God-world relationality, one that inevitably involves a divine vulnerability. For these themes elsewhere in Fretheim's work, see his *The Suffering of God: An Old Testament Perspective*, OBT (Philadelphia: Fortress, 1984) and *God and World in the Old Testament: A Relational Theology of Creation* (Nashville: Abingdon, 2005).

57. Many other passages could be noted in this regard. So, for example, in Num 12, the complaint against Moses eventuates in a divine curse, implying the closest of connections between God and "my servant Moses" (Num 12:8).

In my judgment, another profound example of the comingling of the divine and human agents, and thus their participation, one with the other, may be found in the short account about the shining of Moses's face in Exod 34:

> Moses came down from Mount Sinai. As he came down from the mountain with the two covenant tablets in his hand, Moses didn't realize that the skin of his face shone brightly because he had been talking with God. When Aaron and all the Israelites saw the skin of Moses's face shining brightly, they were afraid to come near him. But Moses called them closer. So Aaron and all the leaders of the community came back to him, and Moses spoke with them. After that, all the Israelites came near as well, and Moses commanded them everything that the LORD had spoken with him on Mount Sinai. When Moses finished speaking with them, he put a veil over his face. Whenever Moses went into the LORD's presence to speak with him, Moses would take the veil off until he came out again. When Moses came out and told the Israelites what he had been commanded, the Israelites would see that the skin of Moses's face was shining brightly. So Moses would put the veil on his face again until the next time he went in to speak with the LORD. (Exod 34:29–35, CEB)

The key interpretive question concerns the verb translated in the CEB as "to shine brightly."[58] In Hebrew, this verb (*qrn*) is apparently a denominative from the noun *qeren*, which means "horn." Several of the ancient versions (especially the LXX, which uses *doxazō*, "to glorify"; cf. the Peshitta and Targum Pseudo-Jonathan, Targum Neofiti, and Targum Onqelos) also understand the sense of the verb to be the shining that is reflected in CEB and so many other modern translations (e.g., NRSV, NJPS). The Vulgate, however, has *cornuta esset facies sua*, "his face was horned"—an image made most famous, perhaps, in Michaelangelo's sculpture *Moses* in the church of San Pietro in Vincoli in Rome, but common in many depictions of Moses in religious art.

While Moses's horns in artistic renderings may strike contemporary viewers as a bit devilish, the Latin translation of the Hebrew text deserves consideration, the venerable "shining" approach notwithstanding. This is not only due to the relationship between the verb *qrn* and the noun *qeren* already noted, but also due to the widely known fact that in ancient Near Eastern art divinities were often portrayed with horns.[59] Indeed, various anthropomorphic figures, especially in series or larger

58. See the studies by William H. C. Propp, "The Skin of Moses's Face—Transfigured or Disfigured?" *CBQ* 49 (1987) 375–86 (popularized in "Did Moses Have Horns?" *BR* 4/1 [1988] 30–37, 44); and also *Exodus 19–40: A New Translation with Introduction and Commentary* (AB 2A; New York: Doubleday, 2006) 620–23. Propp's own suggestion is that Moses's face became dry or hard in some fashion such that it was disfigured, an "example of a symbolic wound incurred during a rite of passage" (623). While novel, I do not find this option compelling, mostly given the overall sense and content of the unit (despite Propp's correct attention to the text's emphasis on "skin").

59 Pictures may be found in *ANEP.*

tableaus, are often *only* identifiable as deities by means of horns, with the equation usually running as follows: the more horns present, the higher up the god in question is in terms of power or pantheon structure. Gary Rendsburg has noted a similar artistic detail in depictions of the pharaoh in Dynasties 18–19 (ca. 1550–1186 BCE).[60] Pharaohs during this period sometimes wore a ram's horn on their face, apparently to signal their deification.

Both the Mesopotamian portrayal of gods with horns and the Egyptian depiction of the pharaoh with a horn (apparently also under divine influence) lend contextual support to the notion that Moses's face was, in fact, horned and not just shining. To be sure, the two possible understandings of *qrn* aren't entirely unrelated, since the gods who wore horns on their heads were also often depicted with radiant light.[61] In any event, in both cases (or a combined one) the possibility that Moses's face is *qrn*-ed suggests a truly close encounter with the divine—an interaction that is so close, in fact, that qualities of the deity are, as it were, rubbing off on Moses and being physically manifested by him. His face looks this way, after all, "because he had been talking with God" (*bĕdabbĕrô ʾittô*; 34:29). Moses has been exposed to divinity in close quarters, for extended periods, and so is now taking on divine characteristics himself.[62] It is no wonder, then, that the people are in awe of Moses, or fear him (34:30). Such language is mostly proper with reference to the Lord,

60 Gary A. Rendsburg, "Moses as Equal to Pharaoh," in *Text, Artifact, and Image: Revealing Ancient Israelite Religion*, BJS 346 (Providence: Brown Judaic Studies, 2006) 201–19, esp. 216–18.

61 See, for example, Menahem Haran, "The Shining of Moses's Face: A Case Study in Biblical and Ancient Near Eastern Iconography," in *In the Shelter of Elyon: Essays on Ancient Palestinian Life and Literature in Honor of G. W. Ahlström*, edited by W. Boyd Barrick and John R. Spencer, JSOTSup 31 (Sheffield: Sheffield Academic Press, 1984) 159–73, who relates Moses's shining face to the Mesopotamian concept of *melammu*: a brilliant light that radiated from the gods, particularly from their heads (see *Enuma Elish* IV 58). The weapons of the gods, too, and other things belonging to the gods, could also radiate *melammu*. The gods were able to grant melammu to others, particularly kings, but could also take it away (see ibid., 168). Finally, *melammu* was often combined with *pulḫu*, which was the awe created or inspired by the god or monarch (see ibid., 172 n19; and A. L. Oppenheim, "Akkadian *pul(u)ḫ(t)u* and *melammu*," *JAOS* 63 [1943]: 31–34). Propp notes: "in Mesopotamian iconography, a stack of horns bears some relationship to the gods' radiant aura called *melammu*" (*Exodus 19–40*, 620) and cites the horn = light equation of Ps 132:17. While the details of Propp's unspecific "some relationship" remain elusive, the relationship seems (once more) to resist an overly precise distinction between energy and essence (see n33 above and n62 below).

62 This, too, might be seen as a kind of "externality," à la Gross (*Divinization of the Christian*, 66) or something to do with energies, à la Glazov ("Theōsis, Judaism, and Old Testament Anthropology," 19) but it is one that is related to the divine being and so related to essence if not also inwardness, individuality, and transcendence. Indeed, the question raised by Gross of the book of Wisdom: "Is this not a genuine deification of the soul—even though it is not so described—to the entire extent in which its position as creature, which, of course, never disappears, allows?" (*Divinization of the Christian*, 68) seems equally applicable to Moses in Exod 34. It might not be going too far, therefore, to say that what one finds in this chapter, may be the Old Testament equivalent of receiving the stigmata, perhaps especially if Propp's interpretation of the *qrn*-ed nature as disfigurement/wounding is deemed accurate. See further below.

but Moses's intermediary function in this unit makes him God's stand-in and so it comes as no surprise that the people are afraid; nor is it surprising that, as they earlier asked Moses to serve as covenant mediator (20:18–21; see Deut 5:5) so now some other or new thing must come between Moses-with-Godlike-features and the people—namely, the veil.[63] This, too, underscores how Moses's communion, or perhaps better, participation, with God is of the most intimate sort, since the human participant in the divine reality is manifesting divine characteristics and must be managed accordingly.[64]

Another, not unrelated way to understand this unit is via the idea of the ruler's two bodies. *The King's Two Bodies* is the title of a famous book by Ernst Kantorowicz, in which he argued that the king was understood to have two distinct bodies in the medieval period: the body politic and the natural body.[65] The notion of a monarch having two bodies was known centuries, indeed millennia, before many of the sources Kantorowicz cites, however, and this was particularly true for Egypt, which also knew of two bodies for the king.[66]

Pharaoh's two bodies correspond to the ones also identified by Kantorowicz in his much-later corpus—namely, the physical, natural body of the specific monarch in question (Egyptian *niswt*) and the "body" or office of Pharaoh that the specific individual inhabited (Egyptian *ḥm*). There has been a good bit of debate in Egyptological circles with regard to the Egyptian king's status: whether he was, in fact, a god or not, or somehow instead semi-divine, and it seems that attitudes on this matter may have varied through the course of Egyptian history or segments of Egyptian

63. See Propp, *Exodus 19–40*, 621: "If this is the true meaning of *qāran* ["to shine, be luminous"], the veiled, shining Moses may be regarded as a walking Tabernacle, manifesting and yet concealing Yahweh's splendor."

64. Rendsburg goes so far as to say, even in the case of the encounters between Moses and Pharaoh earlier in Exodus, that "for the purposes of this story, Moses is elevated to divine status. This is the plain meaning of the two passages cited at the outset [Exod 4:16; 7:1]" ("Moses as Equal to Pharaoh," 203). Rendsburg asserts (though without explicit support) that "in Israel the elevation of a human being from human status to divine status certainly was heretical," but that this "standard theology of the Bible . . . is set aside in the case of Moses's appearance before Pharaoh" (ibid., 202–203). Note also Fretheim, *Exodus*, 311: "Moses now functions as a divine messenger . . . We are told in 33:11 that God speaks to Moses face-to-face. Yet it is twice stated that God's face cannot be seen in all its fullness, even by Moses (33:20, 23). One might then say that *Moses's shining face is the fullness of the face of God which is available to the community*" (his emphasis). See Propp, *Exodus 19–40*, 623: Moses's face, "branded by Yahweh—whether horned, beaming or hardened—becomes the Mask of God."

65. Ernst H. Kantorowicz, *The King's Two Bodies: A Study in Mediaeval Political Theology* (Princeton: Princeton University Press, 1997 [orig: 1957]).

66. See Siegfried Morenz, *Egyptian Religion*, translated by Ann E. Keep (Ithaca: Cornell University Press, 1996 [orig: 1960]) 37–40; and, briefly, Brent A. Strawn, "Pharaoh," in *Dictionary of the Old Testament: Pentateuch*, edited by T. Desmond Alexander and David W. Baker (Downers Grove: InterVarsity, 2003) 631–36, esp. 633.

society.[67] Whatever the case, it seems at least safe to say that "the king *reveals* the deity by being a visible incarnation of it."[68] Furthermore, even if the physical person of the king (*niswt*) was not (always) considered divine, at least while he was still alive, he nevertheless inhabited a divine office (*ḥm*) since kingship belonged first to the gods before it was handed down to humans.[69]

Seen in the light of this background, Moses, too, might be seen as two-bodied: "this man, Moses" (Exod 32:1) on the one hand, and, on the other, the Moses who is close confidant of the Lord, who begins to take on divine qualities (ones also depicted among *pharaohs* of the 18th and 19th Dynasties!). Moses, too, that is, may be seen as human and (semi-)divine, just like the pharaoh was.[70] One way to parse this would be to say that Moses is becoming a new kind of pharaoh—not a tyrannical, despotic one, but a new and ideal type: an "Israelite pharaoh," the ultimate intermediary and priest between YHWH and YHWH's people,[71] one who even inaugurates a new kind of office, that of the prophet, even if the Torah is clear that none who come after, whatever office they hold, can quite compare to the first to hold the post (see Deut 18:15–22 and 34:10).[72]

Yet another way to parse this situation would be in terms of divine participation: that Moses is becoming more and more like God. It is worth observing in this regard that the passage about Moses's horns comes quite late in the book of Exodus. Moses is progressing, that is, in his participation and his upward journey toward perfection in virtue—that is how Gregory would put it at any rate. At the start, Moses's participation with God, while synergistic to be sure, had mostly to do with God's mission and was regularly accompanied by other "helps": God's staff, Aaron, the pillar and cloud, and so on. Later in Exodus, however, the participation seems far more direct and intimate, more physical, and perhaps, therefore, more ontological or essential.

---

67. See the previous note and the essays in *Ancient Egyptian Kingship*, edited by David B. O'Connor and David P. Silverman (PdÄ 9; Leiden: Brill, 1995).

68. Morenz, *Egyptian Religion*, 41 (his emphasis); see also O'Connor and Silverman, eds., "Introduction," in *Ancient Egyptian Kingship*, xxv.

69. Strawn, "Pharaoh," 632 (with literature).

70. For Moses and royal imagery, see Danny Mathews, *Royal Motifs in the Pentateuchal Portrayal of Moses*, LHBOTS 571 (New York: T. & T. Clark, 2012) whose thesis is that the "Pentateuchal authors adapted tropes and traditions, well-attested elsewhere in biblical and other ancient Near Eastern sources, to identify Moses as an exalted, even divinized figure." This formulation (and his book as a whole) reveals that Mathews is not primarily or exclusively concerned with *Egyptian* kingship, though his work is helpful to the point at hand.

71. For the pharaoh as high priest, if not, in principle, the *only* priest of Egypt, see Morenz, *Egyptian Religion*, 40.

72 See Miller, "Moses My Servant," esp. 302: Moses is "the mediator of the divine word, the spokesman for the God to the people. He has that function and distinction in a way that no other figure has....Thus Moses's words are coterminous with God's words."

If so, we might posit a kind of participation equation—namely, that participation in mission precedes incorruptibility, not unlike incarnation precedes resurrection. If the latter parallel with the ministry of Christ seems too far-fetched for some readers, it seems nevertheless quite clear that the narrative of Exodus begins with a sharing in *divine work or activity* and only later progresses to a sharing in *divine attributes or quality*. Whatever the case, paying attention to the narratival and dramatic contours of participation in Exodus suggests something that is more dynamic than generalized and too-static notions of "deification."[73]

In the final analysis, deciding whether Moses's participatory development in Exodus makes him look more like Pharaoh or more like God may be a distinction without significant difference, since, in the case of the Egyptian monarch at least, the divine and human categories bled together a good bit, especially at certain points in the history of ancient Egypt.

Before moving on, I wish to note a possible (major) point of contact between the life of Moses here and the so-called new Finnish interpretation of Luther, which, according to Braaten and Jenson, sees faith as "a real participation in Christ" such that "in faith a believer receives the righteousness of God in Christ, not only in a nominal and external way, but really and inwardly."[74] They continue: "if through faith we really participate in Christ, [then] we participate in the whole Christ, who in his divine person communicates the righteousness of God. Here lies the bridge to the Orthodox idea of salvation as deification or *theosis*."[75] The story of Moses's shining face at the end of Exodus seems to be a type of biblical instantiation of such theosis, replete with the communication of the divine person to the human person who, as a result, participates in the divine. To be sure, the story in Exodus, given its specific content, context, and nature is not about participation "in Christ" or receiving "the righteousness of God in Christ" (but see above and further below), but it is important to observe that the Exodus story chastens what appears in Braaten and Jenson to be a denigration of external manifestations of participation ("not only in a nominal and external way, but really and inwardly"). In the case of Moses's face, proof of participation is in fact "external"—visible to all (*sans* veil, at any rate)—and not solely internal, even as this externality is not simply "nominal" but "really" manifest.[76]

73. My thanks to Anthony Briggman and Mark McInroy for their discussion on this point, which may also connect, in its own way, to the study by Bruce L. McCormack, "Participation with God, Yes; Deification, No: Two Modern Protestant Responses to an Ancient Question," in *Orthodox and Modern: Studies in the Theology of Karl Barth* (Grand Rapids: Baker Academic, 2008) 235–60.

74. Braaten and Jenson, *Union with Christ*, viii.

75. Ibid.

76 See n62 above.

Participation Democratized

One final text from Exodus deserves discussion: it is Israel's successful completion of the tabernacle in Exod 35–40. These chapters repeat, in close but not entirely verbatim fashion, the instructions first given in Exod 25–30. What comes between these two units is, of course, the golden calf debacle where nearly all is lost and things are saved only by Moses's bold intercession. The repetition of details in Exod 35–40 is quite necessary, then, even if mind-numbing to modern readers,[77] because it demonstrates precisely obedient execution of the commands issued in Exod 25–30. What one finds at the end of Exodus, that is, is Israel "at full stretch."[78] Israel has been disobedient to the extreme: opening a deep fissure at the very moment of covenant-making—a fissure that threatens to destroy everything—but after the delicate negotiation of Mosaic intercession and divine forgiveness (33:12—34:9),[79] Israel shows itself faithful . . . repeatedly, obsessively, *minutely*.

One way to gloss such faithfulness is to see it as a kind of participation: Israel here participates in the divine life and mission in the world by faithfully executing God's commands and constructing a place for God's presence, to which, according to later texts, God's people and even the nations will come and pray (see 1 Kings 8; Isa 2:1–5; 56:3–8; Mic 4:1–4; Matt 21:13 and parr.). To be sure, the divine commands are mediated through Moses, but that is nothing new; furthermore, it is all Israel that performs the work (see Exod 39:32, 42–43). And even if Israel participates somehow only through, with, or in Moses, we know that Moses's participation, in Exodus, is with God, from front to back (see 1 Cor 11:1).[80]

It should be underscored that the specific commandments in question concern the tabernacle, the very meeting place—a tent of meeting!—for God and Israel. It is no small thing that Exodus culminates not only with Israel's faithful completion of God's commands concerning this site of divine-human interactivity, but also

---

77. It needn't be so: see Brent A. Strawn, "Keep/Observe/Do – Carefully – Today! The Rhetoric of Repetition in Deuteronomy," in *A God So Near: Essays on Old Testament Theology in Honor of Patrick D. Miller*, edited by Brent A. Strawn and Nancy R. Bowen (Winona Lake: Eisenbrauns, 2003) 215–40 for how repetition can sharpen the memory and play out ethically. See also the insightful study of Amy H. C. Robertson, "'He Kept the Measurements in His Memory as a Treasure': The Role of the Tabernacle Text in Religious Experience" (PhD diss., Emory University, 2010) which raises the possibility that the repetition found in the tabernacle texts may have served a meditative function, especially for those readers living away from or long after the destruction of the tabernacle (and temple).

78. I use this language for Exod 35–40 in Strawn, "Exodus," 53–55.

79. For an analysis of the poetry in this unit, see Brent A. Strawn, "YHWH's Poesie: The *Gnaden-formel* (Exod 34:6b-7), the Book of Exodus, and Beyond," in *Biblical Poetry and the Art of Close Reading*, edited by J. Blake Couey and Elaine James (Cambridge: Cambridge University Press, 2018) 237–56.

80. See the arresting comment by Anderson, *Christian Doctrine and the Old Testament*, 37: "Through the prophets, God has invited Israel into his own person."

with the successful filling of that tabernacle with God's own presence (40:34). If the beginning of Exodus raised questions about God's *absence* and *non*-participation, there is no question, as the book concludes, that God desires close, intimate relationship with all Israel, not just with Moses. And if participation in Exodus is largely begun with Moses's call and mediated throughout the book through Moses, there can be no doubt that at the end, divine-human participation is fully democratized or communalized: made available to all.[81]

Conclusion: On Participatory Reading with Christ and/in God

There are no doubt other details that could be lifted up from the life of Moses in the book of Exodus (and beyond), (re)read, and (re)assessed with an eye toward participation. Gregory's own treatment is lengthy and I have left aside most of the many details he discusses while only barely mentioning many items that would repay far greater scrutiny.[82] While this admission is obvious to the reader of the present essay, I hope that at least some of what has been discussed here is useful in thinking about or rethinking the contribution of the Old Testament to the idea of participation. Furthermore, while I have not drawn extensive connections between the biblical texts I have focused on and more recent theological discussions of participation, I trust that the relationships are clear enough, along with the various implications that may be drawn and that might be developed further, especially for those with great interest in the subject. At the very least, the present analysis has attempted to

---

81. This is also true in Leviticus and not only in the holiness code of Lev 17–26, which extends holiness to the entire community, but to no small degree also in the first part, which, while having the flavor of a technical priestly manual, nevertheless lets readers see "behind the curtain" or "backstage," as it were. Propp, *Exodus 19–40*, 621–22 cites A. H. McNeile, *The Book of Exodus*, Westminster Commentaries (London: Methuen, 1908) cxxiii on how the shining of Moses's face might also pertain to all of Israel: "Moses alone stood in a relation to God close and intimate enough for such a transfiguration to be possible or bearable; the people durst not gaze even upon the reflexion. But Moses was the representative of his nation, and the glory upon his face was a pledge and symbol of the abiding of the divine glory upon the whole people."

82. I am thinking particularly of the intercessions of Moses, as well as his profile as suffering servant. For both things, see Miller, "Moses My Servant," 307–10, esp. 308, on the great intercessors of the Old Testament and how they are most passionate when the sin is greatest ("It is as if they know that the mercy of God is equal to and indeed more intense than the judgment of God"); and 310, on Moses's failure to enter the promised land, in Deuteronomy, on account of Israel (1:37; 3:23–28; 4:21–22) ("Moses does not share the fearful perspective of the people, but he shares existence with them and so must suffer with them . . . .We do not have here a full-blown notion of the salvation and forgiveness of the many brought by the punishment of the one, but we are on the way to that....reminding all hearers that the special way in which judgment becomes grace in the work of this God is when the Lord's own servant receives the judgment 'on your account'"). One might also see more generally the studies by John Barton, "Imitation of God in the Old Testament," in *The God of Israel*, edited by Robert P. Gordon, UCOP 64 (Cambridge: Cambridge University Press, 2007) 35–46; and by Cyril S. Rodd, *Glimpses of a Strange Land: Studies in Old Testament Ethics* (Edinburgh: T. & T. Clark, 2001) 65–76.

account for some aspects that Gregory, for one, doesn't reckon with as much as he might have—among these, I would mention above all *the problem of divine (!) and human non-participation, human resistance to participation*, and *the democratization or communalization of participation*.[83] But, again, more could be said—both generally on the subject-matter and on the specific details mentioned here.

I wish to conclude with one final connection between the life of Moses, Gregory's account, my own study, and the idea of participation. On the one hand, this connection is almost too obvious to mention; on the other hand, its obviousness may be its genius (and hope) insofar as it provides what may be the main and most achievable way to participate with God. It is simply this: *we participate with God in no small way by reading Scripture.* In *The Life of Moses*, Gregory selects the story of Moses and then reads it as a model for progress in the life of virtue. But, as noted earlier, in another of his major studies on the same topic, *On Perfection*, Gregory chooses Paul as the exemplar to study. Paul, Moses, it makes no difference.[84] The point, or, rather, the method, is to read with the saints so as to participate, via such reading, with them and their exemplary lives in God so as to grow in grace, perfection, even divinity.[85]

Although much has been written of late on how stories—narrative proper, that is—are somehow ideal to facilitate such existential engagement, my own sense is that generic specificity and the valorization of narrative at this point are greatly overstated. One *may* and perhaps often *does* read stories in existentially engaged, participatory ways, but one may just as well *not* and, more to the point, *need not* do so. Other genres—but above all others, poetry—seem just as likely to facilitate

---

83. The latter, at least, is probably implicit in Gregory, however, since he believes readers of *LM* can in fact make progress in virtue by following Moses's example. In any event, perhaps some of the problematic texts I have lifted up do not rise to serious problems for notions of participation. Perhaps they are simply bits of the "bare history of the man" that Gregory would say need not detain us overmuch (*LM* I, 21; see further above). But these, too, are part of the life of Moses in Scripture and I have not sought to challenge Gregory with these details so much as *follow* him: attending closely to *all* aspects of Moses's life as recounted in Scripture and subjecting them to contemplation. Again, several of these texts may well be of a sort that would urge Gregory to move on quickly in the "sequence," but, even if he leaves some of these matters aside in *The Life of Moses*, it seems reasonable to believe that Gregory would be agreeable to a deeper contemplation of them if that were possible—and that is the task I have at least tried to begin in my remarks here.

84. Still, given the often-beleaguered state of the Old Testament in many Christian circles, it should be underscored that Moses, not just Paul, is worthy of such attention and contemplation. On the dire state of the Old Testament today, see Brent A. Strawn, *The Old Testament Is Dying: A Diagnosis and Recommended Treatment* (Grand Rapids: Baker Academic, 2017).

85. For recent studies, see Meadowcroft, "One Like a Son of Man"; and Meadowcroft, "Daniel's Visionary Participation." Note also the comments of Angus Paddison, "Scripture, Participation and Universities," in *Scripture: A Very Theological Proposal* (London: T. & T. Clark, 2009) 122–44.

participatory reading.[86] Still further, it is not just the genre, nor the process of reading alone; in communities of faith, there are other things that accompany and facilitate the best reading practices—things like prayer, for instance.[87] Of course, it has long been thought that the most profound type of reading, spiritual reading (*lectio divina*) is, in fact, a kind of prayer.[88]

I end with two remarks on this score. The first is that, according to Luke 4:16–21, Jesus also read Scripture—specifically, of course, the Old Testament—in this participatory sort of way. According to Luke, Jesus read the words of Isa 61 as applying immediately to him and to his ministry. Isaiah was a guide, therefore, not unlike Moses or Paul for Gregory, whose words were to be trusted and enacted in the life lived with and toward God. It is no small matter, furthermore, that the text Jesus selected to read speaks of God's spirit being upon him (see Luke 4:18; Isa 61:1).

The second remark builds from this first one, especially with the tantalizingly Trinitarian evocations of Luke 4 still in mind (even if those are, as yet, seriously underdeveloped and only inchoately present). It is to return to where I began with the possibilities of "participating in Christ" by reading the Old Testament via Trinitarian pre-understandings or predispositions. The passage from Luke suggests that even Jesus participated with God's spirit through reading Isaiah. Jesus' reading in Luke 4 also indicates that the model found in Gregory—reading for participatory engagement with the life and mission of God—is already at work *in* the pages of Scripture, not simply a task to be performed *on* the pages of Scripture. But, of course, the latter performance on Scripture (or from it) is very much possible, assuming that the participation is willed and enabled (see above). So, per Gregory and per Luke 4, one may participate in God *through reading* and, in Trinitarian mode, *such reading also participates in Christ* (and the Spirit!). And so, in this fuller perspective, Moses, too, can be said to be participating in Christ when he participates in God. Perhaps that is why Moses is present at the transfiguration (Matt 17:3 and par.) and why he can be an exemplar for the *Christian* soul (per Gregory) as well as the Jewish soul (per Philo). But insofar as (or at those times when) a Christian reads in these sorts

86. See Lieber, "The Rhetoric of Participation," 145: "In his *piyyutim*, Yannai, one of the first and foremost liturgical poets of Judaism, brings both the Torah portion and the liturgy vividly alive for his community. His listeners did not merely hear the stories of the Torah. In a diversity of ways, they *experienced* their own sacred history, and they did so *in the context of prayer*—a ritual that, in and of itself, *offers access to another realm*. Through techniques of form, such as refrains and patterned repetition, the community had the opportunity to *physically participate* in these poems. And by means of rhetorical devices, Yannai was able to *involve the community emotionally and intellectually as he collapsed the distance* along both horizontal and vertical axes: between past and present and between heaven and earth" (emphases added).

87. See the previous note.

88. See esp. Mariano Magrassi, *Praying the Bible: An Introduction to Lectio Divina* (Collegeville, MN: Liturgical, 1998).

of participatory ways, they also participate in Christ, who also read in the same way, and so they also participate in God, since these three are one—one also, perhaps, in the grandest vision, with the human reader-prayer-participant (see John 17:21).

Let the final words be Gregory's, with a gloss indicating that the finding of which he speaks is dependent in no small way and perhaps entirely on *reading*:

> As your understanding is lifted up to what is magnificent and divine, whatever you may find (and I know full well that you will find many things) will most certainly be for the common benefit in Christ Jesus. Amen. (*LM* II, 321)

RESPONSE TO STRAWN

J. Nathan Clayton

Brent Strawn has produced an engaging study of the theme of Moses's participation with God. I have found responding to his argument and taking part in dialog about it to be a stimulating exercise. In what follows, I will first provide a very brief summary of the paper, to highlight some of the points I find especially salient. Second, I will offer some broad-based comments related to the method displayed in this analysis. Third, I will lay out a few specific questions dealing with some of the key points developed in the main sections of Strawn's essay.

In his introduction, Strawn notes that, for many in the scholarly guild concerned with study of the Old Testament/Hebrew Bible, even to attempt a study of participation with Christ in the Old Testament texts is a non-starter—a restriction based on what he calls the "shadow of historical criticism." Strawn concedes that, a priori at least, the possibility of a fully Trinitarian reading of the theme of divine participation in the Old Testament is decidedly a difficult enterprise (seeing that such a reading would either be based on post-textual [doctrinal] or on pre-textual intellectual dispositions [related to the preunderstanding of the reader]). However, Strawn still suggests that the texts of the Old Testament themselves do, in fact, contribute to the theme of divine participation, even if scholarship (1) has been "lackluster" in examining this theme and (2) has been especially concerned with matters of background study when it has approached this topic. Hence, Strawn proposes: (1) to examine one "extended instance" of divine-human participation in the Old Testament—that of Moses, and (2) to do so by first examining the Cappadocian church father Gregory of Nyssa (4th century CE) and his well-known treatise entitled the *Life of Moses*.

The main sections of Strawn's essay move along two major paths. First, he orients his reader to Gregory's *Life of Moses*. In doing this, Strawn especially highlights three principal points related to Gregory's study of Moses: (1) Gregory defines true virtue in terms of a progressive human participation with God; (2) Gregory affirms that imitation of scriptural examples is a key way forward for humans seeking this life of virtue; and (3) Gregory argues that Moses is the most significant of such Scriptural examples for the Christian to imitate.

Second, then, with Gregory as a guide and inspiration, Strawn proceeds to examine what he views as key moments of divine-human participation in the life of
Moses. Strawn first argues that before Moses's divine calling in Exod 3, there is much
non-participation with God, even if Moses's life anticipates such participation in its
"post-call" future. Moses's call by God in Exod 3 becomes the foundation of his full
participation with God. For Strawn, this call is one of the most profound and foundational salvific acts in all of Scripture, ultimately, as we find "nothing short of divine
participation in Moses's call." In fact, Strawn draws out four key observations from
the narrative of Moses's call: (1) divine-human participation in Moses's life comes at
God's initiative; (2) the "I am who I am" divine name given to Moses in Exod 3:14
points to an elusive divine-human encounter, where God's name is "given and yet
not given"; (3) God's call to participate in the divine mission is perhaps resistible, but
not ultimately so; and (4) Moses's example (of initially resisting God's call and then
responding to it) is also a reminder that participation with the divine can be varied
in its experience and efficacy.

Further, Strawn then examines the place of agency in Moses's life, by interacting
with a 2014 essay by Terence Fretheim, who argues that God never acts unilaterally
in Exodus, as a divine-human synergy is consistently present. The point for Strawn
is to show how in the Pentateuch, as a whole, God's actions are so enmeshed with
those of Moses that, in the end, the divine-human synergy between God and Moses
could be seen as "interconfused."

Two more major issues round out Strawn's study of Moses in the Pentateuch.
First, he highlights the issue of the comingling of the divine and the human in Exod
34. The Hebrew verb *qrn* in 34:29 is usually translated as "shone brightly," in reference to the skin of Moses's face after meeting God on Mount Sinai. Strawn, in
contrast, points to the Vulgate's translation that means instead "his face was *horned
[cornuta]*." A basic linguistic connection between the biblical Hebrew verb *qrn* and
the noun *qeren* (horn) is noted, as well as the known fact that deities in the ancient
Near East were often represented with horns. Understood in ancient Near Eastern
context, this possible connection between the language of "shining" and "horns"
represents further evidence for Strawn that "the qualities of the deity are, as it were,
rubbing off on Moses and being physically manifested by him." The notion of the
two bodies of a ruler is also brought to bear on this part of the discussion: whereby
the ruler's physical body is set in contrast to the larger political body, or office, inhabited by the ruler and representing the divinity on earth. This is expressed in various historical periods, such as in ancient Egypt or medieval Europe, and can help
shed light on Moses's progressive participation with the divine in the Pentateuch.
Specifically, in this way, Moses could be seen as "becoming a new kind of pharaoh,"

not of the tyrannical type, but a new, ideal type that would represent "the ultimate intermediary and priest between YHWH and YHWH's people."

Second, and finally, Strawn briefly discusses the Israelites' faithful and obedient completion of the tabernacle in Exod 35–40 (with its well-known, almost verbatim repetition of the initial divine instructions in chapters 25–30). Despite the episode of the sin of the golden calf in Exod 32, Israel's participation with God is "democratized" with the establishment of the tabernacle and the mediation of Moses, by the conclusion of Exodus (and in contrast to the early chapters of the book, where divine participation should be viewed as divine absence or as non-participatory).

By way of an initial response to Strawn's essay, let me begin with a brief personal story. In the summer of 2017, I had the opportunity to travel for a study tour of Israel and Jordan. During that trip, I was able to hear from, and interact with, a Jewish rabbi from Jerusalem. He was happy to spend time with our Christian group and he also wanted to help us see some contrasts. At one point, he noted: "Your prism for interpreting your Old Testament is the New Testament and Christ, my prism for interpreting my Hebrew Bible is the rabbinic tradition."

This statement stands, for me, as a recent and vivid reminder that, yes, by virtue of our being human knowers and readers, when it comes to our approach to the Old Testament and its relationship to the New, we all carry interpretive prisms with us, whether we realize it actively or not. In that vein, I think one way of highlighting a fundamental issue that is addressed in Strawn's paper is with this question: "Is there any validity to a reading of the life of Moses, as it is presented to us in the canonical text of the Pentateuch, that could contribute, at least in general terms, to the broader canonical theme of human participation with the divine—of human participation, even, with Christ?"

If one is not that familiar with the academic traditions of the broader guild of Old Testament/Hebrew Bible scholarship, it is understandable to miss that even *asking* this question is, indeed, considered "out of bounds," as it is noted at the opening of the essay.

From a broad methodological point of view, I am encouraged that Strawn has *not* deemed this question out of bounds. I am a Christian who holds evangelical convictions concerning the nature of Scripture, salvation, the Christian life, and the like. My academic interests, also, are centered with the Old Testament generally— Hebrew grammar and exegesis, ancient Israelite history, rhetorical and discourse analysis of the canonical text, Old Testament theology, and biblical theology generally. For me, this kind of study can properly nurture the development of a biblical theology that is rooted in these ideas: (1) God has acted supernaturally in human history, and (2) in the canonical texts of the Old and New Testaments, God has left for us a coherent, textual witness to that salvific historical engagement.[1] If any of this is valid, then our study of Scripture *should* have as an ultimate goal the nurturing and the developing of the life of the Church, and questions such as the ones dealt with in this essay should be addressed.

All of this is to state that, in the main, I find the analysis in this piece to be sober, generally persuasive, and even creative in its use of sources, for an Old Testament study. Also, for Strawn to come to the conclusion that "we participate with God in no small way by reading Scripture" is, to me, a welcome perspective on the ultimate purposes of engaging OT (and NT) texts—since this is argued in the context of seeing Moses's participation with God as an actual model for Christians to imitate. Again, it is far from a given that many who engage in the professional study of the Old Testament would ever come to (or be willing to entertain the possibility of) such conclusions regarding the nature of the divine-human relationship as mediated through Scripture, generally, or through the textual traditions centered on Moses in the Pentateuch, specifically.

At the same time, I have a couple of minor methodological qualms about the structure of the study. First, I think the relationship between the main sections of the study could be clarified further. Essentially, I would question Gregory of Nyssa's *Life of Moses* as the actual starting point. In my view, it would seem more natural, and logical, to begin with an exegetical and rhetorical analysis of the key passages in Exodus that contribute specifically to the theme of Moses's participation with God and *then* proceed to show how Gregory's study, in the fourth century, actually reflects on the Moses/YHWH relationship that has been shown to be present in the biblical text in the first place. It seems to me that this sequence would, in fact, help show how much later historical-critical scholarship of the OT/Hebrew Bible is missing key theological dimensions of Exodus and of the Pentateuch as a whole.

Second, when it comes to Strawn's discussion of texts in Exodus and in the Pentateuch, the basis on which certain texts are chosen for analysis could also be clarified. I am simply stating that his readers could perhaps be served by noting the warrant for the choice of certain passages over others. Also, following a more systematic canonical trajectory through Exodus, especially, could be helpful.

So, those are some of my broad-based reactions to this study. Now to a few specific questions with each of the main sections of his paper. The introduction lays out the issues well. For example, as noted above, I appreciate the willingness to push back on what Strawn calls the "shadow of historical criticism." At the same time, at

---

1. For a recent discussion of this kind of stance in biblical theology, see Edward Klink III and Darian R. Lockett, *Understanding Biblical Theology: A Comparison of Theory and Practice* (Grand Rapids: Zondervan, 2012) 59–75.

least for me as a reader, this pushback raises a question in my mind that I am not sure I see answered. While it is clear to me that the final form of the canonical text is taken seriously as the locus of exegesis, it is somewhat less obvious to me as a reader where our author stands on the maximalist/minimalist debate regarding the nature of Old Testament history. Does the "historicity" of the biblical character of Moses matter here? Would this have any impact in the discussion of Moses's participation with God? Strawn's appeal to some historical data from the second millennium BCE could, perhaps, be further strengthened by making his position on the historicity of Moses and the exodus a bit clearer. For example, in his detailed study of the historical reliability of the Old Testament, Kenneth Kitchen has noted that, for the period of Moses and the exodus in general, despite some historical "negatives," and "neutrals," a number of "positives" can be stated with confidence.[2] Ultimately, for Kitchen, the fact that the exodus and Sinai events, as described in Scripture, do correspond not only with "attested realities," but also, "with known usage of the late second millennium B.C. and earlier *does favor acceptance of their having had a definite historical basis.*"[3]

Next, I find the use of Gregory of Nyssa's *Life of Moses* surprising. Methodologically, as noted above, I think finishing the study with an appeal to Gregory's work could be more effective. Ultimately, however, I think appealing to Gregory is surprising not because it is unwarranted, but because it's not *typical* to see interaction with patristic sources in Old Testament studies. In my view, Strawn's use of Gregory confirms the benefit of Thomas Oden's past invitation (and practice) to engage with classic Christian exegesis and theological study (especially from the early church period) without "getting embroiled in everextending modern historical interpretation and debates."[4] Hence, I welcome this kind of engagement in Old Testament study with patristic sources.

At least for Old Testament study, this is a reminder that pre-critical exegesis and theological reflection stand unencumbered with much more recent rationalistic, humanistic, and anti-supernatural approaches—what Brent calls, I think rightly, "excessively historicizing/literalizing approaches."[5] This reminds me that it was probably more natural for someone like Gregory in the fourth century to be willing to examine Moses's participatory life as an example to imitate—even as Gregory remains a human reader of Scripture.

---

2. K. A. Kitchen, *On the Reliability of the Old Testament* (Grand Rapids: Eerdmans, 2003) 310–11.

3. Ibid., 312. Emphasis added.

4. Thomas C. Oden, *The Word of Life. Systematic Theology: Volume Two* (New York: HarperCollins, 1992) xi.

5. See Strawn's n19.

Second, then, this section also leads me to wonder, generally, how much we miss in our reading of the Old Testament and of Moses, of the full, divine intent of the text. In his introduction, Strawn mentions the possibility of a Trinitarian reading, and interpretive disposition, as being "post-textual" or "pre-textual." However, in light of the consistent nature of God, couldn't this Trinitarian reality be present in the text *itself*? Indeed, could not Trinitarian notions exist in the OT text, even before the book of Exodus, at least in embryonic form? Perhaps it would be warranted to observe Trinitarian notions in Genesis, in texts like Gen 1–3 and its nuanced allusions to the nature of the Godhead, or with the visitors of Gen 18? My point is to suggest that we could be missing a deeper attainment of textual meaning by being overly concerned about forcing doctrine on the text—when theological doctrine should itself be rooted in the biblical text. Hence, is it warranted in any way to find any Trinitarian clues in the text, and how might this impact our reading of the nature of God and his interactions with Moses from the immediate canonical setting of the Pentateuch? How much do we, or should we, know about the nature of God when we come as readers to the opening chapters of Exodus?

Finally, I found myself engaging in most detail with the third and main section of the paper and the exegetical analysis presented there. I think this section provides some clear insight into how we may go about reflecting on Moses's participation with God. This certainly calls for further engagement, and also, for thinking about other sections of the OT canon that contribute to the theme of divine-human participation. For the sake of brevity, I will raise just three questions from this final section.

First, with the discussion of the pre-call texts in Exod 1 and 2, is it too strong of a claim to state that *failure* can originate from the divine? Yes, it is clear that God is absent in most ways, at least from certain *human* perspectives, at the opening of the book. But even as Strawn's essay notes, in Exod 1:21, God is still present, in blessing, as He gives families to the God-fearing Hebrew midwives, which seems to connect, at least generally, to the ongoing *toledot* ("generations") structure in Genesis, through which God moves his blessing and redemptive promise forward, especially through His presence and engagement with the patriarchal generations.

Second, in the discussion of Moses's call and its uniqueness, is it possible that too strong a separation is made from the earlier Pentateuchal narratives? For example, Strawn writes in this section that "a divine-human synergy is initiated here in a way unlike anything that has come before in the Old Testament." It is clear that Moses's call is unique in many, if not most, ways. But is there any benefit here to observing a more organic canonical connection with the divine-human "synergy" in the Abram/Abraham texts, for instance—such as in Gen 12, 15, or 17?

So to my third and final question. This is in relationship to two issues that connect quite directly to ancient Near Eastern realities in this discussion: (1) the shining of Moses's face in Exod 34:35 and the issue of *qrn/qeren* (to shine/horn) and (2) the issue of the "two bodies," where the Egyptian Pharaoh could be viewed as revealing the deity as a visible incarnation, and where Moses could be seen as an "Israelite pharaoh," taking on almost God-like qualities (such as in the discussion of Deut 34:10–12). Could this be understood more precisely as an example of a Yahweh-centered *polemic*—where God is infusing certain known second millennium religious notions of divine/human participation in the ancient Near East with His new revelation to, and engagement with, Moses?

All in all, Strawn has presented an intriguing study of Moses's engagement with God that shows, particularly in conversation with Gregory's early study of Moses, how this theme ought to be a fruitful one in further analyzing the broad biblical and theological topic of the participation of the human with the divine.

CRUCIFORM OR RESURRECTIFORM? PAUL'S PARADOXICAL PRACTICE OF PARTICIPATION IN CHRIST

Michael J. Gorman

Cross-shaped or resurrection-shaped? That is the question before us regarding Paul's understanding of participation in Christ. But first, some introductory comments.

"Participation" is back in vogue, theologically speaking, and across the theological spectrum as well as within the various theological subdisciplines and loci—as this volume of *Ex Auditu* and its contributors testify. This is not to say that we all agree about either terminology or, more importantly, substance. But participation is on the table in a major way, and I think this development is one of the most exciting and fruitful directions in theology in recent decades.[1]

This great interest in participation extends of course to Paul, an interest jump-started in recent times by E. P. Sanders and partially fleshed out by James Dunn, Richard Hays, and others before it quite literally exploded.[2] Witness, for instance, the 2017 Society of Biblical Literature annual meeting sessions on the apostle: three of them, encompassing a dozen scholarly papers, focused on participation. Despite this common interest, there is disagreement among Pauline scholars on a variety of topics, including what participation in Christ means concretely. Within this context, I would like to make some personal but relevant remarks.

Perhaps not surprisingly, my computer lists nearly 2,000 files containing some form of the word "cruciform," meaning "cross-shaped." Still more significant, however, is the fact that my computer reveals more than 3,000 files with some form of the word "participate" and more than 3,000 containing some form of the word

---

1. In addition to purely academic works, a number of scholarly books also have significant pastoral implications. See, for example, J. Todd Billings, *Union with Christ: Reframing Theology and Ministry for the Church* (Grand Rapids: Baker Academic, 2011).

2. See E. P. Sanders, *Paul and Palestinian Judaism* (Philadelphia: Fortress, 1977); Richard B. Hays, *The Faith of Jesus Christ: The Narrative Substructure of Gal. 3:1—4:11,* 2nd ed. (Grand Rapids: Eerdmans, 2002 [orig. 1983]) esp. a section titled "Participation in Christ as the Key to Pauline Soteriology" (xxix–xxxiii); Richard B. Hays, "What Is 'Real Participation in Christ'? A Dialogue with E. P. Sanders on Pauline Soteriology," in *Redefining First-Century Jewish and Christian Identities: Essays in Honor of Ed Parish Sanders,* edited by Fabian E. Udoh et al (Notre Dame: University of Notre Dame Press, 2008) 336–51; James D. G. Dunn, *The Theology of Paul the Apostle* (Grand Rapids: Eerdmans, 1998) 390–441.

"mission."[3] These three words—cruciform, participation, and mission—constitute a fair summary of what I have been doing in my exegetical and theological work, especially in Paul, but also in the rest of the New Testament.

My three monographs on Paul (an accidental trilogy), as well as the two introductory texts I have written, have all developed these three themes, though each of the three monographs highlights one theme in particular. *Cruciformity: Paul's Narrative Spirituality of the Cross* (2001) obviously focuses on cruciformity; *Inhabiting the Cruciform God: Kenosis, Justification, and Theosis in Paul's Narrative Soteriology* (2009) stresses participation; and *Becoming the Gospel: Paul, Participation, and Mission* (2015) highlights mission.[4]

Volumes one and three have been nearly universally well received, but volume two (*Inhabiting the Cruciform God*)—in which the word theosis appears not only in the subtitle but also as the content of the book's primary thesis—has been subject to more criticism. One way of stating that thesis is as follows: "For Paul, to be one with Christ is to be one with God; to be like Christ is to be like God," which is to say that "for Paul cruciformity . . . is really theoformity, or theosis."[5] Additionally, in the longest chapter of that book, I contend that for Paul justification is *participatory* and *transformative*, the beginning of "an experience of participating in Christ's resurrection life that is effected by co-crucifixion with him."[6] Two of the main questions about *Inhabiting* that have repeatedly emerged are the following: (1) Is justification really an act of participatory transformation, an event of co-crucifixion and co-resurrection with Christ? (2) Is "theosis" an appropriate designation for what happens to those who participate in the life of the triune God by being so crucified and raised with Christ?

It is tempting to pursue one or both of those questions in this essay, but I have already addressed them in various places and ways. For example, although I believe strongly that theosis language is *appropriate* in discussing Paul and should not be abandoned, I do not think the term itself is *necessary* if other language can suffice. However, I do insist that everything Paul is about, including justification, must be understood as transformative participation in Christ the image of God, and hence as transformative participation in the very life of God.[7] Instead, therefore, I would

---

3. For the record, there are also some 2,700 files with a form of "resurrection." Of course, many of these files overlap, containing two or more of these semantic fields.

4. All three published by Eerdmans (Grand Rapids).

5. Gorman, *Inhabiting the Cruciform God*, 4. That is, it is appropriate to use "theosis" to describe Paul's understanding of transformative participation in the "kenotic, cruciform character of God through Spirit-enabled conformity to the incarnate, crucified, and resurrected/glorified Christ" (162).

6. Ibid., 40.

7. For theosis as an appropriate term, see, for example, Gorman, "Paul's Corporate, Cruciform,

like to focus on a question that has arisen from my work as a whole: Is it adequate to focus on the "cruciform" character of participation in Christ? Or, in other words, what happened to the resurrection and its implications for Christian practice? Is participating in Christ not also resurrection-shaped, that is, "resurrectiform" or "an-astiform" (a term based on the Greek word for resurrection, *anastasis*)? This sort of question has been raised by such scholars as Stephen Finlan (proposing "anasti-form"), Andrew Boakye (proposing "resurrectiform" or "reviviform"), and Rachael Tan.[8]

At first, this might seem a bit like asking Martin Luther if he would want to balance his *theologia crucis* with a hearty theology of glory. "*Mē genoito!*"—"May it never be!"—he would perhaps answer.[9] But I wish to take this question with utmost seriousness and probe it carefully. My thesis will be, on the one hand, a qualified affirmative response: cruciform participation in Christ is also, paradoxically, partici-pation in Christ's resurrection. And yet, on the other hand, I will insist that we must maintain Paul's emphasis on the cross and therefore grant the word "cruciform" a certain priority. Therefore, rather than using a term like "resurrectiform" in con-junction with "cruciform," I will argue that we need a different term that better cap-tures the crucifixion-resurrection dynamic, or dialectic, of participation in Christ according to Paul. As we will see, this contention is not merely a minor episode of "wrangling over words" (2 Tim 2:14), but a significant exegetical and theological claim about the substance of Paul's theology and spirituality—and their contempo-rary significance.

Missional *Theosis* in Second Corinthians," in *'In Christ' in Paul: Explorations in Paul's Theology of Union and Participation*, edited by Kevin J. Vanhoozer, Constantine R. Campbell, and Michael J. Thate, WUNT 2.384 (Tübingen: Mohr Siebeck, 2014) 181–208. In *Becoming the Gospel* (e.g., 7–8) however, I stress that the term is not necessary. With respect to justification, see *Inhabiting*, 40–104, as well as my forthcoming chapters on justification in *Participating in Christ: Explorations in Paul's Theology and Spirituality* (Grand Rapids: Baker Academic, 2019).

8. Stephen Finlan, "Can We Speak of *Theosis* in Paul?", in *Partakers of the Divine Nature: The History and Development of Deification in the Christian Traditions*, edited by Michael J. Christensen and Jeffery A. Wittung (Grand Rapids: Baker Academic, 2007) 68–80; Andrew Boakye, "Inhabiting the 'Resurrectiform' God: Death and Life as Theological Headline in Paul," *Expository Times* 128.2 (Nov. 2016) 53–62; Andrew Boakye, *Death and Life: Resurrection, Restoration, and Rectification in Paul's Letter to the Galatians* (Eugene, OR: Pickwick, 2017); Rachael Tan, "Conformity to Christ: An Exegetical and Theological Analysis of Paul's Perspective on Humiliation and Exaltation in Philip-pians 2:5–11" (Ph.D. diss., Southern Theological Seminary, 2017; http://digital.library.sbts.edu/handle/10392/5331).

9. This phrase appears fourteen times in Paul's letters (all in Romans, 1 Corinthians, and Gala-tians) generally to answer rhetorical questions. See, for example, Rom 6:1–2.

The Proposal that Participation is "Anastiform"/"Resurrectiform"

Of the three scholars mentioned above who explicitly or implicitly propose language such as anastiform or resurrectiform, we will focus briefly on Andrew Boakye's article "Inhabiting the 'Resurrectiform' God: Death and Life as Theological Headline in Paul." The title is a "deliberate adaptation" of the title of my book *Inhabiting the Cruciform God.*[10]

In his essay, Boakye first states his basic agreement with what he rightly understands to be three of the primary cross-centered claims of *Inhabiting*:

1. "'justification is by crucifixion, specifically co-crucifixion, understood as participation in Christ's act of covenant fulfillment'";

2. "'co-crucifixion leads to co-resurrection which draws those of faith into a cruciform lifestyle' (i.e., informed by the cross) for which Jesus was template and Paul was example";

3. "God's cruciform nature gave shape to Jesus' self-giving act."[11]

While these claims, according to Boakye, are "hermeneutically sound" and, "pastorally, [offer] a sharp upward call," the more fundamental claim of my book, which "equates being 'in Christ' with 'inhabiting the *cruciform* God'"[12] (emphasis his) troubles Boakye. He therefore offers "two lines of critique." The first critique, somewhat ironically (given the article's title and thesis), challenges my own use of resurrection language for Paul's understanding of present existence in Christ; Boakye finds the notion of present resurrection with Christ only in post-Pauline (to his mind) letters, namely Colossians and Ephesians, so he prefers the language of "revivification" with respect to Paul's theology.[13] The second critique mistakenly attributes the phrase "resurrection shaped" to me as a description of Paul's view of life in Christ, while correctly noting that I do speak of "co-resurrection." Boakye then affirms my thesis that "'inhabiting the God of life-in-death and power-in-weakness'" is "the heart of 'Paul's cruciform spirituality.'"[14] Accordingly, Boakye argues, we "better comprehend both the church's ethical program and Paul's ministry career as 'resurrectiform'"

---

10. Boakye, "Inhabiting the 'Resurrectiform' God," 53. Some of this article is restated in Boakye's *Death and Life*, 13–14.

11. Boakye, "Inhabiting the 'Resurrectiform' God," 53. In points 1 and 2 in the numbered list, Boakye indicates he is quoting me, but only point 1 is a direct quotation; in 3, he is also paraphrasing me, as he rightly indicates.

12. Ibid.

13. Ibid., 54.

14. Ibid.

since "a resurrection requires a death, [while] the reverse is not true."[15] He expands this thesis as follows:

> It seems to me precisely because power comes from weakness (Gal 2:19; 2 Cor 12:9), life from death (Gal 5:24–25; 2 Cor 4:11) and victory from suffering (Gal 3:4; Rom 8:17), [that] emphasizing crucifixion over resurrection . . . *creates a hierarchy that Paul never intended.* This brief paper will explore whether the ministry of Paul and the lives of the rectified are actually resurrection shaped.
>
> I propose that a simple survey of Paul's death-life lexicon will elucidate just how resurrection shaped the life and ministry of Paul was, and how profoundly ideas of resurrection inform the lives of those rectified through faith in Christ.[16]

Boakye then offers a spirited defense of this thesis, with a particular focus on 2 Corinthians. His major claim, building on a brief examination of the language of life and death in Paul, is that "The twinned concepts of life *and* death is [*sic*] critical to Paul's depiction of God's work to rectify the world, Paul's evaluation of his own role within that work and how he remedies aberrant theology and behaviour in the Jesus assemblies."[17] He then appeals to 2 Corinthians to defend this three-part claim.

In other words, with respect to salvation, ministry, and spirituality, cruciformity needs to be balanced with "resurrectiformity."[18] Although I basically agree with much of the substance of what Boakye says, I want to maintain that Paul actually does create a hierarchy of sorts, privileging the cross in several ways, and not least in 2 Corinthians. In making this argument, I am not "marginalizing" the resurrection as Boakye implies at the end of his essay;[19] nor am I only attending to "half" of Paul's

---

15. Ibid. In *Death and Life*, 14, Boakye states that the term "reviviform" would be more accurate, but since he does not employ that term in the article, or elsewhere in the book, we will generally stay with "resurrectiform" in this essay.

16. Boakye, "Inhabiting the 'Resurrectiform' God," 55 (emphasis added). In a note in the middle of this passage, Boakye mentions Finlan's neologism "anastiform" and affirms Finlan's critique of my work: that we leave out half of Paul's message if we only call life in Christ cruciform (Finlan, "Can We Speak of *Theosis*?", 74–75).

17. Boakye, "Inhabiting the 'Resurrectiform' God," 56.

18. Boakye uses this noun twice (ibid., 59).

19. Ibid., 62.

message, as Finlan claims (Boakye concurring),[20] or attending only "partially" to Paul's theology of conformity to Christ, as Rachael Tan argues.[21]

However, rather than turning this essay into a direct response to Boakye (or Finlan or Tan), I will instead think theologically with Paul about the resurrection and the resurrectional character of participation in Christ, doing so partly in dialogue with these scholars. Unlike them, however, I think it best, as stated above, not to use terms like "resurrectiform" or "anastiform" in parallel with "cruciform" to refer to the *form*, or narrative structure, of participation in Christ according to Paul. Rather, it is better to speak of participation in Christ as having a resurrection *quality*—or perhaps even a resurrection *ethos and effect*. There may not be a suitable term with the "ring" of "resurrectiform," but—as we will see—the neat parallelism between "cruciform" and "resurrectiform" might actually be misleading. Thus, I will propose that terms like "resurrectional" or "resurrection-suffused," in conjunction with "cruciform," are better, more accurate descriptors of Paul's paradoxical understanding of participation in Christ.[22]

---

20. Writes Finlan: "In chapter 3 [of Philippians], the believer's re-formation or conformation begins with sharing in Christ's sufferings and death, and *then* with participation in resurrection. Conformity with Christ, then, is first 'cruciform,' and then 'anastiform'.... *Theosis* has to do with 'anastiform' experience, both in this life and the next. If we want to call Paul's gospel 'cruciform,' as Michael Gorman does, we must also call it 'anastiform,' or we leave out half his message" ("Can We Speak of *Theosis*?", 74–75). At first Finlan appears to find a sequential pattern of cruciform conformity followed by ("then . . .") anastiform conformity, but then he says that theosis is an anastiform experience both now and later. He understands this "anastiform" existence primarily as transformation into a Spirit-led instead of a fleshly life (72–74), describing it also as "living as though already in the kingdom of God and receiving eternal light and truth" (77). He further describes theosis as "being "transformed into Christlikeness," which "always involves both cruciform and *anastiform* living, but points to a thoroughly *anastiform* destiny" (78). For Boakye's agreement, see his "Inhabiting the 'Resurrectiform' God," 55 n12.

21. Tan ("Conformity to Christ," 179) agrees with me that Paul advocates conformity to Christ (rather than mere imitation of him) but then remarks, "Although cruciformity captures the meaning of conformity *partially*, it could mislead one to focus only on the cross (*crux*) without the resurrection, dying without the rising, and sufferings without the power. It is clear from our exegesis that Paul's conformity includes *both* the power of Christ's resurrection *and* the participation in his sufferings. He wants to know Christ, his mindset, his attitudes, and everything related to Christ. No doubt the cross is central to Paul's theology and forms the basis of conformity, but conformity is more than that. It is this comprehensive aspect which pervades the whole of life that is highlighted in this passage [Phil 3:7–11]."

22. In the second edition of Gorman, *Apostle of the Crucified Lord: A Theological Introduction to Paul and His Letters* (Grand Rapids: Eerdmans, 2017) I was more appreciative of such terms, though with the same basic understanding offered here: "To die with Christ is also to be raised to new life— resurrection life (Rom 6). Some scholars have suggested that we speak not only of *cruciform* existence in Paul but also of *resurrectiform, reviviform*, or *anastiform* existence.... This is true, but it is true only paradoxically: cruciform existence is anastiform, and vice versa. It is also true only partially and provisionally, for full resurrection life will be known only in the future, in the eschaton" (*Apostle*, 2nd ed., 151–52, with references to Boakye and Finlan in a note).

First Response: Cautious Affirmation

Even with that thesis, my first response to the concerns of Boakye, Finlan, and Tan is generally affirmative. Participation in Christ is of course participation in the resurrected Christ and is therefore in a profound sense "informed" by the resurrection.[23] There are several important commonsense and specifically Pauline perspectives that justify both their concerns and my affirmation of what I think they are trying to convey with terms like "resurrectiform."

First, of course, is the commonsense assumption that one cannot truly participate in any meaningful way in the life of a dead person. If Christ has not been raised from the dead, Paul might say, our (so-called) participation is in vain.

Second, the God Paul knows and worships in Christ is the living God, the God of resurrection, the God of new creation who "gives life to the dead and calls into existence the things that do not exist" (Rom 4:17).[24] Thus the God of Paul's gospel and Paul's ministry on behalf of God is life-giving; this is in part what Boakye means by "resurrectiform" and what I mean by "resurrectional"—resisting the "form" language in connection with resurrection because (paradoxically, as we will emphasize later) the character or "shape" of this resurrecting God revealed in Christ is cruciform.[25]

Third, Paul himself grounds our salvation not only in the cross, but also in the resurrection. For instance, in Rom 4:24–25 Christ's death and his resurrection are so inseparable that they essentially constitute one saving event, and elsewhere Paul both assumes this inseparability and sometimes articulates it (e.g., Rom 8:34—Jesus is the one "who died, yes, who was raised, who is at the right hand of God, who indeed intercedes for us").[26] Moreover, 1 Corinthians 15 makes it clear that there is no salvation, no hope, and no purpose without both Christ's resurrection and ours, but that with resurrection comes purposeful life now and permanent eschatological life in the future.

Fourth, Paul can characterize the gift of salvation effected by Christ's death and resurrection as "life" and even, in some sense, as resurrection. In Rom 5:18, Paul declares that "one man's act of righteousness leads to justification and life for all." Although this life is predicated on Jesus' singular act of righteousness (his death),

23. See Boakye's phrase cited above that for Paul "the resurrection inform[s] the lives of those rectified" ("Inhabiting the 'Resurrectiform' God," 55). I have, in fact, recognized my own need to give greater emphasis to the resurrection. The second edition of *Apostle* attempts to do precisely that.

24. See 2 Cor 1:9, which Boakye rightly explores while also briefly noting Rom 4:17 ("Inhabiting the 'Resurrectiform' God," 56).

25. Boakye is right to stress that "2 Corinthians houses a deeply embedded nucleus of revivification language exemplary of Paul's self-perception of the political, social, and theological dynamics of ministry" (ibid., 62).

26. See also, for example, 1 Thess 4:14; Rom 5:10.

it is clear that the result is the opposite of death (see 5:15) and thus that the "life" effected by Christ's death is a form of resurrection. This is also the strong implication of the Abraham story: that despite Abraham's body being "as good as dead" and his wife's womb being barren (Rom 4:19), the God of Abraham (and of Paul) is the one "who gives life to the dead" (Rom 4:17)—the God of resurrection, new creation, and new life.

Fifth, in my view the ongoing experiential side of salvation (ethics, spirituality) involves participating not only in Christ's death, but also in his resurrection. This is especially clear in Paul's treatment of the implications of baptism: "Therefore we have been buried with him by baptism into death, so that, just as Christ was raised from the dead by the glory of the Father, so we too might walk in newness of life" (Rom 6:4).[27] Thus Paul can say that we are "those who have been brought from death to life" (6:13) in anticipation of eternal life (Rom 6:23); that is, present resurrection life ("newness of life") is a foretaste of future resurrection life ("eternal life").[28]

---

27. Despite the claims of certain interpreters, including Boakye, that Paul does not promote a present resurrection but restricts resurrection language completely to the future, Daniel Kirk, Ann Jervis, and others have demonstrated that Paul sees believers as participating in Christ's resurrection now, this present participation taking the form of new life. See, for example, J. R. Daniel Kirk, *Unlocking Romans: Resurrection and the Justification of God* (Grand Rapids: Eerdmans, 2009); L. Ann Jervis, "Time in Romans 5–8," in *The Unrelenting God: Essays on God's Action in Scripture in Honor of Beverly Roberts Gaventa*, edited by David J. Downs and Mathew L. Skinner (Grand Rapids: Eerdmans, 2013) 139–49 (esp. 145); Frederick S. Tappenden, *Resurrection in Paul: Cognition, Metaphor, and Transformation*, ECL 19 (Atlanta: SBL Press, 2016).

28. This seems to be Finlan's point in speaking of both present and future anastiform existence. Although Boakye prefers the term "revivification" to "resurrection" in describing my fourth and fifth points, we are in essential agreement about the importance of life in Christ having a resurrection-like quality. For a methodologically unique approach to this issue that arrives at conclusions similar to mine, see Tappenden, *Resurrection in Paul*. Tappenden writes, "For Paul, resurrection is an ongoing event whereby both Christ's death and Christ's life are continually manifested in the Christ-believing body" (226). Present resurrection is the result of the presence of the divine spirit, who effects "a trajectory of transformative embodiment" (155) in a "single resurrection event" (155) from baptism to eschatological completion: "the already risen interior thus awaits the achievement of the not yet risen exterior" (157). For Tappenden, this ongoing, participatory, transformational resurrection is expressed in "certain patterns of embodiment" (177) that involve dying with Christ: (1) "life in death" (190–207), which is complementary to life through death (199, 234), and (2) "ecstasy, ethnicity, and resurrection" (207–25). Although the latter pattern may seem closer to Finlan, Boakye, and Tan than to me, Tappenden stresses that in all aspects of this experience, "the nature of the enspirited earthly body's present experience of resurrection ... is characterized by a process of ongoing outer death and inner life" (226). (Although Tappenden does not use the word theosis, his insistence on participation in Christ as a single resurrection—an ongoing process and trajectory—is actually quite theotic in nature.) In my words, I would say that the *shape* of resurrection life in the present is cruciform, and that theosis involves cruciformity.

The Priority of Cruciformity in Paul's Understanding of Participation

Nevertheless, although I agree with my critics that we need to keep the cross and resurrection together, and I affirm that we need to speak of participation in Christ's resurrection, I suggest that it is imperative that we maintain the priority of cruciformity and of the term cruciform to describe the shape, or structure, of life in union with Christ. Moreover, because throughout Paul's writings there is a discernible cruciform substance, even a pattern, that describes participation in Christ, but not a discernible "resurrectiform" substance or pattern, there really is no parallel between cruciform and "resurrectiform" life.[29] Rather, the profound Pauline paradox of participation is that the cruciformly structured life in Christ is, simultaneously, participation in Christ's resurrection. This is the case in two closely connected senses that we might cautiously call "spiritual" and "missional": experiencing newness of life (spiritual) and being a channel of life for others (missional). That is, the cruciform life is suffused with the power of the resurrection; it is resurrectional, but not resurrectiform.[30]

I will substantiate this claim by looking at a few key texts from Paul's letters, specifically the Corinthian correspondence and Philippians. Many other texts could be considered to corroborate the argument.

1 Corinthians 2:2 in the Context of 1:18—2:5: The Theophanic Cross

In 1 Cor 2:2 Paul claims that he had "decided to know nothing among you [the Corinthians] except Jesus Christ, and him crucified," which should probably be translated as "nothing among you except Jesus the Messiah, that is, Jesus the *crucified* Messiah" (cf. 1 Cor 1:23). How could Paul possibly make this claim about his allegedly myopic focus on Christ crucified in the letter that contains his most sustained exposition of the resurrection of both Jesus and believers (1 Cor 15)?

On the one hand, the most immediate context suggests that 1 Cor 2:2 is a rhetorically charged claim, bordering on hyperbole, in which Paul contrasts his own

29. The closest we get to a resurrection "pattern" in Paul is the dynamic of life in death (so Tappenden), but that is more of a principle in search of a concrete pattern than it is an actual pattern. The concrete pattern itself, as we will see below, is specific and cruciform.

30. In the original essay discussed at the North Park Symposium, there was no explicit definition of "resurrectiform." By denying the appropriateness of the term "resurrectiform" to describe Paul's theology and spirituality, I have in mind a theology and spirituality of present glory, triumph, and/or power that minimizes or even dismisses the centrality of ongoing participation in Jesus' crucifixion. Indeed, as just noted in the text, the central Pauline paradox is that the resurrection life is cross-shaped (cruciform) from start to finish, meaning until the *parousia* or the bodily resurrection. It is possible that the response by Markus Nikkanen may have been slightly different had I made this implicit understanding of resurrectiform more explicit.

message with the showy rhetorical practices of certain unnamed preachers who may have "come proclaiming the mystery of God to you in lofty words or wisdom" (2:1). In other words, we should perhaps not take Paul literally. On the other hand, however, if we expand the context just a bit to include the entire rhetorical unit of 1:18—2:5, it becomes clear that we *should* take Paul very literally. In this unit, Paul makes astonishing claims about Christ crucified both as divine self-revelation and, hence, as epistemological criterion for discerning the activity of God.

By claiming that Christ crucified constitutes the power and wisdom of God (1:24) Paul is saying that the cross is not only a Christophany but also, and in a sense more fundamentally, a theophany. As such, the cross is the criterion for knowing how and where God works, that is, both *among* the weak (the Corinthians: 1:26–31) and *through* the weak (Paul: 2:1–5). The implicit corollary of this epistemological criterion for discerning the means by which God works, and the space in which God works, is that we participate in God's sort of activity—which is of course the work of God's Spirit (2:4, 6–16)—by means of, and in spaces of, human weakness. (This corollary will become both more fully developed and turned into a memorable slogan in 2 Corinthians: "whenever I am weak, then I am strong" [2 Cor 12:10]).

In other words, the word (*logos*; 1 Cor 1:18) of Christ crucified is not a minor part of Paul's gospel or an optional supplement; nor is it even merely a prelude to the more important reality of the resurrection. Rather, the cross tells us something about Christ, about God, about God's Spirit's work in the world, about us, and about our benefitting from and participating in God's work that even the resurrection does not tell us. That is, Christ crucified is the *sine qua non* of the substance of the gospel because of its theophanic, christophanic, pneumatophanic, anthropophanic, and ultimately ecclesiophanic character.[31]

To be sure, the word of the cross is no gospel, and it has no soteriological consequence, apart from the resurrection. The mini-creed that Paul inherited, passed on to the Corinthians, and quotes back to them (1 Cor 15:3ff.) names both the crucifixion and the resurrection as the fulfillment of Scripture and the basis of salvation. Without the resurrection, says 1 Cor 15, everything else Christians say and do is meaningless. Paradoxically, however, the cross maintains a priority in emphasis throughout the rest of 1 Corinthians. This is because for Paul the resurrection validates his fundamental claim that the cross is both how and where God acts savingly for the world. The salvific, theophanic, and paradigmatic character of

31. Which means that Christ crucified reveals the character of God, Christ himself, the Spirit, the human person, and the church. See my essay, Michael J. Gorman, "The Cross in Paul: Christophany, Theophany, Ecclesiophany," in *Ecclesia and Ethics*, edited by E. Allen Jones III et al (London: T. & T. Clark, 2016) 21–40.

the cross obtains only because the resurrection validates it as such. We participate in Christ, in the Spirit, in the life of the Triune God by participating in the reality that the resurrected Christ in whom we live and move and have our being is the crucified Christ, and none other. In the words of Andy Johnson, Jesus is "stamped forever with the legacy of being crucified."[32] Similarly, in the last century Ernst Käsemann wrote that the cross is "the signature of the one who is risen."[33]

The resurrected Christ does not displace the crucified Christ as the place of divine life and of our participation in that life. On the contrary, we participate in Christ truly only when we know this Christ as the crucified Messiah, the one whose obedient faithfulness to God and self-giving love on the cross determine the shape of our own lives, individually and corporately, in the power of the Spirit. (This is essentially the message of 1 Cor 13, which message is applied to various concrete situations throughout the letter.)[34] For Paul, as we shall see further below, that cruciform life is—paradoxically—the resurrection-suffused life, and vice versa.

Phil 2:5–8: The Cross as Divine Self-Revelation and Paradigm

We turn next to Philippians, and specifically to its famous christological poem (often called a hymn) within the context of the letter. Of many things that could be said about this rich text, we will highlight two aspects: its reaffirmation of the christophanic and theophanic character of the cross, and the corollary participatory, paradigmatic character of Christ crucified for the Philippians and for all Christians.

Christophany as Theophany

It is widely recognized that Phil 2:6–11 contains some of the most significant christological affirmations in the New Testament. It has even been called the place "where Christology began."[35] Although the precise significance of nearly every phrase has been debated, there is no argument about the poem's overall importance. Moreover, everyone agrees that three key main verbs in vv. 6–8 characterize Christ's actions: (1) he did not regard (or consider) equality with God as something to be grasped

---

32. Personal correspondence, Sept. 1, 2017, based on his own published work.

33. Ernst Käsemann, "The Saving Significance of the Death of Jesus in Paul," in *Perspectives on Paul*, trans. Margaret Kohl (Philadelphia: Fortress, 1971; repr. Mifflintown, PA: Sigler, 1996) 32–59, here 56.

34. Particularly important is the phrase "does not insist on its own way" (*ou zētei ta heautēs*) in 13:5, which is echoed in 1 Cor 10:24, 33 and in Phil 2:4.

35. Ralph P. Martin and Brian J. Dodd, eds., *Where Christology Began: Essays on Philippians 2* (Louisville: Westminster John Knox, 1998).

or exploited;[36] (2) he emptied himself; and (3) he humbled himself. The climax of this downward mobility, this course of ignominies, is crucifixion, a perfectly Roman conclusion to a perfectly un-Roman trajectory from the highest heights to the lowest depths.[37]

We may refer to vv. 6–8 of the poem as narrating a Christophany—a revelation of Christ, of the Messiah. But a good case can also be made that this Christophany is also a theophany—a revelation of God. The critical words in support of this claim are the first few of v. 6: *hos en morphē theou hyparchōn* (literally, "who, being in the form of God"). The participle *hyparchōn* ("being") needs to be interpreted: does it imply a rather neutral sense of simultaneity—"while being (i.e., while he was) in the form of God"? Or perhaps it has a concessive sense—"although being (i.e., although he was) in the form of God"? This has been the interpretation of nearly every modern English translation;[38] it is not incorrect, but it may be incomplete. There is another significant option: a causal sense, namely, "because of being in the form of God" (= "because he was in the form of God . . .").

Building on the suggestions of others (including C. F. D. Moule, N. T. Wright, and Stephen Fowl) I have elsewhere made an extended argument for this translation of the participle in a causal sense—"because"—as a fundamental aspect of what the poem conveys about Christ (in addition to the concessive sense: "although").[39] That is, Christ did not do what he did *in spite of* being in the form of God and equal with God, but precisely *because* he was in the form of God and equal with God. This causal ("because") interpretation has been convincing to some significant recent interpreters of this text.[40] If it is correct (and I am quite convinced that it is), then the poem tells us something profound not only about Jesus and what it means to be the Messiah, but also about God and what it means to be divine. God, it says, is by

36. Greek *harpagmos*, a term that occurs only here in the NT, the meaning of which is much debated.

37. See especially Joseph H. Hellerman, *Reconstructing Honor in Roman Philippi: Carmen Christi as Cursus Pudorum*, SNTSMS 132 (Cambridge: Cambridge University Press, 2005).

38. NASB has "although"; CEB, ESV, NAB, NET, NLT, NRSV, and RSV all have "though." NIV has the neutral "being in very nature God," as do (for instance) several major French translations.

39. Maintaining both "although" and "because" is not a case of wrongly trying to have one's cake and eat it too; it is rather a matter of the text's surface structure ("although") and its deep structure ("because"). See Gorman, *Inhabiting the Cruciform God*, 9–39.

40. See, for example, Ben C. Blackwell, *Christosis: Engaging Paul's Soteriology with His Patristic Interpreters* (Grand Rapids: Eerdmans, 2016) 11–12, 205–6; Jordan Cooper, *Christification: A Lutheran Approach to Theosis* (Eugene, OR: Wipf & Stock, 2014) 56; John M. G. Barclay, "'Because he was rich he became poor': Translation, Exegesis and Hermeneutics in the Reading of 2 Cor 8.9," in *Theologizing in the Corinthian Conflict: Studies in the Exegesis and Theology of 2 Corinthians*, edited by Reimund Bieringer et al., BTS 16 (Leuven: Peeters, 2013) 331–44 (esp. 339–40); Tan, *Conformity to Christ*, 79.

nature self-emptying (kenotic), self-humbling, self-giving—vulnerable and "downwardly mobile."[41]

The specific narrative structure of this downward mobility is a critical dimension of Paul's understanding of Christ and, as we will see below, of participation in Christ. As I have shown elsewhere on numerous occasions,[42] this narrative pattern is as follows:

> Although [x] (possessing status)
>
> not [y] (pursuing self-interest)
>
> but [z] (being self-giving/seeking the good of others).

Furthermore, as we have just seen, this "*although* [x] not [y] but [z]" pattern is also to be understood as "*because* [x] not [y] but [z]." The narrative pattern reveals the fundamental character—the "life story," so to speak—of God and of God's Messiah. This counterintuitive pattern about the nature of being truly divine and messianic both reinforces and unpacks what we observed in 1 Cor 1:18—2:5. Of course the story does not end with crucifixion, but with exaltation; the two-step, sequential structure of the poem as a whole is from crucifixion to exaltation. But it is the cruciform x-y-z pattern of the first part that becomes normative for present life in Christ.

Christophany as Paradigm for Participation

Throughout Philippians, this "although/because [x] not [y] but [z]" Christ-paradigm of humility, self-emptying, concern for others, and even suffering to the point of death is consistently described and prescribed, as many interpreters have recognized. (It occurs throughout the rest of Paul's letters, too, including as a description of Paul's own ministry in 1 Cor 9, summarized in vv. 4–5, 15, 19.)[43]

First of all, in the poem's most immediate context, Paul prescribes genuine participation in Christ/in the Spirit (which means in Christ/Christ's body, the *ekklēsia*)

---

41. In the response to my paper by Markus Nikkanen and, in the subsequent symposium discussion, there was some theological and exegetical concern about this claim. The main point to be made, theologically, is that the triune God is a communion of persons whose nature is self-donating love. I use "self-emptying" here in a metaphorical sense as one way to describe this love (as does Philippians, I suggest). For a similar view in connection with the church's missional participation in God/Christ, see Stephen R. Holmes, "Trinitarian Missiology: Towards A Theology of God as Missionary," *International Journal of Systematic Theology* 8 (2006) 72–90. Holmes writes, "Just as purposeful, cruciform, self-sacrificial sending is intrinsic to God's own life, being sent in a cruciform, purposeful and self-sacrificial way must be intrinsic to the church being the church" (89).

42. See, for example, Gorman, *Cruciformity*, 90–91, 168–73, et passim; and Gorman, *Apostle*, 2nd ed., 80–81, 125–26, 310, 507–9.

43. For 1 Cor 9, see esp. Gorman, *Apostle*, 2nd ed., 80–81, 310. For other letters, see Gorman, *Cruciformity*, and various chapters in *Apostle*, 2nd ed.

in terms that echo the poem and its narrative structure of not seeking self-interest but that of others:

> 1If then there is any encouragement in Christ, any consolation from love, any sharing in the Spirit, any compassion and sympathy, 2make my joy complete: be of the same mind [see 2:5], having the same love, being in full accord and of one mind. 3Do nothing from selfish ambition or conceit [or "empty glory"; see 2:7, 11], but in humility [see 2:8] regard [see 2:6] others as better than yourselves [*heautōn*]. 4Let each of you look not to your own interests [*ta heautōn*] but to the interests of others. (Phil 2:1–4)[44]

Moreover, near the end of the letter (4:2) Paul prescribes cruciform harmony ("to be of the same mind"; *to auto phronein*) for Euodia and Syntyche, who are in some sort of dispute, by using the language of unity from 2:2 ("be of the same mind . . . of one mind; *to auto phronēte . . . to hen phronountes*) and from the introduction to the poem describing the mind of Christ (2:5; *phroneite*).

Furthermore, Paul describes living examples of such cruciform participation by briefly narrating stories of himself and others that borrow the ideas and even the language of the poem. Paul's own desire to die and be with Christ is held in check by his Christ-like commitment to put the needs of others first (1:21–26). His own suffering (1:7, 12–24) is clearly for him participation in Christ's sufferings (3:10). And his "conversion"[45] autobiography echoes the Christ-poem in multiple ways, not least in the threefold repetition of the verb that characterizes Christ's fundamental act of "considering" or "regarding":

- [Christ Jesus] did not regard (*hēgēsato*) . . . (Phil 2:6)
- Yet whatever gains I [Paul] had, these I have come to regard [*hēgēmai*] as loss because of Christ. More than that, I regard [*hēgoumai*] everything as loss because of the surpassing value of knowing Christ Jesus my Lord. For his sake I have suffered the loss of all things, and I regard [*hēgoumai*] them as rubbish [or "filth," "excrement"], in order that I may gain Christ. (Phil 3:7–8)

In addition, Paul says of Timothy, "I have no one like [lit. "equal in soul to" (*isopsychon*)] him" (2:20) and "he has served [*edouleusen*] with me in the work of the gospel" (2:22), statements which together echo the description of Christ as the one equal *(isa)* to God (2:6) who took on the form of a slave (*doulou*; 2:7). And of Epaphroditus Paul writes that he "came close to death [*mechri thanatou*] for the work of Christ" (2:30), using the exact phrase from the poem that announces Christ's

---

44. Some aspects of the echoes from the poem are discernible only in Greek, such as the twofold use of the reflexive pronoun in 2:3–4 (*heautōn*) and in 2:7–8 (*heauton*). The Greek of 2:4 also echoes that of 1 Cor 13:5, noted above.

45. I use the term "conversion" in the sense of dramatic transformation, not to mean a change of "religion."

obedience unto death: "he . . . became obedient to the point of death [*mechri thana-tou*]—even death on a cross" (2:8).[46]

Where is the resurrection in the midst of all this death and death-like living? If we are looking for the term itself in the poem, we will be looking in vain, for it speaks of Christ's exaltation (2:9), not resurrection. Even this event in the Christ-narrative is something in which believers will share, however, as Christ "will transform the body of our humiliation that it may be conformed to the body of his glory" (3:21). Thus the two-step structure of the poem, from humiliation to exaltation, becomes the present-future pattern of believers, a pattern that is fundamentally synonymous with the pattern of death-resurrection that we also find in Philippians 3 (and else-where) for both Christ and Christians:

> to know Christ, that is (a) the power of his resurrection [*anastaseōs*] and (b) the participation [*koinōnian*] in his sufferings by (b') being conformed [*sym-morphizomenos*] to his death, if somehow I may attain (a') the resurrection [*exanastasin*] from the dead. (Phil 3:10–11; my trans.)

The chiastic (abb'a') structure of this text suggests that knowing the power of Christ's resurrection refers, at least in part, to the future resurrection from the dead. As in Rom 8:17 (God's adopted children are "joint heirs with Christ—if, in fact, we suffer with him so that we may also be glorified with him"), the sequential pattern of suffering and death followed by future resurrection is evident here. But the close grammatical connection between knowing that resurrection-power and participat-ing in Christ's sufferings also strongly suggests that we paradoxically experience the power of Christ's resurrection, as well as his sufferings, *as we are conformed to Christ's death.* For Paul, participating in Christ ("be[ing] found in him"; Phil 3:9) consists of knowing him in two inseparable senses: (1) experiencing the power of his resurrection now even while (2) sharing in his sufferings and thus being con-formed to his death. In other words, participating in Christ's resurrection *now* and participating in his sufferings and death *now* are simultaneous—indeed, in many ways, overlapping—realities. That is, *present participation in Christ is resurrection-empowered and resurrection-suffused but cross-shaped.* This simultaneity of crucifor-mity and resurrectionality is the point also of 2 Cor 12:10—"whenever I am weak, then I am strong." Indeed, it is the present cruciform life, which is paradoxically but profoundly an experience of knowing Christ's resurrection-power, that leads to future bodily transformation and resurrection, that is, to resurrectiform life. The *simultaneous* reality of *cruciform* existence being *resurrectional* existence is paired with the *sequential* reality of *cruciform* existence leading to *resurrectiform* existence.

46. For a fuller discussion, see Gorman, *Apostle*, 2nd ed., 489–91.

The key to present participation in Christ, then, is participatory *simultaneity*—sharing in Christ's death and resurrection at the same time—and the shape of that sharing is *cruciform*. This cruciformity can take the form of actual suffering (as it did for both the Philippians and Paul) as well as the more general form of kenotic, self-giving love. In fact, the two forms of cruciformity can coexist in the same person or community, as they did in Christ. That is why Paul consistently commends and advocates cruciform existence throughout the letter (and throughout all his correspondence), even calling participation in Christ's suffering a "grace": God "has graciously granted (*echaristhē*) you the privilege not only of believing in Christ, but of suffering for him as well" (Phil 1:29).

Yet one more thing needs to be said about this cruciform participation: it is—once again, paradoxically—far from morbid. Indeed, as everyone recognizes, Philippians is a letter of joy (see 1:4, 18, 25; 2:2, 17–18, 28–29; 3:1; 4:1, 4, 10). This too is undoubtedly part of what Paul means by knowing the power of the resurrection: joy in the midst of suffering. Paul might even paraphrase the letter to the Hebrews (on the assumption he did not write it!) by saying this:

> looking to Jesus the pioneer and perfecter of faithfulness, who for the sake of the joy that was both given to him in the midst of suffering and set before him as the end-result of suffering, endured the cross, disregarding its shame, and has taken his seat at the right hand of the throne of God. (Heb 12:2; NRSV alt.)

For Paul, then, participating in Christ is constituted by a pattern of death and resurrection that is both sequential and simultaneous. In this present life—corresponding to Christ's earthly life—the fundamental shape of participation is cruciform, but this cruciform participation is empowered by the resurrection—or, more accurately, by the (Spirit of the) resurrected crucified Messiah (see Gal 2:19–20; Rom 8:9–11). The Christian experience of *sequential* death and resurrection is grounded in the narrative sequence of the Christ-story, while the Christian experience of *simultaneous* death and resurrection is grounded in the reality that the Resurrected One remains the Crucified One. Accordingly, whether it is Paul, Timothy, Epaphroditus, Euodia and Syntyche, the Philippian community in ancient Macedonia, or us, the power of the resurrection is manifested in similar ways: through cruciform participation in Christ.

2 Corinthians 3–5, Focusing on 4:7–12: Resurrectional Cruciformity

The claims of Philippians about the simultaneity of cross and resurrection, with the stress on cruciform life in Christ, could hardly be more robustly affirmed than they are in 2 Corinthians. This symbiosis of cross and resurrection is revealed as Paul describes the ministry of himself and his colleagues (chaps. 1–7), as he redescribes that ministry in contrast to the activity of the "super-apostles" (chaps. 10–13), and as he encourages the Corinthians themselves to practice joyful, Macedonian-like cruciform generosity (chaps. 8–9).

At the same time, Andrew Boakye's argument for the importance of the "resurrectiform" dimension of Paul's theology is made primarily from this letter. Our goal will be to discern what Paul says on these matters and how best to articulate them theologically, proposing once again that Paul advocates resurrectional cruciformity rather than a resurrectiform existence. Constraints of space require us to focus on one critical text, 2 Cor 4:7–12.[47]

Paul has just told the Corinthians that he and his colleagues are ministers of a gospel about the glory of God, the glory of Christ (4:1–6; cf. 3:1–18). He has also told them that the role he and his co-workers play in proclaiming this gospel is to preach Jesus' lordship and to practice Jesus' servanthood (4:5). The paradox inherent in the comingling of a story of glory and a story of shame (servanthood/slavery) needs now to be spelled out in terms of its existential implications for apostolic ministry. How Paul and his coworkers live (and therefore also all ambassadors of Christ should live, he implies) is as much a part of their ministry as what they say, for ministers embody in themselves the slave-like existence of their Lord (see Phil 2:6–8; 1 Cor 9). Paul's life of affliction in the service of others is proof of his status as slave rather than Lord, as well as a demonstration of a fundamental theological claim of the letter, already previously made in 1 Corinthians (esp. 1:18—2:5): that God's power operates in and through human vulnerability and weakness (see esp. 2 Cor 1:3–6 and 12:9–10).

The paradoxically coupled images of slavery and glory propel the rest of this section of 2 Corinthians (through 5:10). Paul senses the tension between a gospel of glory and a life of slavery and affliction. He resolves it by finding the conjunction of death and resurrection in Jesus to be the pattern of his own life. Moreover, if the claims of 4:7–12 are not at odds with the bold claim of 3:18—that contemplating the glory of the Lord changes people into the likeness of the Messiah—then all believers, apostles or otherwise, are being called to participate in a transformation into glory that comes about only by becoming vessels of death-through-life.

Paul begins 4:7–12 with an image of having treasure in clay jars that functions as the thesis of the paragraph (4:7).[48] He then proceeds to give a brief but eloquent

47. According to Boakye, in 2 Cor 4:11–12, "the resurrectiform shape of the Pauline gospel exhibits the cruciformity of which Gorman speaks" ("Inhabiting the 'Resurrectiform' God," 58).

48. Some translators and other interpreters consider 4:7 to be the conclusion to the previous paragraph, but the parallel language of 4:1 ("since . . . we are engaged in [lit. "since we have"] this ministry") and 4:7 ("But we have this treasure"), together with the stark shift from the images of glory

catalog of apostolic sufferings (4:8–9).[49] Paul then interprets this ministerial experience of affliction as a paradoxical dynamic of life being made manifest in death (4:10–12). Weakness has a purpose, as Paul will say in three different ways with three parallel purpose ("so that"; Gk. *hina*) clauses in vv. 7, 10, and 11.

The "treasure" named in 4:7 is clearly first of all the gospel of the glory of God in the face of the Messiah Jesus (4:4, 6), while the "clay jars" are the lives of those in and through whom the gospel is proclaimed.[50] The treasure is also, in a profound sense, Jesus himself, whose dying and life Paul and his colleagues "carry" and make visible. With this clay-jar image, and then throughout the paragraph, Paul points out the necessary (and, in his case, actual) correspondence between the narrative shape of the gospel about Jesus and the narrative shape of ministerial life: power in weakness, life through death (not merely power *and* weakness or life *and* death). Paul also makes it clear that this is the *only* way that truly divine power—the power of cross and resurrection, of new covenant and new creation—can be manifested in and through human beings. As Paul had previously told the Corinthians (1 Cor 1:18—2:5) the gospel reveals that this is simply the way God works, whether in the crucifixion of Jesus (1:18–25), the calling and composition of the Corinthian community (1:26–31), or the ministry of Paul (2:1–5).

Cruciform existence, then, is paradoxically the manifestation of divine power—indeed, of resurrection power. The mission of God is accomplished in and through suffering and weakness, or else the power of the cross is no power at all, and the gospel that Paul preached is utter nonsense. Theosis, or participating in the life of God through dwelling in Christ and being empowered by the indwelling Spirit of the Father and the Son, is a foretaste of future resurrection that is presently—paradoxically—cross-shaped. This (present) theosis is necessarily both cruciform and missional, for God in Christ was letting loose the divine power of creation to recreate people into a new people of the new covenant ready and able to continue the manifestation of God's work in Jesus in the world. That is, they were to be a people who would practice resurrection (to use the words of Eugene Peterson and Wendell Berry) by embodying the cross.[51]

and light in 4:6 to the image of clay jars in 4:7, suggests that 4:7 begins a new discourse unit.

49. Lisa M. Bowens ("Investigating the Apocalyptic Texture of Paul's Martial Imagery in 2 Corinthians 4–6," *JSNT* 39 [2016] 3–15) argues convincingly that the language used in 4:8–9 occurs elsewhere in military contexts and thus implies apocalyptic conflict.

50. Paul may also be alluding to the prophetic image (e.g., Isa 29:16; 45:9; 64:8; Jer 18–19) of God's people as God's pottery, as he does in Rom 9:21–23.

51. Boakye reads this passage somewhat similarly, finding in it both cruciformity and resurrectiformity, in his words ("Inhabiting the 'Resurrectiform' God," 58–59). But what he fails to articulate sufficiently clearly is that it is precisely Paul's cruciform ministry that is the vehicle and mode of God's resurrecting activity, such that calling Paul's ministry resurrectiform rather than resurrectional risks

Power (*dynamis*), then, is the critical word in Paul's thesis statement in 2 Cor 4:7. Paul does not merely aver that the treasure *is* contained in clay jars so that its divine source will be evident (so NIV, NRSV, RSV), but rather implies that the treasure *must* be in clay jars because clay jars are fragile and thus "weak," and when the gospel of God is contained in other kinds of vessels—vessels of power, such as those of the "super-apostles" described in chapters 10–13—the gospel is distorted and the power of the gospel becomes the power of someone or something else. Yes, the gospel is the power of God for salvation (Rom 1:16), but only when it is contained within, and channeled through, jars of clay.

Paul expressed the necessity and purpose of such oddly construed divine, resurrection power, and its *modus operandi*, in the three parallel "so that," or purpose (*hina*), clauses noted above, followed by a summary statement:

Verse	Weakness/Death	Power/Life
4:7	But we have this treasure in clay jars, **so that**	it may be made clear that this extraordinary power belongs to God and does not come from us:
4:10	always carrying in the body the death [or "dying"] of Jesus, **so that**	the life of Jesus may also be made visible in our bodies.
4:11	For while we live, we are always being given up to death for Jesus' sake, **so that**	the life of Jesus may be made visible in our mortal flesh.
4:12 (summary)	So death is at work in us,	but life in you.

The three parallel purpose clauses and the summary statement all proclaim that cruciform existence has a paradoxical purpose: the manifestation of the transformative power of God and the "life" of Jesus: the transformative, resurrection power of Jesus to bring life out of death, as 4:12 says in conclusion. That is, through the cruciform ministry of weakness and suffering, the transformative, life-giving power of God manifested in Jesus' resurrection is unleashed in the life of Corinth and beyond. To be sure (once again, paradoxically), this resurrectional life brought forth in Jesus will be cruciform, for cruciformity is not just for apostles, as Paul has said clearly elsewhere (e.g., in Philippians) and will make plain in chapters 8 and 9 when he discusses the collection for Jerusalem.[52]

---

underemphasizing this paradox.

52. In *Christosis* (e.g., 203) Ben Blackwell likewise stresses both that the life of Jesus—and of God—is manifested in the apostolic dialectic of life through death and that this form of revealing the divine life is not restricted to apostles.

All of this is because the exalted, living, life-giving, resurrected Lord is identical to the crucified Messiah. The life he produces corresponds to the life he led and the death he died. There are not two things operating, crucifixion *and* resurrection, or death *and* life, but rather life *in* death, power *in* weakness, resurrection *in* crucifixion (cf. 12:9–10). God's uncanny, paradoxical power works this way both *in* us and *through* us, Paul says.[53] This cruciform life is not only one of participating in Christ's sufferings, as catalogued in 4:8–9 and elsewhere, but also one of participating in Christ's love, as the catalog in 1 Corinthians makes clear (4:9–13): "When reviled, we bless; when persecuted, we endure; when slandered, we speak kindly" (1 Cor 4:12b–13a)—words that echo Jesus' own teaching and praxis. Christ's suffering on the cross was the ultimate manifestation of a life of cruciform love; so too, participation in his life will be manifested as love that will likely culminate in suffering.[54]

The similarity of the apostle's sufferings to those of Jesus is reinforced by the Greek verb Paul uses in the phrase "we are always being given up [or "handed over"] to death" (2 Cor 4:11): *paradidometha*, a passive form of the verb *paradidōmi*. This verb is frequently used in all four Gospels, in both passive and active forms, to signify Jesus' betrayal and his being handed over to the authorities.[55] Paul knew at least an oral tradition about Jesus' deliverance to death that used this verb: "For I received from the Lord what I also handed on (*paredōka*) to you, that the Lord Jesus on the night when he was betrayed [or "handed over"; *paredideto*] took a loaf of bread" (1 Cor 11:23). The apostle also uses the verb to signify Jesus' own active self-giving in death (Gal 2:20),[56] as well as his being delivered to death by his Father (Rom 4:25; 8:32). The verb is used additionally in texts about Jesus' followers being handed over to authorities.[57] In fact, in Acts, Paul is both one who hands disciples over to others (Acts 8:3; 22:4) and, later, one who is handed over (Acts 15:26; 21:11; 28:17).

Although *paradidōmi* does not always signify "hand over to death," that is clearly the sense of most of these texts, especially those concerning Jesus, but also those focused on the disciples.[58] What is significant for reading 2 Cor 4:11 is that

53. Similarly, see Paul's use in 2 Cor 2:14 of the Roman triumph as an image of apostolic ministry. Paul depicts himself as the conquered captive (death) who is "in Christ" (resurrection/life). In Christ, he is both defeated and victorious, dying and living.

54. I agree with Billings, *Union with Christ*, 142n52 that "cruciform" with respect to Christ characterizes his entire life, not only its culmination.

55. See, for example, Matt 10:4; 17:22; 20:18–19; 26:2, 15, 16, 21, 23–25, 46, 48; Mark 3:19; 9:31; 10:33; 14:10, 11, 18, 21, 42, 44; 15:1, 15; Luke 9:44; 18:32; 21:12; 22:4, 21, 22, 48; 24:7; John 6:64, 71; 12:4; 13:2, 11, 21; 18:2, 5, 30, 36; 19:11, 16a; 21:20; see also Acts 3:13.

56. See Eph 5:2, 25. See also Gal 1:4, where the related verb *didōmi* is used.

57. For example, Matt 10:19; Mark 13:11–12; Luke 21:12; see also Acts 12:4.

58. Occasionally there is a contextual reference to prison and/or punishment rather than death per se, but the word "death" or "kill" often appears in the context, and/or the context usually implies that

Paul tells his story of apostolic suffering in the language that both he and the evangelists used to narrate Jesus' own deliverance to death and in the language that those same writers employed to describe the similar fate of Jesus' followers, including Paul himself. To be handed over to death constantly ("always" in 4:10–11) then, is to share repeatedly in the fate of Jesus, which has now become the fate of his disciples—as Jesus himself predicted, according to the Gospel writers: "take up [your] cross daily" (Luke 9:23).[59] But since death cannot literally happen repeatedly, Paul is obviously talking about the death-like practices and near-death experiences that he describes and prescribes, both here and elsewhere.

The best word to characterize this is not imitation, as if Paul were deliberately seeking these situations and inviting others to do the same. Rather, the passive voice of *paradidometha* suggests that he and his colleagues are being acted upon, and thereby being conformed to the story of Christ. Thus "participation" and "conformity" characterize Paul's experience better than "imitation."[60] This does not, however, mean that Paul is an unwilling participant in these sufferings; nor does it mean that the only forces at work in his life of conformity to the sufferings of the Messiah are those of his enemies. Rather, as we see here (and in the subsequent sentences: 4:14–15), Paul views the sufferings as beneficial—even life-giving—for others, and he believes he is empowered to endure them by God. Indeed, God is mysteriously at work in and through these sufferings.

In 2 Corinthians, of course, Paul also speaks about transformation "from glory to glory" (3:18; my translation), implying some type of present glory. But the context of that verse, especially the following sentences in chapter 4 that we have just examined, suggest that Paul has in mind a present, *cruciform* glory and Christ-likeness that will eventually become an eschatological, fully resurrectiform glory.[61] As in 2 Corinthians, so also in Philippians, Romans, and elsewhere: present glory is power in weakness, life in death, glory in suffering. But it is nonetheless glory: cruciform glory; it is nonetheless participation in the life and power of God in Christ by the Spirit: cross-shaped participation. In other words, there is real participation in divine power, in the resurrection, even in glory, but this participation is paradoxically marked by what appears to be the *opposite* of power, resurrection, life, and glory. The

---

death is the goal of the handing over.

59. See also, of course, the many predictions of literal suffering and persecution, and cf. 1 Cor 15:31.

60. Similarly, Douglas A. Campbell, *The Deliverance of God: An Apocalyptic Rereading of Justification in Paul* (Grand Rapids: Eerdmans, 2009) 914–24.

61. In Rom 8:30, similarly, Paul can speak of glorification in the past tense because in Christ the process of restoring humanity into the image and glory of God—into Christ-likeness—has begun (see Isa 55:3, 5–7).

apostolic practices of being afflicted and persecuted, of nonretaliation and blessing when cursed, and so on are fundamentally, then, experiences of glory: *the glory of the cross.* They are spiritual practices, cruciform practices, *theotic* practices.[62]

To repeat for emphasis: that such paradoxical resurrection-suffused participation in the cross is not limited to apostles is clear in numerous ways. Not only do we have the testimony of other letters with similar paradoxical dynamics, such as Philippians (discussed earlier), but we also have the explicit witness of 2 Corinthians itself (esp. chaps. 8–9) as noted above. Moreover, elsewhere Paul speaks autobiographically of being in Christ in ways that are appropriate for all believers (e.g., Gal 2:19–20), and he invites others—specifically the Corinthians—to imitate him and his cruciform mode of participation in Christ (1 Cor 4:16; 11:1; cf. Phil 4:9; 2 Thess 3:7–9).[63]

Conclusion: The Pauline Participation Paradox—
Resurrectional Cruciformity

Many other texts in Paul could be considered to see how the themes we have explored in parts of Philippians, 1 Corinthians, and 2 Corinthians are so thoroughly enmeshed in Paul's articulation of his theology and spirituality.

For instance, Romans 6 speaks of both dying and rising with Christ as liberation from sin (or "Sin," understood as a cosmic power), but the freedom of "newness of life" (6:4; cf. 6:13)—of being alive to God (6:10–11)—is paradoxically one of dying to sin (6:11) and of self-giving to God (6:13–23). Or consider Romans 8, a robust text on participation in Christ; it contains numerous "in" passages indicating a spirituality of mutual indwelling ("in" Christ and vice versa; "in" the Spirit and vice versa; 8:2, 9–11); numerous words that begin with a form of the Greek prefix *syn* (meaning "with," "co-"; 8:16–17, 22, 26, 28–29); and the metaphor of adoption as God's children (8:14–25), which has frequently been associated with theosis, or deification, in the Christian tradition. Indeed, no passage on participation in Paul is more filled with exuberant life in the Spirit than Romans 8—it radiates resurrection power (8:11). At the same time, however, Paul makes it clear that life in Christ, life in the Spirit, is cruciform in several ways, especially ongoing dying to the flesh (8:1–6) and suffering, both with all creation and for the gospel (8:17–39).

---

62. This paragraph has been adapted from Gorman, *Apostle*, 2nd ed., 443, and Gorman, "Paul's Corporate, Cruciform, Missional *Theosis*," 190–92. Paul's association of the cross with glory is reminiscent of the Gospel of John (e.g., John 12:23; 13:31–32; 17:1).

63. See 1 Thess 1:6; 2:14. See also Jeffrey W. Aernie, "Faith, Judgment, and the Believer: A Reassessment of 2 Corinthians 5:6–10," *CBQ* 79 (2017) 438–54.

These texts, among others, reinforce the central claim of this essay: for Paul, resurrectional life in Christ is the cruciform life, and vice versa. This is the paradox of participation for Paul. Furthermore, I have argued that it is best to use "cruciform" for the shape, structure, or form of this present life in Christ, avoiding the additional use of the parallel term "resurrectiform" or "anastiform" for present participation in Christ. Rather, I propose using terms like "resurrectional" or "resurrection-suffused" (meaning "resurrection-enabled" and "life-giving") for present participation, reserving any other "-form" language for the fully transformed eschatological future (e.g., "resurrectiform," "reviviform," "anastiform"). Hence "resurrectional" or "resurrection-suffused" characterizes that which enables and sustains cruciform participation in Christ and that which results from such participation: abundant life (cf. John 10:10). Yes, we have been crucified *and* raised with Christ—raised to newness of life; revivified, if you prefer. But the fundamental shape of present resurrection life is cruciform.[64] We participate in the resurrected Christ by continually carrying his death in our mortal but resurrection-empowered bodies, both "personally" and "missionally." Such is the Pauline paradox of participation in Christ. *To be in Christ is to embody continuously and simultaneously Good Friday and Easter.* This is resurrectional cruciformity.[65]

Paul's paradoxical spirituality of resurrectional cruciform participation in Christ is a matter of critical importance. The gospel is not the gospel of Paul, or of God, if it loses its focus on the cross—rightly understood as the theophany of God's self-giving, life-giving love. "To be truly human is to be Christlike, which is to be Godlike, which is to be kenotic and cruciform."[66] Life in Christ is not truly life in Christ when it loses its cruciform shape of participation precisely in that divine love and life. I illustrate this assertion with one extreme but important example.

Shortly after the Charlottesville white-supremacist rally in August of 2017, I watched a documentary about a KKK group in which the filmmakers were permitted to witness a ceremonial cross "lighting." As the ceremony began, the hooded KKK members encircled a tall wooden cross. The "grand knight" (if that is the correct title) began the ceremony by announcing that this was to be a cross lighting, not

---

64. In his symposium response to the paper, Markus Nikkanen expressed particular surprise that I (to his mind) failed to see the resurrectiform nature of life in Christ since I hold to Pauline authorship of Ephesians, which speaks of life in Christ as being "raised ... up with him and seated ... with him in the heavenly places" (Eph 2:6). My reply was to point to Eph 5:1–2 ("Therefore be imitators of God, as beloved children, and live in love, as Christ loved us and gave himself up for us") which both demonstrates the cruciform, earthly character of life in/with Christ "in the heavenly places" and implicitly claims that cruciformity ("as Christ loved us and gave himself") is theoformity ("imitators of God").

65. We might say that the former (Good Friday) supplies the *pattern*, while the latter (Easter) supplies the *power*, for participation in the resurrected crucified Messiah.

66. Gorman, *Inhabiting the Cruciform God*, 39.

a cross burning. He then approached each member with a burning torch, lighting each one's own torch in turn as he asked, "Do you accept the light of Jesus Christ?"—to which each member replied, "I do." The grand knight then set the cross aflame, announcing to all that they together were proclaiming the cross of Jesus Christ.

My gut reaction was to call aloud words like heresy, abomination, and blasphemy. To be sure, these folks believed they were proclaiming the cross. I suspect they also believed they were proclaiming a risen, living savior; perhaps some of them even sing about such a savior on a regular basis. But their ceremony and their lives are neither resurrection-suffused nor cross-shaped. And their sort of distortion of Christian faith plagues the world, not only in Charlottesville, but also elsewhere; it is death-dealing rather than life-giving.

Let me be clear: I am not in any way accusing any of the scholars proposing "resurrectiform" language of deliberately pushing the church in the wrong direction. I am, however, saying that Paul advocates a specific form of spirituality and discipleship that is as critical for our time as it was for Paul's—and for Dietrich Bonhoeffer's. *In fact, the very integrity of the church and of the gospel are at stake.* "Cheap grace," Bonhoeffer famously wrote, "is grace without discipleship, grace without the cross, grace without the living, incarnate Jesus Christ."[67] The corollary of this bold assertion is that the only way we know the living, incarnate Christ is through cruciform discipleship. For Bonhoeffer, as for Paul and for me, "form" language is critical. Speaking of the "form of the incarnate one" that "transforms the church-community into the body of Christ," Bonhoeffer wrote, "The form of Christ on earth is the form of death [*Todesgestalt*] of the crucified one. The image of God is the image of Jesus Christ on the cross. It is into this image that the disciple's life must be transformed . . . It is a crucified life (Gal 2:19)."[68] It is, said Jesus, taking up one's cross, not enjoying one's eschatological glory.[69]

May the church be faithful in its calling to be resurrectional by being cruciform.[70]

---

67. Dietrich Bonhoeffer, *Discipleship*, vol. 4 of *Dietrich Bonhoeffer Works*, trans. Barbara Green and Reinhard Krauss (Minneapolis: Augsburg Fortress, 2001) 44. There are, unfortunately, numerous preachers advocating some (alleged) form of resurrection life without any ongoing cruciform existence.

68. *Discipleship*, 285.

69. I owe this reminder to Michelle Rader, my research assistant. See also Michael J. Gorman, *The Death of the Messiah and the Birth of the New Covenant: A (Not So) New Model of the Atonement* (Eugene, OR: Cascade, 2014) esp. 32–50, 78–98, 106–8, 114–18.

70. I am grateful to Andy Johnson and Michelle Rader for their feedback on a draft of this essay; to Markus Nikkanen for a thought-provoking response at the symposium; and to colleagues and other participants in the symposium for their equally stimulating conversation.

RESPONSE TO GORMAN

Markus Nikkanen

Michael J. Gorman's essay is both a clarified account of his view of Paul's narrative spirituality and a response to his recent critics who have suggested that Gorman does not pay enough attention to Christ's resurrection.[1] In his essay, Gorman insists that for Paul participation in Christ is cruciform: the believer participates in the narrative of Christ's self-giving and conforms to the crucified Christ. According to Gorman, "cruciform participation in Christ is also, paradoxically, participation in Christ's resurrection." Nevertheless, Gorman parts ways with his interlocutors by suggesting that participation in the narrative of Christ's resurrection belongs to the believer's "fully transformed eschatological future." While "present participation in Christ is resurrection-empowered and resurrection-suffused," it cannot be called "resurrectiform."

The intention of my appreciative albeit critical response is not to say that Gorman is wrong about cruciformity. Many Pauline texts urge conformity with the death of Christ, and Paul's own *mimesis* of Christ suggests that participation in Christ is cruciform. Nevertheless, Paul does not urge conformity *solely* with the crucified Christ. As will be argued, Paul sometimes focuses on the narrative of the resurrection of Christ and urges conformity with the risen Christ. This indicates that present participation in Christ is both cruciform and resurrectiform, although the former takes precedence in many texts.

The following response poses theological,[2] exegetical, and terminological questions in regard to (1) Gorman's foundational claim about God being self-emptying

---

1. See Stephen Finlan, "Can We Speak of *Theosis* in Paul?," in *Partakers of the Divine Nature*, edited by Michael J. Christensen and Jeffery A. Wittung (Grand Rapids: Baker Academic, 2007) 68–80; Andrew Boakye, "Inhabiting the 'Resurrectiform' God: Death and Life as Theological Headline in Paul," *Expository Times* 128.2 (2016) 53–62; and Rachael Tan, "Conformity to Christ: An Exegetical and Theological Analysis of Paul's Perspective on Humiliation and Exaltation in Philippians 2:5–11" (PhD Dissertation, Southern Theological Seminary, 2017). See also David Moffitt's review of Gorman's recent book, *The Death of the Messiah and the Birth of the New Covenant* (Eugene, OR: Cascade, 2014) where Moffitt criticizes Gorman for under-developing the themes of resurrection, ascension, and exaltation in his discussion of the atonement. David M. Moffitt, review of *The Death of the Messiah and the Birth of the New Covenant: A (not so) New Model of the Atonement*, by Michael J. Gorman, *JTS* 68.1 (2017) 468–71.

2. I wish to express my gratitude to PhD candidate Jared Michelson (University of St Andrews,

and downwardly mobile *by nature*, and in regard to (2) Gorman's main proposal that present participation in Christ is cruciform, not resurrectiform.

Is the Triune God Self-Emptying and Downwardly Mobile by Nature?

According to Gorman, "for Paul cruciformity . . . is really theoformity, or theosis."[3] This dense statement has profound theological implications. By identifying cruciformity with theoformity, Gorman asserts that the story of Christ crucified is no other than God's own story, and that to be in the shape of the cross is to be in the shape of God himself.[4] Indeed, Gorman insists that "God . . . is *by nature* self-emptying, self-humbling, self-giving—vulnerable and 'downwardly mobile.'"[5] Gorman's claim, however, leads to two sets of difficult theological questions:

The first set has to do with intra-trinitarian relationships and the relationship of the Trinity with the created order. If God is *by nature* downwardly mobile, how does this downward movement play out in intra-trinitarian relationships from all eternity? Or does the triune God need the world in order to be downwardly mobile? Is there, perhaps, development in God so that he becomes self-emptying and downwardly mobile in Christ?

The second related set of questions concerns the communication of Christ's divine and human attributes. Is Christ's human nature suffused with his divine nature so that his human nature shares in the divine attributes, or does his divine nature remain beyond his human nature? Is the experience of the cross restricted to Christ's person, or does the Father suffer on the cross with Christ (Patripassianism)? Indeed, can cruciformity be legitimately labelled as theoformity?

Theologically, it is not necessary to regard the cross as a revelation of God's self-emptying and downwardly mobile *nature*. The cross is more properly a revelation of God's love *and* righteousness *under the conditions of sin, finitude, and creatureliness.* Such a view of the cross as a revelatory event does not demean God's loving nature in any way, for to say that "God is love" is not the same as to say that God is *by nature* self-emptying and downwardly mobile. Indeed, there is no need to define "love" as "empathy" which easily leads to the view that altruistic behaviour is essential to love.[6] Love can be defined as "desire for union with the other," as Thomas Aquinas

---

Scotland) for his help in thinking through some of the theological issues involved in Gorman's work.

3. Here Gorman cites his book, *Inhabiting the Cruciform God: Kenosis, Justification, and Theosis in Paul's Narrative Soteriology* (Grand Rapids: Eerdmans, 2009) 4.

4. For Gorman's definition of cruciformity, see Michael J. Gorman, *Cruciformity: Paul's Narrative Spirituality of the Cross* (Grand Rapids: Eerdmans, 2001) 4–5.

5. The emphasis is added.

6. Gorman seems to equate God's love with self-emptying and downward mobility. Love, however,

did. Consequently, the downward mobility one finds in the cross can be viewed as an outcome of God's love (and righteousness) under certain conditions—not as an essential characteristic of God's love and therefore essential to God's nature.

Exegetically, it is not clear that Gorman has succeeded in providing Scriptural warrant for his foundational claim about the nature of God. The texts central to his claim are 1 Cor 2:2 and Phil 2:6:

> *ou gar ekrina ti eidenai ev humin ei mē Iēsoun Christon kai touton estaupōmenon.*

> I decided to know nothing among you except Jesus Christ—that is, Jesus Christ crucified (1 Cor 2:2).[7]

> *hos en morphē theou huparchōn ouch harpagmon hēgēsato to einai isa theō.*

> Although he was (or: because he was) in the form of God, he did not consider his equality with God as something to be exploited for his own advantage (Phil 2:6).[8]

In regard to the first text, Gorman rightly recognizes Paul's "rhetorically charged claim, bordering on hyperbole." But then he discards the hyperbole and asserts that Paul needs to be taken "very literally" since Paul "makes astonishing claims about Christ crucified . . . as divine self-revelation" in the wider context. But are these claims not as rhetorically charged as Paul's decision itself, and is it not possible that Paul's heavy emphasis on the cross in 1 Corinthians is due to the pastoral and missional strategy he uses to overturn the value system and identity claims of Roman Corinth?[9] There is more work to be done here if Paul, indeed, needs to be taken "very literally."

---

can be defined either as "empathy" or as "desire for union with the other." The first definition regards love as altruism and suggests that self-emptying and downward mobility are necessarily part of God's nature if God is love. This definition of love, however, is affected by Anders Nygren's influential but refuted differentiation between *eros* and *agape*. Nygren famously took God's love to be the altruistic *agape* love. The second definition comes from Thomas Aquinas and is free from the idea that love necessarily entails self-emptying and downward mobility.

7. The translation is from Gorman, *Cruciformity*, 1 where he correctly takes *kai* as epexegetical.

8. The translation presents the two major options based on Gorman, *Inhabiting*, 11, 20.

9. The reason why Paul proclaimed "Christ crucified" in Corinth has been a matter of scholarly debate for a long time. Opinions have ranged from Paul changing his missional strategy as a reaction to the rejection of his gospel in Athens (Acts 17) to Paul's message being the same always and everywhere. While scholars usually reject a drastic change in Paul's thinking, the idea that Paul's emphasis could have changed according to the group to which he was preaching is common. For a review of the different views on why Paul preached "Christ crucified" in Corinth, see Todd D. Still, "Why Did Paul Preach 'Christ Crucified' in Corinth?," in *Texts and Contexts: Gospels and Pauline Studies*, edited by Todd D. Still (Waco, Texas: Baylor University Press, 2017) 73–82. Without diminishing the importance of Christ's death on the cross for Paul's theology and spirituality, and without lessening his focus on the cross in 1 Cor 1:17–2:16, I suggest that Paul's emphasis on cruciformity and the death of Christ in 1 Corinthians is partly due to his attempt to overturn the Corinthian, status-oriented

In regard to the second text, Gorman proposes that it has both a surface struc-ture and a deep structure. The surface structure describes Christ emptying himself *although* he had the form of God whereas the deep structure shows it was precisely *because* Christ was in the form of God that he emptied himself. While Gorman is correct that the present active participle *huparchōn* can be translated concessively or causally, it is unlikely that the participle has both meanings at the same time.[10] Moreover, nothing in the text forces a causal translation, and the mere possibility of *huparchōn* being causal is not evidence that it is.

Realizing this in his *Inhabiting the Cruciform God*, Gorman seeks to support the causal translation with other Pauline texts.[11] The proposed parallels, however, fail to convince: even if 1 Thess 2:6–8 and 1 Cor 9:1–23 were ultimately about Paul foregoing his rights *because* of his true identity as an apostle of Christ and not simply about setting a Christ-like example of foregoing one's rights for the sake of others and the gospel, why should one infer from these texts (which describe a human response to being in Christ) that the christological discussion in Phil 2:6 needs to be read causally?[12]

Consequently, Gorman's foundational claim about God's essentially down-wardly mobile and self-emptying nature remains in need of more theological and exegetical clarification. This weakens the force of Gorman's second proposal about the priority of the language of cruciformity. After all, Gorman resists "the 'form' language in connection with resurrection because . . . the character or 'shape' of this resurrecting God revealed in Christ is cruciform."[13]

Is Present Participation in Christ Cruciform, Resurrectiform, or Simply Christ-shaped?

According to Gorman "cruciform participation in Christ is also, paradoxically, par-ticipation in Christ's resurrection." By this he means that present participation in

---

mindset. Similarly Still, "Why Did Paul Preach 'Christ Crucified' in Corinth?," 77, who suggests that Paul's focus on the cross in Corinth had to do with the overemphasis on Christ's parousia Paul had encountered in Thessalonica, talks about multiple factors and states that "[t]here were clearly forces in that city that shaped that shaped his preaching."

10. Contra Gorman, *Inhabiting*, 22–23 who suggests that based on "the Pauline narrative affirma-tion 'although…' also means 'because…', whether used autobiographically or christologically." The concessive participle, as Wallace states, "is semantically the opposite of the causal participle." See Dan-iel B. Wallace, *Greek Grammar Beyond the Basics: An Exegetical Syntax of the New Testament* (Grand Rapids: Zondervan, 1996) 634. See also Wallace's defense of the concessive option on the same page.

11. Gorman, *Inhabiting*, 23–24.

12. Ibid., 22–25.

13. In other words, Gorman thinks that participation in Christ must be cruciform *because* God is cruciform.

Christ has a resurrection "quality," and that it can be described as "resurrectional," "resurrection-suffused," or "resurrection-enabled." Present participation in Christ, however, cannot be called "resurrection-shaped" or "resurrectiform" since conforming to the risen Christ is reserved for the believer's "fully transformed eschatological future."

Is this temporal sequence—cross-shaped participation in the present time followed by a resurrection-shaped participation in the eschatological future—exegetically and theologically viable? I wish to raise three issues:

First, *the terminology used in the discussion needs to be clarified*. Much depends on the definition of "resurrectiform" and "resurrectiformity." Neither Gorman nor his interlocutors define these terms clearly, and there is a real possibility of talking past each other.[14] Do these terms imply the kind of triumphalism Gorman rightly opposes in the conclusion of his essay or do they refer to the believer's participation in the narrative of Christ's resurrection from the dead to be part of God's new creation?

My response to Gorman's essay is predicated on the idea that the latter is the correct way to understand resurrectiformity. After all, Christ's resurrection is the beginning of God's new creation in him, and, as the believers participate in Christ, they participate in the narrative of rising from the dead to live as God's new creation. In my opinion, resurrectiformity has nothing to do with the kind of triumphalism that rejects cruciformity. Rather, to be resurrectiform is to be the *kainē ktisis* of 2 Cor 5:17 that lives a new and properly ordered life to and under God.

But how does Gorman use the key terms? He defines "cruciformity" as *narrative spirituality*, a *process* of conforming to the crucified Christ, and supplements this definition with the idea of conforming to a self-emptying, self-humbling, and self-giving God.[15] One would assume, then, that the term "resurrectiformity" could be used similarly to point to a *process* of conforming to the risen Christ. This does not, however, seem to be the case, since "resurrectiform" participation is possible only in the "fully transformed eschatological future." According to Gorman, the ones who are "resurrectiform" have already reached the goal, they have already been fully conformed to the risen Christ. These, to me, are confusing uses of terms that sound similar: with one there is a process involved (cruciformity) whereas the other indicates a state (resurrectiformity).

Second, *the idea of temporal sequence needs to be reconsidered in light of the Spirit's agency*. At the moment, Gorman's view of present participation in Christ

---

14. Even Gorman himself expresses uncertainty over what his interlocutors are trying to convey with terms like "resurrectiform."

15. Gorman, *Cruciformity*, 4–5.

implies an insufficient view of the Spirit's agency and power. Why is it possible for the Spirit to empower and direct the believer to conform to the crucified Christ but not to the risen Christ? Indeed, why do cruciformity and resurrectiformity even need to be understood in terms of a temporal sequence in the believer's life, and not as a parallel processes?[16] After all, both Christ's death and his resurrection remain in the past from the believer's point of view, and the believer can access these events only through the Spirit who unites the believer with the *risen* Lord and transforms the believer into his image (see Rom 8:29; 1 Cor 12:13; 2 Cor 3:18).[17] Indeed, what other Christ is there than the risen Christ? Can Christ be divided?[18]

Gorman pushes back on the idea of dividing Christ by proposing that present participation in Christ has a resurrection quality. According to him, "cruciform participation in Christ is also, paradoxically, participation in Christ's resurrection." Nevertheless, he divides the narrative of Christ by placing half of it in the eschatological future—supposedly away from the reach of the believer and of the Spirit! Paul does not, however, make such a division: in 2 Cor 5:17 Paul indicates that anyone who is in Christ is already part of the new creation and urges the Corinthians *to conform* to this reality in the risen Christ.[19] Moreover, it is the Spirit that transforms the believer into the image of the risen Lord (2 Cor 3:18).

Third, *the resurrectiform language of Colossians and Ephesians needs to be taken seriously.* Since Gorman does not doubt the Pauline authorship of Colossians and Ephesians, it is unclear how he can consider "resurrectiform" an unfit description of present participation in Christ.[20] In both of these letters the believer conforms to

16. Gorman suggests that there is no "discernible 'resurrectiform' substance or pattern" and therefore "there really is not a parallel between cruciform and 'resurrectiform' life." In light of the texts discussed in this response, this suggestion does not sound true. Just as the believers conform to Christ's death by humbling themselves and giving themselves for others, so the believers conform to Christ's resurrection in regarding themselves and other believers as part of God's new creation and in living renewed lives wholly surrendered to God.

17. Consider, for example, Rom 8:11, 13 where the Spirit of the one who raised Jesus from the dead dwells in the believer. Consequently, resurrection life comes to all who by the Spirit put to death their sinful deeds. It is important to notice that Paul is not referring here merely to a time in the eschatological future but to *the process of being conformed to the risen Christ at the present time.* In addition, it is worthwhile to notice that for Paul the eschatological time has already begun in Christ, and the believer lives in between the now and the not yet.

18. See Calvin, *Institutes* 1.11.6.

19. 2 Corinthians 5:14–16 makes this clear by suggesting that the believers should live for him who died and rose for them (*mēketi heautois zōsin alla tō hyper autōn apothanonti kai egerthenti*). Consequently, the ones that are in Christ are part of the new creation (5:17) and do not know each other *kata sarka* (5:16). The believers conform both to Christ's death and his resurrection.

20. In discussion, Gorman affirmed the Pauline authorship of Colossians and Ephesians. While whether Colossians and Ephesians were written by Paul himself or "Pauline devotees" cannot be decided here, it is good to notice that scholarship is currently a moving target on the issue, and more and more scholars are willing to consider the letters authentic. Andrew Boakye (one of Gorman's

the risen Christ, and ethics proceeds from the idea that the believer has been raised with Christ and lives anew to God. For example, in Col 3:1–5 Paul claims that having been raised with Christ has brought about a new identity in Christ. Consequently, the believer is commanded to put to death everything that does not belong to this new identity. Rising with Christ *and* its necessary antecedent, dying with Christ, are understood as the narrative *starting place* of the believer's present participation in Christ as the believer looks toward the eschatological transformation that brings the process of conforming to Christ's death and resurrection into fulfilment. Similarly, in Eph 2:5–6 Paul reveals that the believer, who used to be dead in his or her sins, has been made alive with Christ, raised with him, and even seated with him in the heavenly realms. Ephesians 4:22–24, then, fleshes out the idea of having been made alive in Christ by urging the believer to put on the new human that has been created according to God in righteousness and holiness. Paul does not consider it problematic to urge conformity with the risen Christ although he well knows that this conformity will not find its fulfilment until the eschatological future.

The adequate response to these texts is not to say that one finds cruciformity in both of the letters. That is not in dispute here. Instead, Gorman needs to explain in light of the data presented here, why present participation in Christ cannot also be described as resurrectiform. After all, Paul is urging conformity with the risen Christ and grounding his ethical imperative in the idea that the believer has been raised with Christ. The believer is clearly participating in the narrative of Christ's resurrection, and this means that present participation is more than merely "resurrection-suffused" or "resurrection-enabled" for Paul.

Conclusion: Christ-shaped present participation

Unlike Gorman suggests, present participation in Christ is both cruciform and resurrectiform according to Paul. There is one Christ, and he cannot be divided. Consequently, the believer is meant to embody the whole redemptive story of Christ:[21] he or she conforms to the self-giving, suffering, and death of Christ on the cross but

interlocutors) suggests that Colossians and Ephesians were written by "Pauline devotees." See Boakye, "Inhabiting the Resurrectiform God," 54. The mere idea of "Pauline devotees," however, suggests authorship that knew Paul's theology and spirituality from top to bottom. This begs the question, whether, for example, Rom 6 and Col 3 are so very different from each other? After all, Rom 6:4 is not merely speaking about an eschatological age in which the believer will finally be fully conformed to the risen Christ. Instead, Paul assumes co-rising with Christ and uses the risen Christ as a template for the believers' present spirituality.

21. Robert W. Jenson, *Systematic Theology Vol. 1: The Triune God* (New York: Oxford University Press, 1997) 190 writes: "Crucifixion and Resurrection together are the church's *Pasch*, her passing over from being no people to being God's people, her rescue from alienation to fellowship, her reconciliation."

also to the newness and orderliness of Christ's resurrection. To quote paradoxically Gorman himself, "*To be in Christ is to embody continuously and simultaneously Good Friday and Easter.*"[22]

22. The emphasis is original.

UNION(S) WITH CHRIST: COLOSSIANS 1:15–20

Grant Macaskill

This essay concerns the representation of diverse relations within the text of Col 1:15–20 and, particularly, the way that this is developed using the classic Pauline language of union, of being "in Christ" or "in him." My reasons for examining this representation are both positive and negative, both constructive and critical. Constructively, it is important that we probe the complexity of the concept of union with Christ, recognizing that it is not necessarily reducible to one thing; it is not, in the theological sense of the word, "simple." That is to say, "in Christ" language (or related structures and images) is used in a range of ways, of a range of things, and is not confined to the salvific relationship between the believer, or the church, and Christ. Attentiveness to this might problematize some of our ways of thinking of union with Christ, but it might also problematize our way of thinking about other doctrines, such as providence or creation, which might in our traditions be *functionally*[1] sub-Christian, inadequately conceived with respect to the person of Jesus Christ and insufficiently integrated with the gospel. For, while one of the points that I want to press is that we should not homogenize these different uses of the imagery or language, I also want to stress that these multiple "unions with Christ" are described with a common grammar because there are correspondences between them. I will suggest that these correspondences are obviously centered on the common mediatorial role of Christ, which is, perhaps less obviously (or more contentiously) a covenantal role. Constructively, then, I want to highlight the place of union with Christ and the role that covenant should play in accounts of providence and creation. This has quite far-reaching implications for our doctrinal systems and pastoral reflections, because the doctrines of creation and providence are "distributed":[2] they are properly considered to function in multiple locations of doctrine (straddling theol-

---

1. I use this word to indicate that while *in principle* our theological systems might be good and proper, *in practice* we can neglect the proper linkages between concepts or can line the elements up in ways that are inappropriate, giving a certain independence or proportion to things that ought rightly to be derived from theology proper or Christology, and proportioned with respect to these things.

2. The word "distributed" is one that I take from John Webster's "On the Theology of Providence," in *The Providence of God*, edited by Francesca Aran Murphy and Philip G. Ziegler (London: T. & T. Clark, 2009) 158–77. It indicates that the doctrine is not self-contained, but functions as an aspect of other doctrines, across the theological system broadly. See David Fergusson, *Creation* (Grand Rapids: Eerdmans, 2014) 52.

ogy proper and economy) and serve to link the related doctrines at work in each of those locations.

Negatively, or critically, it is important to probe the complexity of the representation in Col 1:15–20 because a confusion of these different kinds of union, particularly as they have been handled in the theological tradition, can lead to a kind of naïve universalism. Now, to be clear, I am not claiming that attentiveness to this point by itself rules out universalism; what it challenges is a particular line of argumentation for a particular kind of universalism that flattens the distinction between kinds of union with Christ.

While I am using the language of "union with Christ" of this, the distinction that I have in view has been explored using the looser language of "participation" by Norman Russell, in his magisterial study of *The Doctrine of Deification in the Greek Patristic Tradition* (Oxford: Oxford University Press, 2002). Russell identifies a distinction between "dynamic" and "passive" participation in the life of God through Christ, with the passive forms reflecting a shared ontology or nature (all creation participates in the created nature of the mediator; human life distinctively shares in his human nature) and the dynamic forms reflecting the activity of the Spirit and the experience of partaking in the sacraments (in which only the members of the sacramentally delineated church participate). Broadly, I think Russell's language is helpful in the analysis of the Fathers, but in terms of the biblical material itself, I think the covenantal character of union with Christ gives us a more precise set of analytical categories.

Preliminary Decisions

Before turning to consider some of the key details, I need to give a brief summary of some of the interpretive decisions that I have made in the background to this discussion.

The most important of these concerns the use of the expression "image of God" (*eikōn tou theou*). While the use of this phrase may remind the reader of the story of Adam and Eve, this is not the only relevant (or even the principal) background to the use of the expression in Col 1:15, and it must be treated with care. The background to this passage is a composite or hybrid one and we need to allow the right elements of the complex to have the basic or framing significance. As I have noted elsewhere,[3] the "iconic" status of Jesus is here unqualified by prepositions: where in Gen 1:27–28 humankind is made "in (or according to) the image and likeness of

---

3. Grant Macaskill, *Union with Christ in the New Testament* (Oxford: Oxford University Press, 2013) ch. 5.

God," Jesus simply "is" the image.[4] Any Adamic connotations are stretched quickly by the language that follows: Adam was not the "firstborn" of creation, and can be understood as such only by some very creative handling of the term "first born" (*prōtotokos*).[5] It is also difficult to see how an Adamic background might explain the explanatory force of the subsequent *hoti* statement: "for (*hoti*) in/by him all things were created." The parallel expression "through him" (*di' autou*) further problematizes such a background for the character of the relationship in view, for it implies some form of co-agency in the activity of creation, just as the statement that "in him all things hold together" (*panta en auto sunestēken*) implies co-agency in the activity of providence.

In fact, rather than being most clearly linked to Adam theology, much of the imagery and language has more obvious backgrounds in the biblical and Jewish representations of Wisdom, Torah, and the Memra (the Aramaic word for "the Word" that is frequently added to the targumim): all are represented as the "first" of God's creative works and as maintaining a role in creation and providence. We can point to the representation of Wisdom in Prov 8 for a good example of this. Within the Jewish traditions, both biblical and non-biblical,[6] this has an important integrative drive that centers on Torah: because the cosmos was created through Wisdom and Torah, the "wise" who are saved and live in adherence to the law live according to the grain of the universe.[7] Hence, creation, ethics, wisdom, and law are essentially unified. As an aside, past scholarship has often seen the traditions represented by Wisdom and Torah as competitive, usually linked to some notion of competing "schools," but more recent scholarship has tended to see them as associative.[8] As such, rather than

4. While we can argue for a closer identification of humankind and the image through, for example, claiming the *bet* to be a *bet essentiae,* evidence from Jewish traditions suggests that, if anything, the prepositional character of humankind's imaging of God is understood to emphasize the ontological distance between God and humanity. See further below.

5. In his response to this paper, Constantine Campbell notes the association of the word with the concept of pre-eminence, allowing it to point to the distinctive position of Adam within creation. I note below the way that the text emphasizes such pre-eminence, but still consider the representation of the image as the one "by whom" and "through whom" all things were made to stretch any Adamic connotations; they are much more similar to the widespread traditions of the creative activity of Wisdom that are encountered in Judaism.

6. As texts, the witnesses to these traditions are quite late, being found in the rabbinic texts and the targumim, but these are widely considered to preserve traditions that were widespread in the Second Temple period. For a good example of a work that negotiates the parallels between New Testament material and the textually later rabbinic corpus, see Christopher Rowland and Christopher Morray-Jones, *The Mystery of God: Early Jewish Mysticism and the New Testament* (Leiden: Brill, 2009).

7. This phrase is drawn from the title of Stanley Hauerwas's Gifford Lectures, *With the Grain of the Universe: The Church's Witness and Natural Theology* (repr., Grand Rapids: Baker, 2013). Hauerwas himself picks the expression up from John Howard Yoder.

8. See Michael Fox, "Three Theses on Wisdom," and Stuart Weeks, "Wisdom, Form, and Genre," both in *Was There a Wisdom Tradition? New Prospects in Israelite Wisdom Studies*, edited by Mark R.

representing *either* Wisdom *or* Torah as the principal source for ethics, the various sources and traditions consider *both* to express in a unified way the order of God's cosmos.

To be clear, I am not saying that Col 1:15–20 is devoid of allusions to the Eden story, but that these do not serve as the *principal* background to the imagery used throughout this passage; rather, the Wisdom/Torah passages provide these. But even while allowing some measure of allusion to the Adam story, it is important to note that in Jewish contexts the word "image" (*eikōn*) was not exclusively linked to this human being, or more broadly to the first couple. As Rowland notes,[9] we encounter it as a loanword in Aramaic texts for other human beings, such as Jacob, who have seen the glory of the divine form and make it visible to others. It is, then, a word apparently having a fairly technical sense (which is why it is calqued into Aramaic) with distinctively human, *but not necessarily Adamic*, connotations in much Jewish literature. Resisting the tendency to truncate the interpretation of "image" (*eikōn*) to something with principally Adamic significance allows us to recognize the range of ways in which Jesus is represented as performing the mediatorial roles of Wisdom or Torah, but as a human being. Indeed, for reasons that will emerge through this essay, the importance of any Adamic resonance in the passage is precisely in its affirmation of the human particularity of the "image" (*eikōn*).

The Grammar of Union in Colossians 1:15–20

The identity of *eikōn tou theou tou aoratou* ("the image of the invisible God") is established by the relative pronoun *hos* ("who"), the antecedent to which is the expression "the Son of his love" in 1:13. This construction grounds all that follows in the internal relationships of God and we must be careful not to lose sight of this: the separation that some modern translations introduce between vv. 14 and 15, by making 1:15–20 into a new section, obscures it.

The Son-Icon is then described as the "firstborn" (*prōtotokos*) "of all creation" or "of every creature" (*pasēs ktiseōs*) with this statement followed by an explanatory *hoti* clause: "for (*hoti*) in him (*en autō*) all things were created." This is, in turn, followed by a series of pairings that represent the totality of "all things": in heaven and upon the earth, visible and invisible, whether thrones or dominions, whether rulers or powers. Clearly, this totality of "all things" is important to the author.

Sneed (Atlanta: Society of Biblical Literature, 2015) 69–86 and 161–78 respectively.

9. Rowland and Morray-Jones, *The Mystery of God*, 164; see also Silviu Bunta, "The Likeness of the Image: Adamic Motifs and ṢLM Anthropology in Rabbinic Traditions About Jacob's Image Enthroned in Heaven," *JSJ* 37 (2006) 55–84.

Not everyone has seen the *en* to represent a spatial relationship of the kind that we might render as "in him". Some versions, including the ESV, have translated it as an instrumental phrase: all things were created "by him." There are, I think, good reasons to press against this. If the work is Pauline, even if only in a derivative sense (though my own view is that it is genuinely a work of Paul himself) then the obvious parallels with the apostle's extensive use of "in Christ" language to denote a particular union between believers and Christ are significant.[10] In other words, the language used here should be read with an eye to the kind of things that Paul says in, for example, Rom 8. Furthermore, within the letter itself, as Paul Foster has recently noted,[11] there is a well-developed theology of union with Christ which is rendered in the immediate context using the form *en* + dative, with an evidently spatial or inclusive (not instrumental) sense. So, for example, in 1:13–14:

> He has delivered us from the domain of darkness and transferred us to the kingdom of his beloved Son, in whom we have redemption (*en ō echomen tēn apolytrōsin*) the forgiveness of sins (Col 1:13–14 ESV).

The spatial sense here is linked to correspondingly spatial imagery—the transfer from one domain to another—and the ESV here allows for the more traditional rendering "in him." Similarly, as Constantine Campbell notes, the use of "in him" (*en autō*) in v. 16 seems to be set in parallel with the phrase in v. 19, which is undoubtedly spatial (or, more precisely, locative): God was pleased to have his fullness dwell "in him."[12] Adopting the instrumental translation in v. 16 may well be a strategy invoked by the editors to avoid any inference of panentheism but, as we will see, there are other ways of conceiving the spatial or inclusive language used there that maintain the creator-creature distinction and by neglecting these, the translation loses something theologically quite significant.

I will discuss these alternative ways of conceiving the spatial or inclusive language below, in relation to the category of "covenant," but before doing so it is important to take note of the other prepositions that are used in relation to "him" (*autos*). At the end of v. 16, the same word used at the beginning of the verse for the "all things" (*panta*) that were made in him is repeated, but now with two different prepositions designating the relationship to "him": "all things have been created through him and for him" (*ta panta di' autou kai eis auton ektistai*). Now "all things"

---

10. Discussions of the extent and significance of this language are found throughout Macaskill, *Union with Christ in the New Testament*; and Constantine Campbell, *Paul and Union with Christ* (Grand Rapids: Zondervan, 2012).

11. Paul Foster, *Colossians*, BNTC (New York: Bloomsbury T. & T. Clark, 2016) 28–35 and wider context.

12. Campbell, *Paul and Union with Christ,* 180–81.

are represented as being created "through him" (*di' autou*) and "for him" (*eis auton*). There is an interesting shift in the verb tense, from the aorist used at the beginning of the verse to the perfect used here. Without placing too much weight on this, we might consider it to reflect a sense of continued relationship between the things so created and the one *through* whom and *for* whom they were made (the "for" perhaps being key to this continued sense). The range of prepositions reflects a range of relationships, all of which reinforces the sense that however one looks at the world, whichever angle one takes, one sees things that are related to Jesus. They are in him, through him, and for him.

The language here has an interesting parallel in 1 Cor 8:6, which famously expands the Shema of Deut 6:4 to incorporate the identification of Jesus with God:

> Yet for us there is one God, the Father, from whom are all things and for whom we exist, and one Lord, Jesus Christ, through whom are all things and through whom we exist (1 Cor 8:6 NRSV).

Here, in contrast to Col 1:16, the prepositions are used quite distinctly of God, the Father, and Jesus: all things are "from" and "for" the Father, but "through" Jesus. The arrangement, which draws manifestly covenantal overtones from its appropriation of the Shema, distinguishes the mediatorial activity of Jesus from the primacy and ultimacy of God the Father. In Colossians, however, the author is happy to deploy both "through" and "for" with respect to Jesus' relationship to "all things," negating any possibility that Jesus can be considered less than God, while still individuating God (who is distinctly named in 1:19–20 as the agent of salvation) and the Son-Icon.

The identification of the Son-Icon specifically as the "firstborn" of all creation has a significance that is picked up in the next verse, further unpacking the "because" (*hoti*) of v. 16: he is before all things and in him all things hold together. There is here a temporal dimension that echoes the representation of Wisdom in Prov 8 and of the Torah in the rabbinic receptions of that passage, which I will quote below: these things precede or antedate the appearance of other creatures and are basic to the existence and order of these. But the tense is present[13]—the image *is* before all things—and the real priority to which the text drives is not simply pre-existence, but rather the pre-eminence or primacy (*prōteuōn*) named at the end of v. 18.[14] That

13. I wonder whether we might see here the kind of playful use of tenses encountered in Jewish reflection on the Tetragrammaton as encountered in the targumim to Exod 3:14 and Deut 32:39 and as reflected in Rev 1:8 and its parallels throughout that epistle.

14. As noted above (n5), Constantine Campbell responds to my arguments by noting the association of "firstborn" with pre-eminence, reinforcing this by noting the non-temporal significance that "before" (*pro*) can have. The point I make here aligns well with these observations, up to a point: the logic of the passage still, I think, requires a temporal element that we can designate as "pre-existence," allowing the Son to act in his creative capacity. We must, I think, allow that both temporal and

this word is located there is important, for between it come two other concepts: providence and salvation. All things are not just made by the Son, but subsist in him: "in him all things hold together" (*en auto sunestēken*). Again, to render this using a spatial or locative translation acknowledges that instrumentality or agency is not all that is at stake here; there is some sense in which such providence must be understood to take place within the "sphere" of the Son's reality, to use the kind of language employed by Constantine Campbell.

I will suggest below that there is a better term to use than "sphere" or "domain," but only once having noted the effortlessness with which the author moves from speaking about creation and providence to speaking about redemption, which suggests a significant co-ordination of these. There is no sense of awkwardness in the passage, as if radically different ways of thinking about being "in Christ" are squidged together like play-dough. In fact, the passage directs the reader to recognize the correspondences between Christ's relationship to the church and his relationship to "all things": just as he is the firstborn of creation, so he is the firstborn from the dead, and just as he is creatively before all things, so now as the head of the church he is seen in all things to be pre-eminent. In the Greek text, the move from speaking of Christ's creative and providential status and function to his redemptive status and function is in fact seamless, occurring within a chain of repeated uses of "and" (*kai*) that is often masked in translation:

> and (*kai*) he is before all things

> and (*kai*) in him all things hold together

> and (*kai*) he is the head of the body the church (vv. 17–18)

The correspondence between the creative/providential and the redemptive is finally and thoroughly affirmed in vv. 19–20, which bring together all of the key words and prepositions we have seen so far:

> For *in* him all the fullness of God was pleased to dwell, and *through* him God
> was pleased to reconcile to himself all things, whether on earth or in heaven,
> by making peace through the blood of his cross (Col 1:19–20 NRSV).

I labor all of this in order to stress that the author seems determined for us to co-ordinate these different concepts. But it is equally important to stress that the deliberate paralleling of elements is developed in such a way as to demand not just identification, but also differentiation. Jesus is the firstborn of creation, but also the firstborn of the dead: these are not the same thing. Precisely by linking the word

---

positional overtones are at play in the passage.

"firstborn" to two different genitives, the author makes its significance complex. Similarly, he indicates that "all things" are in him, yet "all things" need to be reconciled; they (or, at least, some) are, as yet, estranged. We are intended to identify the "all things" in their mutual relationships to Christ, but not to simplify them into something singular, with a correspondingly singular relationship. Precisely through the deliberate paralleling of terms, those terms and their distinct relations to the Son-Icon are rendered complex.

One further point may now be noted. These complex relations are all connected to the nature(s) or being of the Son-Icon: he is able to sustain the created realm because of his own creatureliness (he is the firstborn of every creature)[15] and is able to bring life to the dead because he shares in their mortality (he is the firstborn from the dead). The relations, in other words, rest upon shared natures. What makes these 'natural' relations creationally, providentially, and redemptively significant is the fact that the figure at the center of this account is, at the same time as being creaturely and mortal, "the son of his love" (1:13, my translation); to relate to him is to be involved in the inner relationships of God.

I want to suggest that the category of covenant, designating the particular kind of ordered relationship existing between God and "God's own," is one that allows us to make sense of all of this. Within the breadth of this category we can differentiate species of participation or union that converge on a single point—now seen to be Jesus—but that are not identical and that require different mediatorial activities. In the next section, I will pursue this with reference to the background imagery at work in Col 1:15–20, but I would make the basic observation here that for a Jewish thinker of the Second Temple period, covenant did not signify just one little bit of Israel's relationship with God, in a simple non-reducible way; it was the whole of that relationship, with all its complexity. Within that, there were distinctive roles on which the covenant bore in different ways, often involving some kind of mediation: adults/parents, children, men, women, priests, high priests, Levites, kings (and so on, and so forth)—each had distinct roles within the covenant community and the covenant itself bore upon them differently. Indeed, it was possible to be outside of the covenant people but to be inside the "sphere" of the covenant, to be "the alien in the midst" of Israel (e.g., Exod 12:48; 20:10) for whom specific requirements or

---

15. Some at the North Park Symposium, including Constantine Campbell (in his response) were concerned that my language here was somewhat Arian in tone. As a result, I have modified this particular sentence by amending "nature or being of the Son-Icon" to "nature(s) or being of the Son-Icon" to indicate that the creaturely human nature belongs to the Son-Icon, to the person of the mediator Jesus Christ, who is both divine and human. On Jesus Christ's creatureliness, though, we must insist. Much contemporary evangelical theology operates with a rather emaciated Christology that does little justice to the true significance of the incarnation; we are a long way from the richness of the accounts that we see in Athanasius or even in Calvin.

provisions of the covenant obtain. I am not suggesting that all of this *directly* influences the imagery of Col 1:15–20, but that in a less direct way it helps us to understand that for Jewish thinkers of the time covenant had the capacity to be a concept at once comprehensive and complex. Not only so, but it might be central at once to the most dramatic eschatological hopes (as in Jer 31:31) and the most mundane of daily realities (as in Deut 22).[16]

Covenant Language and Imagery: Explicit and Implied

There is a wealth of imagery in Col 1:15–20 that is evocative of this covenantal framework. First, it might be suggested that the use of "image" (*eikōn*) invokes the imagery of the temple (which, of course, was functionally central to the covenant between God and Israel): much discussion centers on the empty place within Israel's temple that would, in other religions of the time, have been occupied by an image representing the deity. No graven image occupies this space in Yahweh's temple, for he is the invisible God and cannot be represented in such a way.

Much of the discussion of Gen 1:26–27, of course, has been concerned with the way that Adam and Eve might be understood to fulfil this purpose within the temple-space of the Garden of Eden, at the heart of the cosmos.[17] This may be a valid reading of Gen 1:26–27, but it was not one necessarily self-evident to Jews of the Second Temple period. If anything, Adam was regarded not as an icon, but as a protological high priest within the cultic Eden.[18] Any potentially iconic significance was treated with caution by Jewish readers, including the translators of the Greek versions: man is not the image itself, but is made "according to" or "after" the image.[19] Some later Jewish readers treated the paired Hebrew words *ṣelem* and *dĕmût*

---

16. In his response to this paper, Campbell defends his own use of "sphere" or "domain" language by noting the expression "transferred (us) into the kingdom of the son of his love" (*metestēsen eis tēn basileian tou huiou tēs agapēs autou*) in 1:13. This seems to suggest movement from one domain or dominion into another. I agree with this, but my point is that the concept of "kingdom" (*basileia*) is, for Jewish thinkers, freighted with covenantal significance. To live within the sphere of God's reign is to live within the administration of the covenant, with lives that are ruled down to their most mundane levels. To be in God's kingdom is to live within a settled and mediated relationship with him, in which not just one's liturgy, but also one's farming practices and domestic architecture are subject to divine regulation, because the covenant does not bear only upon the individual.

17. See, for example, Greg Beale, *The Temple and the Church's Mission: A Biblical Theology of the Dwelling Place of God* (Downers Grove: Inter Varsity Press, 2004).

18. See J. van Ruiten, *Primaeval History Interpreted: The Rewriting of Genesis 1–11 in the Book of Jubilees* (Leiden; Boston: Brill, 2000); and "The Garden of Eden and Jubilees 3:1–31," Bijdr, 57.3 (1996) 305–17.

19. Note the Greek translation of Gen 1:26: "according to our image and likeness" (*kat' eikona hēmeteran kai kath' homoiōsin*). See the comments made in Jas 3:9 on people "having been made according to the likeness of God" (*kath' homoiōsin theou gegonotas*).

as a chain, indicating that man is made "in the likeness of the image."[20] The similarity between humanity and God, then, is strictly analogous and somewhat limited, and the idea that man functions in the place of the icon in Second Temple Jewish thought is not as well attested as it is sometimes assumed to be.

So, we should be careful not to assume that we are dealing with an appropriation of the concept of Adam as temple icon. This, though, is not to disavow temple imagery per se. That here we have some kind of temple imagery at work is supported by the language of the "fullness" (*to plērōma*) that is pleased "to dwell" (*katoikēsai*) in Christ. In fact, a growing body of scholarship in recent years has seen the imagery of this passage as reflecting Jewish mystical traditions about the relationship of the divine form, or fullness, to the heavenly temple. This temple imagery is interesting, because numerous links can be understood to exist between temple and cosmos. Much of the scholarship on Gen 1 has highlighted the priestly instincts reflected in the way the story of creation is told: creation corresponds to the orderliness of the temple, with its delineated spaces and personnel. While some have read this through a particular salvation-historical lens,[21] with the temple recovering the original order of the now-fallen creation, serving as a kind of oasis of restoration within a disordered cosmos, most scholarship would see the Gen 1 story as anticipating the temple;[22] that is, rather than the temple pointing back to the creation story of Gen 1, that story points *forward* to the temple that is at the heart of the covenant. The relationship between the two is a figural one.

Within the Jewish mystical traditions that I mentioned earlier, the earthly temple is understood as corresponding to the heavenly one. In some cases, involvement with earthly liturgy is understood to allow participation in the heavenly realm,[23] with the heavenly temple understood as something that supervenes upon the earthly one, set apart from creation but accessible through the activity of worship. In other cases, the heavenly temple is understood macrocosmically: it contains the entire cosmos, so that when the fullness of God dwells in that temple, it "fills all things in every way" (Eph 1:23). This, indeed, is the kind of imagery that some have seen to be at work in Col 1:15–20 and in the related imagery in Ephesians.

The specifics of each view are less important than the broad covenantal-creational affirmation. The temple is the center point for the ordered relationship between God and Israel, and it turns out to be the center point for the ordered

20. b. Ketub. 8a. See Markus Bockmuehl, "'The Form of God' (Phil 2:6) : Variations on a Theme of Jewish Mysticism," *JTS* 48 (1997) 1–23.

21. Most obviously Beale, *The Temple and the Church's Mission.*

22. See W. P. Brown, *The Ethos of the Cosmos: The Genesis of Moral Imagination* (Grand Rapids: Eerdmans, 1999) esp. ch. 1.

23. See especially the *Songs of the Sabbath Sacrifice* from Qumran (4Q400–407 and 11Q17).

relationship between God and all of the cosmos: the lines of order all converge on and run through the holy of holies. Sin is the fundamental disrupting of this, the chaos that seeks (and ultimately fails) to bring an end to divine order. Now, radically, the imagery of the temple is recast in ways that understand Jesus to be the "mystery"[24] that was always at its heart, the image that was never seen until now. That, I think, makes good sense in relation to some of the other strategies that the New Testament writers deploy to identify Jesus and his community with the temple. These strategies are also reflected in this passage through the image of the head and the body, which elsewhere meld with temple imagery.[25] To be clear: temple and covenant are not identical, but they are coordinate concepts, with the meaning of the temple and cult always framed by the covenant. It is further noteworthy that cultic/sacrificial language is used in relation to the reconciled in 1:21—they are "holy in his sight, without blemish and free from accusation." This adds to the broadly covenantal sense of the passage.

The covenant is also evoked through the use of a composite of Wisdom and Torah imagery. The following extract from the Genesis Rabbah (1:1) nicely illustrates the kinds of traditions being taken up in the imagery of Col 1:

> The Torah says, "I was the artistic tool of the Holy One, blessed is He." As is the practice with the world, when a king of flesh and blood builds a palace, he does not build it from his own knowledge, but from the knowledge of an artisan (or: architect). And the architect himself does not build it from his own knowledge, but rather he has plans and diagrams that help him to know how to make the rooms and how to make the narrow gates. In this manner, the Holy One, blessed is He, looked at the Torah and created the world. And the Torah said, *In the beginning, God created* (Gen 1:1) and there is no *beginning* i.e., *reshit* but the Torah, as it is said, *The Lord made me, the beginning of his way* (Prov 8:22)—Genesis (Bereshit) Rabbah 1:1.[26]

What is important about this rabbinic text, which is later than the New Testament but probably contains older traditions, is that involves an intertextual reading of Gen 1:1 and Prov 8, combined quite predictably according to the principles of Jewish exegesis. The parallels with Col 1:15–20 should be obvious. Effectively now,

24. This word is common in the Pauline writings and probably reflects the significance of the Aramaic loanword *raz* that appears to have functioned as a technical term in the Qumran literature. See Grant Macaskill, *Revealed Wisdom and Inaugurated Eschatology in Ancient Judaism and Early Christianity* (Leiden; Boston: Brill, 2007) esp. the discussion of 4QInstruction in ch. 3.

25. See Macaskill, *Union with Christ in the New Testament*, ch. 6.

26. Translation from Brian Ogren, *The Beginning of the World in Renaissance Jewish Thought: Ma'aseh Bereshit* (Leiden; Boston: Brill, 2016) 72–73. The commentary has a vibrant afterlife in later Jewish traditions; Ogren's wider discussion, in which this translation is embedded, concerns its uptake in the Zohar.

the traditional identification of Wisdom and Torah reflected in the Genesis Rabbah is expanded and "re-personalized": where those things were represented using *metaphorically* personal imagery, now they are identified with an *actual* person, Jesus, who is understood to be the ordering principle by which (now, non-metaphorically, "by whom") all things were made. If we take on board the shifts in scholarship that I mentioned earlier, towards seeing the relationship of Wisdom and Torah as associative rather than competitive, then we can see something quite interesting going on: Wisdom and Torah are considered to participate in the reality of Jesus Christ. They are, in this most basic of senses, *evangelical*: they draw their own identity from the gospel. Any approach that sets them fundamentally at odds with the gospel, as I think some members of the so-called apocalyptic school do,[27] is seriously problematic. The corollary of this, then, is that we recognize the congruity of covenant and gospel. But if we are to be faithful to the logic of this passage, we have to allow the right concept to serve as the principal one that conditions or determines all others: creation and covenant derive their significance from Jesus Christ, for he is the substance of the mystery glimpsed through them, but only now disclosed.

I want to suggest that this move, by which the world-ordering functions of Wisdom and Torah are linked to the mystery named Jesus Christ, allows us to differentiate the forms of union that are at work here. In the Jewish mind—and here there is good license to generalize, for the traditions are so widespread—God's relationship to the whole cosmos was covenantal, with the Torah playing a vital mediatorial role that is specified to be (necessarily) creaturely: Torah is made, as the "beginning of [God's] way," the firstborn of creation. God's relationship to the cosmos is thereby seen to be an orderly one, and that order is identified with covenant and Torah, so that those who live in accordance with the covenant live in line with the grain of the universe. Yet, Israel has a *particular* place within that covenant; it bears upon her in a distinctive way. And, as we noted above, within that distinctive covenantal relationship, further particular relationships could be differentiated: all covenantal, all determined by the same covenant, but all different. God's relationship to the forces of nature and to the tiniest occupants of the most obscure parts of the cosmos are "regular," they are "ruled" and the rules are disclosed through the Torah, if only partially. Now, that regulative reality is fully revealed to be the person of Jesus, and is known through him. But—and this is key—just as Israel was set apart within the totality of the cosmos for a special relationship of covenantal union with God,

---

27. See my comments to this effect in Grant Macaskill, "Review Article: The Deliverance of God," *Journal for the Study of the New Testament* 34 (2011) 150–61. I make similar comments with a more theological direction in Grant Macaskill, "History, Providence and the Apocalyptic Paul," *Scottish Journal of Theology* 70 (2017) 409–26.

and knew him in a particular way because of this, so those who *know* Jesus enjoy a particular kind of union with him that is distinct from the kind that the rest of the cosmos enjoys. All of the unions are real, and to treat any of them as if they were not evangelically determined would be wrong, but not all of them involve a union that is characterized by prayer.

It is not by accident that I focus on this language of knowledge and prayer. Consistently throughout Paul's writing, union with Christ is represented in cognitive and noetic terms. Multiple verses could be cited, but let me here simply quote Eph 1:17–18:

> I pray that the God of our Lord Jesus Christ, the Father of glory, may give you a spirit of wisdom and revelation as you come to know him, so that, with the eyes of your heart enlightened, you may know what is the hope to which he has called you, what are the riches of his glorious inheritance among the saints (Eph 1:17–18 NRSV).

The personal focus of this knowledge—it is about knowing "him"—is necessarily communicative, and the prominence of prayer as a theme in the Pauline writings is its natural corollary. Again, multiple texts could be cited, but let me quote another one from Ephesians that links prayer and knowledge:

> For this reason I bow my knees before the Father, from whom every family in heaven and on earth takes its name. I pray that, according to the riches of his glory, he may grant that you may be strengthened in your inner being with power through his Spirit, and that Christ may dwell in your hearts through faith, as you are being rooted and grounded in love. I pray that you may have the power to comprehend, with all the saints, what is the breadth and length and height and depth, and to know the love of Christ that surpasses knowledge, so that you may be filled with all the fullness of God. (Eph 3:14–19 NRSV).

This is a passage rich in temple imagery,[28] but what I am keen to stress is its very personal quality: Paul knows the Father, the Spirit, and Jesus, and wanting others to enjoy this same knowledge, he prays that their comprehension of Christ's love would grow.

Now, why do I stress all of this? I do so because it allows us to differentiate modes of participation, of being "in Christ." Some are distinctively passive, some distinctively non-reciprocal, some distinctively unconscious. But others involve knowledge and the renewing of the mind—they involve prayer. This, as many will know, is precisely the point highlighted by Todd Billings in his defense of Calvin's

---

28. See A. Mark Stirling, "Transformation and Growth: The Davidic Temple Builder in Ephesians" (PhD diss., University of St Andrews, 2012).

understanding of union with Christ against the challenges brought by Radical Orthodoxy and Gift Theology.[29] Far from Calvin's account of salvation being passive in the sense of being devoid of reciprocity, as some Gift theologians allege, Billings highlights that his emphasis on prayer is indicative of real involvement in salvation. It is passive, yes, in the sense that the principal agency is God's and we are objects of his activity, but it is not a salvation lacking in reciprocity: we are saved into a relationship, and that is *really* expressed in the communicative activity of prayer. Conversely, there is a distinct sense in which persons and things can enjoy the benefits of God's covenantally ordered relationship to the cosmos without any such reciprocity: he makes the sun to shine on the evil and the good and the rain to fall on the righteous and unrighteous alike (Matt 5:45). The point here is that while their enjoyment of God is evangelically conditioned—it rests on Christ's role as covenant mediator—it is not necessarily one that can be described using the grammar of soteriology. Humans can remain distinctively non-reciprocal, distinctively anti-covenantal, even as "all things" are being reconciled. Rather than being people of prayer, they can be idolaters.

Covenant, I think, gives us a thicker word for this than the language of sphere (or domain) that some use for the locative "in Christ." I understand why that word would be used, particularly as a way of rendering the locative or spatial significance of the expression and do not consider it to be inappropriate. We might, possibly, see this kind of imagery to be at work in some of the language of age or *aeon*, which is sometimes understood in spatial terms. But given the kind of covenantal associations that I have noted above, and that I have probed in greater detail in my study of *Union with Christ*, I think "covenant" is more appropriate and more helpful than "sphere." It allows us also to highlight the kind of distinctions that are internal to the concept of covenant that I have discussed here: all things may be in Christ, participating in God's work of reconciling all things to himself, but not everything prays. The distinction reflects Russell's differentiation of dynamic and passive participation, but with reference to the kinds of categories that are live in Jewish thought.

Pastoral Conclusions

So much for the theory. In this final section, I want to reflect on some of the pastoral implications that this may have.

First, this emphasis on diverse covenantal union provides a particular conceptual underpinning to our attempts to develop an integrative account of Christian

---

29. J. Todd Billings, *Calvin, Participation and the Gift: The Activity of Believers in Union with Christ* (Oxford: Oxford University Press, 2009).

ethics, one that takes seriously our evangelical commitment to creational care, environment, social outreach, etc. We often seek to ground these too narrowly, I would suggest, on the category of lordship: Jesus is the lord of all life, and so we should take seriously our need to act in all its areas. This is not wrong, but neither is it adequate: it seeks to make the "ruler" motif (to which the concept of lordship is often reduced) do all the ethical loadbearing, when actually there are other motifs that need to be brought into the discussion, including those of covenant and Christ as mediator. To say that Christ "rules" all creation might not necessarily lead us to an acknowledgement of our need to care for the environment, for example, since rule is not always understood in terms of care; to say that all creation is "in him," however, as the object of creative and providential activities that are internal to his identity, is to recognize that we cannot mistreat the creation without treating him abusively. The category of covenant, properly handled, allows us the freedom to use this kind of language assertively, bringing in its full breadth of force, without falling into the confusion represented by panentheism.[30]

This was the key point that I intended to highlight at the beginning of the essay when I spoke of certain doctrines as functionally sub-Christian: they are not adequately conceived with respect to the person of Jesus Christ. There is also, though, a subtle converse or corollary to this, one that John Webster became highly sensitive to in his later theological work.[31] The failure to relate creation and Christology can also lead to a serious distortion of Christology itself, one that we might suggest to be a factor contributing some rather Marcionite qualities to much contemporary theological and biblical scholarship.[32] Unless we allow Christology to incorporate the doctrines of creation and providence, and to speak accordingly of those things that are the objects of God-in-Christ's creative and providential activity, then our Christology will be an imbalanced one.

Second, by framing everything in relation to the Son's pre-existence—creation, providence, redemption—the passage demands that all of our talk about sin and evil is similarly framed. That is, we cannot allow ourselves to talk of sin and evil in a way that is not basically informed by Christology. This is something to which Barth, in particular, was sensitive, exemplified by his readings of Rom 5 in his book *Christ*

30. This recognition might also allow those who acknowledge the need to affirm this to do so without having to resort to a Moltmannian account, which is often where evangelicals end up, but which is rather panentheistic in character.

31. See, for example, Jurgen Moltmann, "Non ex aequo: God's Relation to Creatures," in *Within the Love of God. Essays on the Doctrine of God in Dialogue with Paul Fiddes*, edited by Anthony Moore and Andrew Clarke (Oxford: Oxford University Press, 2014) 95–107.

32. Again, the label has been attached on more than one occasion to Douglas Campbell's *The Deliverance of God: An Apocalyptic Rereading of Justification in Paul* (Grand Rapids: Eerdmans, 2009).

and Adam,[33] and on this point at least he is right. God's dealings with the cosmos and its inhabitants have always been conditioned by the gospel of Jesus Christ; that is one crucial implication of Col 1:15–20. He related to the cosmos *in Christ* when he laid its foundations, he related to the cosmos *in Christ* when he first made humanity according to his image, he related to the cosmos *in Christ* when that paradigmatic first sin took place; all of his dealings are mediated and the same mediator is at the heart of all of them. The pastoral significance of this is, I think, enormous, for our tendency is so often to see our latest and worst sin as placing us beyond the bounds of the gospel. But to see "all things" as bounded by the gospel is to recognize that this way of thinking is fundamentally wrong: God's disposition towards his creatures is always and everywhere gospel-shaped. What remains from this observation is the question of precisely how we relate to him within the covenant. I am sensitive to the risk in all of this of giving any kind of priority to our response to God, as if the precise quality of our faith is the thing that saves us, rather than the one in whom that faith is placed. We must not render faith in such terms. Neither, though, should we render it in terms that negate the reality of the communion that it generates.

Third, this differentiation of kinds of union allows us to see "all things" as evangelically conditioned—their significance always contextualized and determined by the gospel—without collapsing everything into a single, simple universalism. This frees us to assert the first two points made above, which we often shy away from as evangelicals, without fearing that by doing so we have asserted a universalism that downplays the place of faith and repentance. Faith, repentance, and personal transformation are consistently represented throughout the New Testament as features of the one who has been united with Christ unto salvation, for that union involves the personal relationship indicated by the realities of knowledge and prayer. Undoubtedly, the one who knows Christ and prays to (and through) him is conditioned by union with Christ in other ways of which s/he is not always conscious, as a creature, as an object of providential care. But there is a distinct form of union that unavoidably involves prayer and sacrament, by which we become "participants/sharers" (*koinōnoi*), by which we are adopted, by which, through the work of the Holy Spirit in us, we cry "Abba, Father."

---

33. Karl Barth, *Christ and Adam: Man and Humanity in Romans 5* (New York: Harper, 1956); translated by T. A. Snail from *Christus und Adam nach Romer 5* (Zurich: Evangelischer Verlag, 1952).

RESPONSE TO MACASKILL

Constantine R. Campbell

It will come as no surprise to those familiar with his work that I find Grant Macaskill's essay intriguing, well-argued, and insightful. It is careful and creative. Exploring the Christ-hymn of Col 1:15–20, Macaskill offers a fresh reading of this well-known text, with special attention given to the notion of the "image of God" and the possible covenantal overtones throughout the hymn. In this brief response, I will not rehearse the essay's arguments but will go straight to my key reflections. First, I offer affirmation for points that are interesting, compelling, and illuminating. Second, I offer some resistance to a few of the essay's assertions and conclusions.

Macaskill rightly affirms the complexity of the concept of union with Christ. It is not reducible to one theological idea, but represents a range of concepts that are related under the umbrella of connectedness to Christ, whether that connectedness is our own, or the Father's perichoretic mutual indwelling with the Son. This is not a new insight, and goes back at least as far as Markus Barth's 1964 commentary on Ephesians,[1] and has been vigorously argued in my own writings,[2] but it is a conclusion that must be restated and pressed since it is clear that scholars and theologians continue to make the mistake that we are talking about a simple, jejune concept. Union with Christ is neither simple nor simplistic.

First, some affirmations. Macaskill is right to affirm the spatial reading of *en autō* in Col 1:16—*everything was created in him*. While an instrumental reading of *en* is possible, and is adopted by some translations, this side steps the serious conceptual work of understanding what a spatial meaning might involve. Macaskill correctly points to the spatial imagery already at work in the context (e.g., 1:13–14) and I will add that the thrust of the Christ-hymn is concerned with the supremacy of Christ and the reconciliation of all things through him. Given this reconciliation theme and the fact that Christ is the center point of reconciliation, the locative *en autō* provides a strong fit.[3]

---

1. "The impossibility of elaborating a final definition of the meaning of 'in Christ' may well have a simple cause: namely that Paul used the formula *in more than one sense*." See Markus Barth, *Ephesians: Introduction, Translation, and Commentary on Chapters 1–3* (AB; Garden City, NY: Doubleday, 1974) 69 [his emphasis].

2. Constantine R. Campbell, *Paul and Union with Christ: An Exegetical and Theological Study* (Grand Rapids: Zondervan, 2012) 25–27.

3. See Constantine R. Campbell, *Colossians and Philemon: A Handbook on the Greek Text* (Waco: Baylor University Press, 2013) 11; Campbell, *Paul and Union with Christ*, 179–81.

I greatly appreciate Macaskill's thinking about the relationship between the two "firstborn" phrases, "firstborn of all creation" (*prōtotokos pasēs ktiseōs*) and "firstborn from the dead" (*prōtotokos ek tōn nekrōn*; 1:15, 18). Rightly does he state, "we are intended to identify all things in their mutual relationship to Christ, but not to simplify them into something singular, with a singular relationship." This helps us to understand the nature of the reconciliation of all things in Christ (1:20)—this reconciliation need not be understood as singular or simplistic. There are different kinds of reconciliation, with some parties being reconciled willfully, and others against their will. Macaskill's discussion of *prayer* as the marker that identifies "friendly" reconciliation in contrast to "unfriendly" reconciliation is helpful.

One way that Macaskill coordinates the two sections of the Christ-hymn—Christ's relationship to creation and his relationship to the church—is highly intriguing. The temple is able to coordinate these domains since the earthly temple was held to point to God's ordering of the cosmos. In other words, temple imagery has a built-in cosmic referent, and this is indeed an interesting way to coordinate the two parts of the hymn. But of course it depends on being persuaded that the "image" (*eikōn*) of 1:15 should be understood through the lens of temple imagery.

Now we turn to some resistance. Overall, Macaskill's treatment of the notion of "image" (*eikōn*) does not give sufficient attention to its genitive modifier, "of the invisible God" (1:15a). Whatever else might be said about its possible backgrounds, the phrase "image of the invisible God" (*eikōn tou theou tou aoratou*) plainly evokes the juxtaposition of "image" with the invisibility of God. In this way, it seems that the plainest meaning of the phrase has to do with the *revelation* of God. Though invisible, he is revealed by his "image" (*eikōn*) Jesus Christ. Such an understanding resonates with texts such as John 1:18—"No one has ever seen God. The one and only Son, who is himself God and is at the Father's side—he has revealed him." This is not to deny the temple associations that Macaskill finds here, but the emphasis ought to be seen alongside the revelatory function that is explicitly identified in the text.

There are a couple of points related to the language of "firstborn," *prōtotokos*, that require some probing. Macaskill wants to play down the possible Adamic connotations here, as well as for "image" language, pursuing other echoes for the language. He states that "Adam was not the 'firstborn' of creation," but this does not fairly consider the connotations of *status* inherent to *prōtotokos*. The point of being *firstborn* is not temporal —but status-oriented; the firstborn had the privilege of receiving the inheritance. But more important is the neglect of the possible meanings of the genitive "of all creation," in the phrase *prōtotokos pasēs ktiseōs* (1:15b). This can be understood as a genitive of subordination, thus rendering the translation, "the firstborn *over* all creation."[4] This better fits the status connotations of *prōtotokos*, but also allows for an Adamic understanding—Adam may not have been temporally first within creation, but he is presented as first in terms of status. He has authority and dominion over God's creation. In any case, Macaskill wisely takes a nuanced position, not denying an allusion to Adam, while not regarding it as the principal background.

When Macaskill explores what it means that Christ is "the firstborn of all creation" (*prōtotokos pasēs ktiseōs*) we come to a problem that requires further probing. He refers to Christ's "own creatureliness (he is the firstborn of every creature)." While Macaskill would no doubt strongly disavow any association with christological Arianism, this statement seems dangerously close to it. At least, this is precisely an Arian reading of the phrase "firstborn of all creation"—taking the genitive as a *partitive* genitive, thus viewing Christ as a *part* of creation. But this genitive phrase is much more likely a genitive of subordination—Christ is firstborn *over* all creation. The context affirms this reading, since "everything was created by him," and "all things have been created through him and for him" (1:16). Thus, Christ cannot be viewed as *part* of creation, but is the one through whom everything is created. He is firstborn in terms of status over creation, not as the temporally first-born part of it.

Now we come to the notion of covenant, which is an important theme in Macaskill's work. He sees covenant as sufficiently broad as to envelop the various species of participation or union with Christ. And this idea is both the major contribution of Macaskill's essay, as well as its most contentious aspect, in my view. To begin, covenant is understood very broadly by Macaskill, simply encompassing (first Israel's, but also) humanity's relationship with God. It is not restricted to particular covenants and is not delimited by the standard language associated with the cutting of covenants.

Such an understanding of covenant, made popular in scholarship by the likes of N. T. Wright, is controversial, as several scholars will object to such a broad relationship being known by that nomenclature. Some problems inherent to this use of "covenant" include the following. First, the definition is so broad, does it really mean anything? If we simply mean God's relationship to creation, how does it advance our understanding by using the term "covenant"? It is not clear what is gained.

Second, it raises the question of how the specific covenants in the biblical canon relate to this mega-"covenant." If we use a biblical term for a concept for which the bible does not use said term, is the integrity of that term threatened? So that when the term *is* used, its significance has been diluted. For example, the *Oxford English Dictionary* now includes a figurative meaning under the dictionary entry for the

---

4. Daniel B. Wallace, *Greek Grammar Beyond the Basics* (Grand Rapids: Zondervan, 1996) 104; Campbell, *Colossians and Philemon*, 10–11.

word "literally."[5] Our misuse of the word "literally" to mean something figurative has bleached the word to the point at which its integrity has been compromised. How, now, do we say "literally" without being misunderstood to mean "figuratively"? It is all but impossible, and it makes me *literally* want to kill somebody.

While it is observed that a type of mega-"covenant" can be found in Second Temple literature—relating the whole of creation covenantally to its creator—this does not mean that the biblical authors hold to such a broad concept of covenant. The covenants that Paul explicitly depends on are Abrahamic, Mosaic, and Davidic (and some would say Adamic). Does he ever invoke a covenant with creation? It is unlikely. So, how does Macaskill's sense of covenant relate to the specific covenants explicitly presented in the biblical texts?

Third, even if we accept this definition of covenant, and accept that there are hints of it implied in various New Testament texts, should they be prioritized *over* other elements that are explicitly found in the text? For example, Macaskill's temple understanding of "image" relies on its *implicit* significance, but the text *explicitly* links it to the invisibility of God, thereby making the revelatory function of "image" more significant. It is not clear if conceiving it covenantally helps or not.

Regarding this last point, covenant is unhelpfully prioritized in another way too. Macaskill agrees that underpinning the Christ-hymn exists a sphere or domain theology, such that everything is upheld by Christ in the sphere of his reality. This is undoubtedly correct. But then Macaskill goes on to argue that a covenantal understanding is better than sphere or domain. The problem here is that, while the covenantal overtones, or undertones, of the passage require some elucidation to see them, domain or sphere is explicitly and directly highlighted in the verses that immediately precede the Christ-hymn—"He has rescued us from the *domain* of darkness and transferred us into the *kingdom* of the Son he loves" (1:13). "*Domain* of darkness" is how translators render *exousias tou skotous*. So, the problem is *not* in accepting the possibility of covenantal overtones (if we accept Macaskill's broad understanding of the term) but in the argument that it trumps the notion of domain or sphere. This is unconvincing.

In conclusion, Macaskill's paper is stimulating, intriguing, and well argued. The already evocative and rich Christ-hymn of Col 1:15–20 will require rereading and further reflection. Of particular value are Macaskill's suggestions for coordinating its two halves, possibly through temple imagery, his affirmation of the complexity of union with Christ, and his spatial/locative understanding of *en autō*. But the essay's chief points of contention involve reading the text's possible inferences over, and

5. See https://en.oxforddictionaries.com/definition/literally: "Used for emphasis while not being literally true. 'I was literally blown away by the response I got.'"

sometimes against, explicit elements of the text. Seeing the "image of the invisible God" as primarily temple imagery instead of revelatory of the invisible God is one example, and the overarching concept of covenant over the domain of Christ's rule is another.

WHY BOTHER WITH PARTICIPATION? AN EARLY LUTHERAN PERSPECTIVE

Olli-Pekka Vainio

For no one hates his own flesh, but nourishes and favors it.
He is our King and our High Priest,
and we are bone of his bones. (TNC 148)

The doctrine of divine participation has recently received a significant amount of scholarly interest. What has been surprising is the wide ecumenical spread of the authors interested in the topic. For example, Catholics, Lutherans, Pentecostals, and Reformed theologians have expressed their enthusiasm toward a doctrine that some time ago was seen only as an exotic fringe feature of Orthodox theology.[1]

I am writing here as a Lutheran, and as a card-carrying member of the Finnish Luther School, which is famous for its claim that Luther in fact understands justification as deification, and not merely as a purely forensic declaration.[2] Here I do not want to repeat the often-made theses on Martin Luther, but instead I want to focus on "the Second Martin," that is, Martin Chemnitz (1522–1586). Perhaps unknown to non-Lutheran audiences, Chemnitz was, after Luther and Philip Melanchthon, the most influential Lutheran Reformer.[3] Chemnitz's historical influence on Lutheranism has been summarized in the adage: "if Martin [Chemnitz] had not come along,

1. See, for example, Roger Olson, "Deification in Contemporary Theology," *ThTo* 64.2 (2007) 186–200; Todd J. Billings, *Union with Christ: Reframing Theology and Ministry for the Church* (Grand Rapids: Baker Academic, 2012); Cynthia Peters Anderson, *Reclaiming Participation: Christ as God's Life for All* (Minneapolis: Fortress, 2014); Paul M. Collins, *Partaking in Divine Nature: Deification and Communion* (London: T. & T. Clark, 2010); Daniel Keating, *Deification and Grace* (Naples, FL: Sapientia, 2007); and Veli-Matti Kärkkäinen, *One with God: Salvation as Deification and Justification* (Collegeville, MN: Liturgical, 2004).

2. Overviews of the Finnish interpretation of Luther are *Union with Christ: The New Finnish Interpretation of Luther*, edited by Carl E. Braaten and Robert W. Jenson (Grand Rapids: Eerdmans, 1998) and *Engaging Luther: A (New) Theological Assessment*, edited by Olli-Pekka Vainio (Eugene, OR: Cascade, 2010). This essay is to a great extent based on my dissertation, which examines the origins of the Lutheran doctrine of justification: Olli-Pekka Vainio, *Justification and Participation in Christ: The Development of the Lutheran Doctrine of Justification from Luther to the Formula of Concord (1580)* (Leiden: Brill, 2008). The material is used with permission. In this article, I refer to Chemnitz's translated works because they are more accessible than the Latin texts. For those who are interested in the original Latin sources, I offer the full references in Vainio, *Justification and Participation in Christ*.

3. For his biography, see Jacob A. O. Preus, *The Second Martin: The Life and Theology of Martin Chemnitz* (St. Louis: Concordia, 1994).

Martin [Luther] would hardly have survived."[4] His most important achievement was the *Formula of Concord* (1580) an intra-Lutheran confessional examination of the issues that threatened to fragment the newly born Lutheran movement.[5]

Considering our theme, Chemnitz is worthy of close examination because he structured his theology around Christology and, like Luther, he understood justification as participation.[6] Here I hope to illustrate, with the help of Chemnitz, how the idea of participation with the divine nature of Christ is an essential element of Christian soteriology. Chemnitz's Christology also offers a good example of how early Lutherans sought to systematize the biblical message with the help of tradition, as Chemnitz is well known for his extensive use of patristic sources.[7]

Moreover, Chemnitz's work on Christology provides a perspective on the unity of doctrine: all the various parts of the Christian creed form a coherent whole. No part is detached and isolated from the others. A minor change somewhere effects a major change elsewhere.[8] Christology and Trinitarian theology may often sound like unnecessary hair-splitting or a convoluted attempt to square a circle to non-specialists. I grant that many fine works of analytic Christology are not light reading and grasping their meaning requires years of education and training. But Christology is like gravity; it affects everything even if the fine details of it are understood only by a select few and even they understand it imperfectly. There is a difference between understanding *that* something happens as it does and understanding *how* and *why* exactly it happens as it does.

---

4. Lat. "Si Martinus [Chemnitius] non fuisset, Martinus [Lutherus] vix stetisset."

5. Among his best-known writings are his examinations on the doctrine of the Holy Supper, *Repetitio sanae doctrinae* (1561) and *Fundamenta sanae doctrinae* (1570), and his influential work on Christology, *De Duabus naturis in Christo* (1570). The English edition [hereafter TNC] is Martin Chemnitz, *The Two Natures in Christ,* translated by J.A.O. Preus (St. Louis: Concordia, 1971). *Examen concilii tridentinii* (1566–1575) is a colossal examination of the degrees and canons of the Council of Trent. The English edition [hereafter ECT] is Martin Chemnitz, *Examination of the Council of Trent,* translated by Fred Kramer (St. Louis: Concordia, 1972). Chemnitz's lectures on Melanchthon's *Loci Communes* were published posthumously as *Loci Theologici* (1591).The English edition [hereafter LT] is Martin Chemnitz, *Loci Theologici,* translated by J.A.O. Preus (Saint Louis: Concordia, 1989).

6. For the standard, even if a bit old and not necessarily always clear, exposition of the Finnish reading of Luther on this point is Tuomo Mannermaa, *Christ Present in Faith: Luther's View of Justification* (Minneapolis: Fortress Press, 2005). On the critical discussion about the Finnish interpretation of Luther and justification, see Olli-Pekka Vainio, "Luther and Theosis: A Response to the Critics," *ProEccl* 24.4 (2016) 459–74.

7. The idea of the Loci-method was to present the central biblical passages (*sedes doctrinae,* the seats of doctrine) which were then summarized in the form of a coherent exposition of any given doctrine. TNC, especially, is full of patristic citations and the Book of Concord has an appendix, *Catalog of Testimonies,* which tries to prove the truth of Lutheran doctrine with the help of the church fathers.

8. See also Eeva Martikainen, *Doctrina: Studien Zu Luthers Begriff Der Lehre* (Helsinki: Luther-Agricola-Gesellschaft, 1992).

On the True Humanity of Christ

For Chemnitz, Christology and soteriology are interlinked and they both arise from the meaning of Col 2:9–10: "For in him the whole fullness of God lives in bodily form. And you have been brought to fullness in him, who is the head of every ruler and authority."[9] This is the biblical basis for both the doctrine of hypostatic union and justification by faith. To reconcile the fallen world with the Father, God the Son assumes human nature so that he is both truly divine and truly human.

In a section called "On the use of this doctrine" in *Two Natures in Christ* (147–148, 219–220) Chemnitz offers 14 reasons why Christ had to be both divine and human, which primarily concentrate on the qualitative difference between God and humanity, both before and after the Fall. In the light of the well-known theories of atonement, which I will examine shortly, it is interesting that he makes only two references to judicial guilt that requires satisfaction and separates God and the human race. Let me be clear that Chemnitz in no way shuns or disparages satisfaction or penal substitution. What is, however, interesting is how he frames it within a larger theory of the economy of salvation.

In his list, Chemnitz states the following. Assumption is needed because it is Adam's nature that is fallen. Sin and death need to be abolished in this same nature, that is, the human flesh. This takes place so that this sinful flesh is united with the divine nature, which is holy and pure. Christ's merit can be given to us only if our natures are consubstantial. Through assumption, Christ is now not only our brother but the head of the whole human race. Christ also shares with his body his roles as the King and High Priest, through which he administers for us his kingdom and his priesthood.

Moreover, a mere creature could not have borne the wrath of God, and crushed the serpent's head since these actions require divine power. Human nature in itself and in this fallen condition is unable to restore life to our bodies overcome by sin and death. Likewise, a mere human could not enter into the recesses of the Trinity to announce to us the plan of salvation and plead our case in this council. The whole economy of salvation, including conversion, justification, sanctification, and governance of creation, all the way to the resurrection of the dead and establishing the new heaven and new earth is beyond human powers. Finally, only God can preserve these things for eternity. This is the short summary of why Christ had to be both the true God and truly human person. Let us now look at some of these points more closely.

---

9. This is the most used Bible reference in TNC.

Obviously, the "true God" part is not hard to grasp if one follows standard Trinitarian doctrine. God the Son shares the same divine nature with the Father and the Holy Spirit, who seek to bring humanity back to the Triune communion. (TNC 41, 313; ECT II, 56; LT 113) A more interesting question is that of the characteristics of the assumed human nature, which, according to Chemnitz, needs to be true, perfect, capable of experiencing true human emotions, and the same essence as the nature of all other humans.

The reasons for each of these features are as follows. Instead of the assumption being true, it could have been only an apparition so that Christ in his incarnate form would have only appeared to look like a human male (like the appearances of God in the Old Testament, for example, Gen 32:24–30; Dan 3:25, 7:13). However, the consequence of this would have been significant as then the incarnation would not have benefited human beings in any way. Instead of imparting to us the life that is God, he could have given life only "seemingly" (TNC 51).

The perfect human nature includes not only a human body but also a human soul. The old patristic maxim states, "For that which he has not assumed, He has not healed."[10] The assumption of a human soul is crucial because while sin affects our bodies, its origin is in the soul, and by assuming a human soul, he assumes everything typically human (TNC 60, 76).

Because Christ has a human soul, everything he feels, he feels like human beings do. Therefore, his divine nature does not insulate Christ from feelings of pain and suffering during his earthly life. For us it is possible to think that Christ might have experienced pain like split-brain patients do; they feel pain-like sensations but they do not exactly suffer.[11] The experience is mildly annoying but the qualia of pain are lacking. Chemnitz uses the simile of a spear penetrating water: the spear leaves a mark without cutting through anything (TNC 61). Instead, the death of Christ must be a real death, not merely a near-death experience.

The assumed human nature of Christ is the same nature (*homoousios*) as ours, as Heb 2:16 states how God the Son did not "take on him the nature of angels; but he took on him the seed of Abraham" (KJV).

A fascinating topic concerning the assumed nature is its relation to sin. Both Luther and Chemnitz underline that the assumed nature was a sinful, fallen nature. Even in this regard the assumed nature is exactly like ours. A pure nature would not be in need of salvation. Sin, death, and hell must be destroyed in and through the

10. On the origins of the saying in the patristic era, see M. F. Wiles, *Soteriological Arguments in the Fathers, Studia Patristica* (Berlin: Akademie, 1966) 322.

11. On split-brain patients and the sense of pain, see, for example, Ian McGilchrist, *The Master and His Emissary. The Divided Brain and the Making of the Western World* (New Haven: Yale University Press, 2009).

same nature that brought them into this world (TNC 55–6).[12] The nature that Christ assumed in the womb of Mary, who was a sinner like everyone else, was therefore a fallen nature. However, when the Spirit descends on Mary, the assumption takes place, and the human nature is purified (TNC 57, 210; ECT 377). This is an important, but seldom noted point. For Protestants, the cross and vicarious atonement typically take a central place, but this is a limited view of the complete christological account, where salvation already starts at the moment of incarnation.[13] Justification cannot be thought to be an act of mere forensic declaration because sin is not just a legal entity; sin is something that poisons our very bodies and the inmost parts of our being, infecting our thoughts, desires, and actions.

From the assumption onward, Christ carries in him a human nature that he has taken into the process of healing. As a human-divine person Christ is sinless, which means that he is not personally guilty of any sin of commission or omission. However, he participates in the consequences of sin. This takes place first through kenosis: during the incarnation, God the Son does not manifest his divine powers but gives himself over to suffering and death. He is subject to weakness, sickness, suffering, and is also able to die like ordinary humans. Obviously, Christ does not assume every possible disease and individual weakness, like cancer, AIDS, hay fever, or bad hearing; the state of weakness is needed for the ability to experience death and in order to be a true member of the human race (TNC 49–55).

In his *1535 Commentary on Galatians*, Luther makes a bold claim and insists that Christ becomes a sinner: "Christ does not represent his own person; he is no Son of God, born of a virgin, but a sinner."[14] This has caused some concern. Does Luther think that Christ is *really* a sinner? Well, yes and no. In order to save us, he must be our representative in a way that is not merely a bookkeeper's trick. Our sin must be made truly Christ's own. But how can this happen? Chemnitz explains that Christ assumes our sins through imputation (*imputative*) as the Latin version of Isa 53:12 states that Christ "was numbered with the transgressors" (*et cum sceleratis reputatus est*) (ECT 502). By this act of imputation, he now becomes a sinner in the eyes of God.

---

12. The Eucharist unites the receiver of the substances to the assumed nature of Christ in which death is destroyed. Without the consubstantiality of the natures, even the Eucharist would have no effect. If this sounds strange, it is because Luther and Lutherans are "not quite Protestants." See Phillip Cary, "Why Luther Is Not Quite Protestant: The Logic of Faith in a Sacramental Promise," *ProEccl* 14.4 (2005) 447–86.

13. In Orthodox theology, the first two points of contact used by God to draw us back into the divine communion are creation and incarnation. See Andrew Louth, *Introducing Eastern Orthodox Theology* (Downer's Grove, IL: IVP Academic, 2013) 125.

14. *WA* 40 I: 433, 28–30 (my translation) = *LW* 26:277.

The assumption of the human nature is eternal; Christ remains always a human-divine person. Resurrection does not mean adopting some other kind of human nature, but the transformation of human nature according to the image of Christ. Here, it must be noted that *imago Dei* is a concept that in its full sense refers only to Christ. Only he is the true image of God and humans are images of God only in a qualified sense (TNC 46, 150; LT 317, 282). We once bore the divine image, but not anymore. Sometimes, Lutherans went so far as to claim that humans are images of the devil (*imago diabolii*). This is a very strong claim, and it was ultimately condemned as heretical in the third article of the *Formula of Concord*.

But what happened to our nature in the person of Christ? In him, humanity is taken up and exalted into the divine life. Adam's nature sits now at the right hand of the Father, and it is now the heavenly bond that unites heaven and earth forever (TNC 63–4, 77). This is no idle speculation but contains a deeply consoling message for us sinners. Chemnitz writes:

> It is a great comfort that the surest pledge of our salvation and glorification is the human nature of Christ seated at the right hand of the Father where He appears before the face of God on our behalf (Heb 7:25), leading us and joining us to the Father (John 17:24) in order that then we may be made to conform to His glorious body (Phil 3:21). In the very nature by which we are flesh of His flesh and bone of His bones we will come to judgment, in order that we may the more eagerly love His appearing (1. Tim 4:8). By this tie and bond we shall be joined forever to God in eternal life. (TNC 64)

God as God is unapproachable for humans, but in Christ human nature has been taken into the life of God. In Christ, God is not only approachable but God is one of us, and we are sharers of his nature (TNC 79).[15]

Theories of Atonement

Protestant theories of justification typically underline Christ's suffering on the cross. Chemnitz is here no exception. However, after Gustaf Aulén confused the discussion concerning atonement for centuries to come, something needs to be said about how atonement functions in accord with the idea of participation. Aulén's mistake was to set different theories of atonement against each other.[16] For example, he claimed that Luther employs especially the *Christus Victor* theory, which was

---

15. See also Aquinas, *ST* III, q. 1 a. 2.

16. Gustaf Aulén, *Christus Victor: An Historical Study of the Three Main Types of the Idea of Atonement* (Eugene, OR: Wipf & Stock, 2003). For a more recent examination of Luther's view of God and of atonement, see David A. Luy, *Dominus Mortis: Martin Luther on the Incorruptibility of God in Christ* (Minneapolis: Fortress Press, 2016).

incidentally also Aulén's favorite theory of atonement. However, if we analyze systematically Luther's texts on atonement, we do not see the kind of juxtaposition that Aulén presupposes. Luther openly uses various theories of atonement, and so does Chemnitz. For Chemnitz, both the idea of vicarious atonement and *Christus Victor* are complementary accounts of how Christ overcomes sin and death (TNC 221–2).

But let us start with the concept of divine Law. Chemnitz shows his Anselmian colors when he writes how God, after revealing his unchanging will in the law, follows it even if humans are found unable to fulfill it. The mode of salvation therefore needs to be in accordance with the law. This leads naturally to the idea of vicarious suffering and satisfaction; if humans are unable to fulfill the law, God himself fulfills the law in Christ (ECT 500–1, 524; TNC 49, 53; LT 530).

But what exactly is this law that Christ fulfills? It is not just any arbitrary set of demands. When Christ portrays full obedience to the law, this means that God the Son shares the same will with God the Father. The law followed by Christ until death is the Father's will to bring humanity back into the Triune communion. Effectively, the obedience of Christ includes all his activities and actions from the incarnation to his ascension (TNC 223, 490–1). Our own lives are nothing but a series of acts where we have shown disobedience to God; in contrast, Christ's life is nothing but a complete union with the Father's will. Some see here an act of horrific abuse, where a bloodthirsty father abandons his son to unspeakable torture only because the father had come up with a list of rules he clings to.[17] This is not how Chemnitz understands Christ's obedience. Being of the same substance with God the Father, but a different person, God the Son does not have his own list of goods even if he has own will. The incarnate life of God the Son is as it is because he loves the same things as the Father. Without a proper Trinitarian framework, our image of God and atonement cannot be anything other than horrific.

The Trinitarian approach also helps us remove our focus from the wrong kind of fixation on the cross as a punctiliar event. As was already noted, the basis for our deification was established at the moment of assumption. This was the first moment of the Son's obedience and the first moment of the divine economy of salvation. Chemnitz understands the obedience of Christ in a very wide sense, as a process ranging from the moment of descent from the heavens to the womb of Mary to the ascension to the right hand of the Father, and the sending of the Spirit, who continues to guide the Church through its earthly struggles. All of this is an expression of the will of the Father to whom Christ is obedient. It is, of course, right to focus on the death of Christ, because death is the wages of sin, and Christ's death is the

17. For example, John Shelby Spong, *The Sins of Scripture: Exposing the Bible's Texts of Hate to Reveal the God of Love* (San Francisco: Harper, 2005).

testament of his life lived in full obedience. Therefore, it is as a moment unparalleled, but there are other moments with equal, but different significance. The resurrection testifies to Christ's power over sin and death, that is, that he is in fact God the Son. The ascension of Christ is also our ascension (TNC 320, 428). All the events of Christ's earthly life add up to our individual salvation. In fact, our salvation takes place first in his person. Christ heals the fallen nature first in himself, as the head, and then he gives it to the body (TNC 60, 239, 313):

> This is the most comforting and salutary exchange (*salutaris permutatio*), that the Son of God has received from us a human nature and sanctified and blessed and exalted and glorified it in his own person. (TNC 55)[18]

How can the hypostatic union effect such things? This is because God the Son is *homoousios* with God the Father and God the Spirit. In God, there is no separation between essence and existence, and in him all perfections are found in abundance (TNC 42, 270). The most important attribute is vivifying life. This is an attribute of God the Son, which is, through hypostatic union, given to his assumed nature, and, through faith, to us:[19]

> For the divine nature of the Logos, essentially or in essence, in, according to, and through itself, by nature, in its very being, is life giving, omnipotent, and omniscient, indeed it is life and omnipotence itself. But the assumed human nature in Christ is in no way life giving or omnipotent, essentially, or in essence, in and through itself, by nature, formally, or in its very being but only by possession, that is, because it possesses the divine majesty and power of the Logos personally united to itself; and by virtue of the Logos which is wholly united with it, it makes all things alive, knows all, can do all, just as hot iron by virtue of its union with the fire can glow and give heat. (TNC 293)

In the beginning, God breathed life into the human soul (Gen 2:7) but through the fall, the Spirit was driven away. Chemnitz points out how Christ donates the Spirit to his church by breathing (John 20:22). Chemnitz sees here a link between two spirations (TNC 329; LT 165). Here again we see how Trinitarian doctrine informs Chemnitz's soteriology.

---

18. Aquinas also argues in this way. See *ST* III.69.3.1.

19. Chemnitz, *Theses quaedam de unione duarum naturarum in Christo hypostatica: item de offi ciis et maiestate Christi mediatoris, Lipsiae*, printed in *Nikolaus Selnecker: Repetitio doctrina de idiomatum communicatione, & humanae in Christo naturae exaltatione, gloria, & maiestate, Lipsiae 1581*, 86: "... quae ab aeterna fuit ipsa vita vivificans."

The Nature of Participation

The person of Christ has now become, in a very literal sense, the place of salvation. The humanity of Christ is the *nexus conjunctionis* between us and God, and we are justified and saved only in union with Him (LT 188–189). According to Col 2:10, Christ is now the head, and everyone who clings to him and apprehends him grows together with God (Col 2:19):[20]

> Thus Paul concludes that he who grasps and clings to this Head, that is, to this individual human nature which in Colossians 1 he calls the body, flesh, and blood of Christ, at the same time grasps, holds, and possesses the whole fullness of the Godhead. For this fullness dwells in the assumed nature, which is akin to us, of the same substance with us, and personally united with us, because there and in that way He has willed that He be sought, found, apprehended, and possessed. For in His absolute deity we cannot approach Him, since we have been alienated and barred from Him because of our sin. But now, since this fullness has been made akin to us in the flesh, not indeed through a transformation or conversion of the natures and essences but through the personal union, we are permitted to approach Him. And since we have an approach and access to the assumed nature of Christ on account of our consubstantial relationship through faith, we also through this same means have an approach to the whole fullness of the deity of the Logos, which dwells in the assumed nature; and thus we are finally brought to fellowship not only with the Son but also with the Father and the Holy Spirit because of the consubstantiality of the Trinity. (TNC 315–6)

In order for the head to animate the body, it needs to be connected with the body. For this to happen several things need to fall into place. First, the head must be of the same essence as the body, which was enabled at the assumption of the human nature. Second, the head must contain in itself the fullness of God, so that it can possess the vivifying power that can raise the dead. This is enabled because of the divinity of Christ (Col 2:9). Third, this fullness of God must be given to the body, which is possible only if the head and the body are united, which occurs through faith in Christ:

> It is required that the Head not be cut off or separated from the body, but be joined with it, and it is also necessary that the members adhere to the Head in a firm union. Thus it is also imperative that the complete Christ is present in the members according to both natures, and that He graft the members into Himself. (TNC 336)

20. Colossians 2:19 expresses this in a negative sense: "They have lost connection with the head, from whom the whole body, supported and held together by its ligaments and sinews, grows as God causes it to grow."

This merit of Christ has become apprehensible through faith because, due to the mutual sharing of the properties in the person of Christ, he is omnipresent. This is possible because the human nature has now become the sharer of divine ubiquity. The human nature of Christ has been raised to the right hand of the Father, making Christ salvifically present in the word and the sacraments (TNC 27):

> . . . so there is only one salvation for the human race, if we do not deny it to ourselves and if we lean wholly on the engrafted Christ, that we may be found in Him, having that righteousness which God gives to faith in Christ (Phil 3:9); that we may be made the righteousness of God in Christ (2 Cor 5:21); and become branches of the Vine (John 15:5); that we may be able to say, I live, yet not I, but Christ lives in me (Gal 2:20). (TNC 102)

It was sometimes fashionable to claim that the later Lutheranism (that is, everyone except Luther) divorced the person and the works of Christ, and this explains why the forensic interpretation of justification became so popular after Luther's death.[21] Nevertheless, Chemnitz hardly supported such a view. He claims:

> For the power, grace, efficacy, merits and blessings of Christ are not communicated to believers outside of or without His person, as if He Himself were not present, as the adversaries themselves admit. They also admit that it is necessary above all things that Christ himself be given to us, that He become ours and that He be present in, with us, and joined to us, so that from Him and in Him and through Him we might be filled with all the fullness of God. (TNC 472)

Protestants typically understand justification as an event that is not processual, but momentary. Naturally, the proclamation of forgiveness of sins is a punctiliar act but that does not mean that the salvific actions of God do not involve a process that changes the human person:

> In external matters God can touch (*tangere*) or bow (*inclinare*) the hearts, but in spiritual matters the infirmity cannot be cured by so simple a remedy. God can soften the heart, turn it or open it, but because the heart is too hard, He wounds, circumcises, and even grinds it to powder. When this profits nothing, He finally takes it away, gives it a new life (*vivificat*) and even creates a new heart. (TNC 241)

21. Lauri Haikola, Studien zu Luther und zum Luthertum (Uppsala: Lundequistska bokhandeln, 1958). See Theodor Mahlmann, "Die Stellung der unio cum Christo in der lutherischen Theologie des 17. Jahrhunderts," in *Unio: Gott und Mensch in der nachreformatorischen Theologie*, edited by Matti Repo and Rainer Vinke (Helsinki: Suomalainen teologinen kirjallisuusseura, 1996), 72–200.

Conclusions

Let me finally summarize the reason why participation is such an important doctrine. Here I will draw from some of the points made by Chemnitz but I also add a few thoughts of my own based on how Luther and Chemnitz seem to use the doctrine.

First, participation is supposed to be the source of deep consolation. On the last day, our judge will be Christ who bears our fallen nature. Thereby we know that our judge is merciful since he knows our afflictions. Justification as participation is not directed against the forensic imputation of Christ's righteousness. Instead, it explains how the imputation can take place, and it serves the same pastoral aim, which is to clarify how sinners are saved through grace alone and without their own merits.

Second, participation explains how the merit of Christ is also our merit. Because of the double consubstantiality of our nature with the assumed nature of Christ, and the consubstantiality of Christ's divine nature with the nature of God the Father and God the Spirit, we quite literally belong to the family of God. Therefore, participation ties justification to Christology and Trinitarian theology, ensuring that the Christian doctrine is coherent.

Third, participation is a biblical image that is supposed to capture not only our intellect but our imagination. Instead of receiving merely a formal letter of pardon, we are engrafted as branches of a good tree, we have been given a new heart, we are resurrected with Christ, and we are already at the right hand of the Father. This is, of course, something that we cannot experience, and our earthly experience often tells us exactly the opposite. Nonetheless, these images are supposed to offer consolation, even when we see nothing but sin in ourselves. Despite our shortcomings, we are loved by the heavenly Father. On the other hand, these images are supposed to call us to the transformation of our lives according to the divine image. Of course, participation is supposed to be a mystery. It is not necessarily something that we feel or experience. It is not even the case that we should yearn and look for those experiences.[22]

Fourth, if biblical allusions and figures of speech are taken seriously as ontological statements, that is, not merely as figures but as something that underscore the deep connection between humanity and God, participation is the only way to explain the meaning of these images. This is the way Luther thought that true philosophizing is supposed to proceed. Instead of starting with the principles that are

---

22. An excellent, and truly surprising, examination of mystical experience in the life of a Christian is Clive Staples Lewis, *Surprised by Joy. The Shape of My Early Life* (London: Fontana, 1955).

presupposed, one needs to start with the text, or something that is experienced, and build philosophical systems only after this event.

Fifth, the doctrine of participation has ecumenical relevance.[23] During the Reformation it became commonplace to underline the forensic aspects of justification. This emphasis was warranted in its own time, but over the years it led to an impoverished view of justification, and that led to a gap between the Christian traditions. Understanding the participatory elements in the doctrine of justification may help us overcome some of problems that create tension between Christian communities.[24]

---

23. Eero Huovinen, "A Common Teacher, Doctor Communis? The Ecumenical Significance of Martin Luther," in *Encounters with Luther. New Directions for Critical Studies*, edited by Kirsi I. Stjerna and Brooks Schramm (Louisville: Westminster John Knox, 2016) 3–14. I do not claim that participation as such can solve all the problems that are related to different interpretations of justification. There are different ontological models that churches use to explain how participation takes place. See, for example, Reinhard Flogaus, *Theosis bei Palamas und Luther: Ein Beitrag zum ökumenischen Gespräch* (Göttingen: Vandenhoeck & Ruprecht, 1997); Georgios I. Mantzaridis, *The Deification of Man: St. Gregory Palamas and the Orthodox Tradition* (Crestwood, NY: St. Vladimir's Seminary, 1984).

24. In his response, Stephen Chester asks whether the idea of participation has any relevance for ecclesiology. It assuredly does and there is a clear ecclesiological application of what has been said above. Here I just refer to Luther who developed a well-known theory of communal life based on the idea of joyous exchange. As Christ gives himself to us, the church, we are called to imitate him in giving our lives for others without asking anything in return. Luther wrote in *WA* 30 I: 26, 31–37: "We have the same faith, same doctrine and the same sacraments. I share the weakness, same lack of understanding, same brokenness and the same poverty with you. If you are naked, I too am naked until you have been clothed. If you are hungry, I too am hungry and thirsty. If I am happy and brave, I will come to you and share your sorrow and weakness and I will not cease until I have made you like I am. Thus, my joy is your joy, and your sorrow is my sorrow" (my translation). This idea also has relevance outside mere ecclesiology. The renewal of the church was supposed to lead a renewal of societal life. In a way, contemporary Nordic welfare societies are extensions of this Lutheran ecclesiological model even if nowadays the theological motivation of social democracy has been quite aggressively rejected. Also, it must be pointed out that there are several other factors behind the relative success of the Nordic welfare model, such as the fact that Nordic countries are wealthy, small, and relatively homogeneous. Chester also points out that I do not mention faith in this essay. For those interested in this aspect, see my essay "Faith" in *Engaging Luther*, 138–54.

RESPONSE TO VAINIO

Stephen J. Chester

As Dr. Vainio notes at the very beginning of his paper, "The doctrine of divine participation has recently received a significant amount of scholarly interest." At least in relation to the little world of academic theology we are being distinctly modish or fashionable in having a set of discussions on this theme. Further, divine participation appears little in contemporary Protestant preaching and evangelism and is often associated primarily with patristic and Eastern Orthodox theology. The temptation therefore is to dismiss concern with divine participation as merely the result of a preference for what seems novel and exotic over more familiar and biblical categories of soteriology. Against such a backdrop, it is the first great virtue of this paper that it reminds those of us who are Protestant that divine participation is not in fact novel or exotic in theological terms but is deeply embedded in our own traditions. For our sixteenth-century Protestant forbears, divine participation is one of the primary soteriological themes in Scripture.

Further, contrary to what is sometimes claimed, their engagement with this theme does not provide an example of the best instincts and insights of theological giants like Martin Luther being quickly abandoned after their deaths by their own followers. Rather, Vainio demonstrates, the greatest Lutheran theologian of the late sixteenth-century, Martin Chemnitz, grants just as central a place to divine participation in soteriology as Martin Luther had done earlier in the century. Nor, one might add, is this a question of early Lutheranism as somehow exceptional within the broader Protestant movement. Vainio quotes Chemnitz speaking of "the adversaries" (TNC 472) who nevertheless agree that "the power, grace, efficacy, merits and blessings of Christ are not communicated to believers outside of or without His person, as if He Himself were not present . . . They also admit that it is necessary above all things that Christ himself be given to us, that He become ours and that He be present with us and joined to us, so that from Him and in Him and through Him we might be filled with all the fullness of God." The adversaries are Reformed theologians who disagree with Chemnitz about how Christ is present in the church and in the eucharist, but who do not disagree with him in the slightest as to the soteriological necessity of divine participation. If we are Protestant, then we need to re-learn our own tradition in relation to this theme.

The second great virtue of this paper is that in exploring Chemnitz's handling of divine participation, Vainio shows us the way in which it serves to connect together central doctrines of the Christian faith. Certainly, the nature of the participation of the believer in Christ is explored, but only after we have first seen Chemnitz handle Christology, with a particular focus on the human nature of Christ, and on the atonement. The unity of incarnation and atonement as a single divine saving initiative for us is shown again and again. We are very far away here from transactional accounts of salvation that abstract atonement and justification from the story of Jesus Christ. Rather, the Christ who is present in the faith of the believer is the same Christ who lived as a human being and in his crucifixion and resurrection overcame sin and death. This integration of the whole of salvation in the person of Christ and in God's actions in him has important consequences. One, which is not explored in any detail in Vainio's paper, is for the nature of faith itself. Faith does not justify because it is the appropriate response to God's grace and is the right kind of religious disposition to fulfill the human side of a contract between God and humanity. Instead, faith justifies because it grasps hold of Christ and unites the believer with Christ.

Another consequence, which certainly is emphasized in the paper, is that such integration explains how the atonement becomes effective for believers. Chemnitz elaborates with greater doctrinal precision Luther's insistence that for our sake Christ became a sinner. By the assumption of human nature, Christ is able to bear the sins of the world and through our union by faith with the Christ who suffered, died, and rose again his sacrifice and victory are realities in which we dwell. As Luther had put it when commenting on Gal 3:13, there is a joyous exchange in which, having taken on himself the sins of the world, Christ is able to give to the believer his righteousness: "By this fortunate exchange with us He took upon himself our sinful person and granted to us His innocent and victorious person."[1] And when commenting upon Phil 2:7 Luther even insisted that the believer "can with confidence boast in Christ and say: 'Mine are Christ's living, doing and speaking, his suffering and dying, mine as much as if I had lived, done, spoken, suffered and died as he did.'"[2]

Vainio is quick to emphasize that for Chemnitz this type of explanation of how the atonement is effective for believers is not a matter of setting different models of the atonement against each other. Chemnitz is not advocating what we would call a *Christus Victor* model of atonement to the exclusion of the idea of vicarious atonement. Instead, Chemnitz also emphasizes vicarious atonement in the sense that when human beings are unable to fulfill the law, God fulfills the law himself in the life and obedience unto death of the incarnate Christ. Here, Vainio claims that

1. *LW* 26:277 = *WA* 40:443, 23–24.
2. *LW* 33:297 = *WA* 2:145, 16–18.

Chemnitz is again being faithful to Luther's own insights. Overall, I agree with this conclusion but would like to lodge a significant qualification. There are certainly plenty of statements, despite the famous assertions of Gustav Aulén to the contrary, in which Luther too emphasizes vicarious atonement and speaks in terms of Christ's merit and of God receiving satisfaction. Yet, there is a particular nexus of Pauline texts (Gal 3:13, "Christ redeemed us from the curse of the law by becoming a curse for us"; 2 Cor 5:21, "For our sake he made him who knew no sin to be sin, so that in him we might become the righteousness of God"; Rom 8:3, 13, verses which speak of God sending his own son in the likeness of sinful flesh and condemning sin in the flesh so that if by the Spirit we put to death the deeds of the body we will live) that Luther consistently interprets in terms of exchange. When I turn to the writings of Philip Melanchthon, I find that he instead characteristically interprets this nexus of texts in terms of Christ as a sacrificial victim who makes satisfaction for sin and bears the punishment for sin.[3] Thus, while there is no evidence of doctrinal disagreement between Luther and Melanchthon concerning the atonement, I do find a distinct exegetical difference between them at this point. Where does Chemnitz fall, I wonder, in relation to the exegesis of the same texts? Does he interpret this important nexus of Pauline texts primarily in terms of "joyous exchange" or vicarious atonement, or does he employ elements of both?

The final main section of Vainio's paper considers, with Chemnitz's help, the union of the believer with Christ. Here is helpfully addressed one of the most frequent anxieties among Protestants concerning divine participation, which is the danger of collapsing the appropriate distinction between God as Creator and the believer as creature. One very significant point in this regard has already been made earlier in the paper: "The assumption of the human nature is eternal; Christ remains always a human-divine person . . . In him, humanity is taken up and exalted into the divine life. Adam's nature sits now at the right hand of the Father, and it is now the heavenly bond that unites heaven and earth forever" (TNC 63–64, 77). In this sense then, the Creator-creature distinction that we are anxious to preserve has been collapsed by God himself. Yet, of course, we remain anxious about the distinction out of a quite proper sense of our own sinfulness and Chemnitz helps us here too by explaining clearly the manner in which we participate in the divine. He appeals to Col 1:18–20, where Christ is defined as the head of the body, the church, and the firstborn from the dead, and it is asserted that all the fullness of God was pleased to dwell in him. This Chemnitz interprets, in light of the immediately following references to reconciliation through Christ's blood and his fleshly body, as a statement

3. Stephen J. Chester, *Reading Paul with the Reformers: Reconciling Old and New Perspectives* (Grand Rapids: Eerdmans, 2017) 244–55.

that the fullness of God dwelt in Christ's assumed human nature. It is through our union by faith with Christ in this assumed nature that we are united with the full-ness of God and brought into fellowship also with the Father and the Holy Spirit. In contrast, says Chemnitz, "in his absolute deity we cannot approach Him, since we have been alienated and barred from Him because of our sin" (TNC 315–16).

If I am interpreting both Chemnitz and Vainio correctly then the chain of thought implied is as follows: in the person of Christ the divine and human na-tures are not confused and remain distinct but do so in one person without division or separation. Yet the communication of properties between Christ's two natures means that it is accurate to speak of the fullness of God dwelling in Christ's human nature. In an analogical manner, the believer united with Christ by faith shares in Christ's properties, not least Christ's justifying righteousness, in such a way that it is accurate to speak of our salvation as involving divine participation. Yet this does not result in any confusion between the divine and the human, or any collapsing of the distinction between the Creator and creature. The second person of the Trin-ity is not merged or mingled with us, but we are united with him without division or separation so that we share in the reality of who he is. Vainio has stated in his monograph on justification and participation in early Lutheranism that "The parties to this conjunction participate in each other's attributes without changing or losing their own essence. The relation between Christ and the believer must be examined according to the rules of Christology."[4] Or as Martin Luther less technically but perhaps more memorably put it, "faith couples Christ and me more intimately than a husband is coupled to his wife."[5]

As a New Testament scholar, especially a Pauline one, I find this explanation of the nature of divine participation particularly helpful. I do so because it not only integrates doctrines but also integrates the exegesis of texts. Thus, for example, in Gal 2:20 Paul insists that he has been crucified with Christ and that therefore he no longer lives but Christ lives in him. Further, Paul then immediately defines this life as the life he lives in the flesh, i.e., as human, embodied life. If the fullness of God dwells in Christ, then I do not know how to interpret this text other than in terms of divine participation. And yet, in a text like Phil 3:9 Paul insists that when we are found in Christ we will have a righteousness that is not our own through the law, but a righteousness that comes from God and is by faith. This text too speaks of our union with Christ and hence of divine participation, but here, even when Paul speaks eschatologically of being found in Christ his emphasis is on the alien

---

4. Olli-Pekka Vainio, *Justification and Participation in Christ: The Development of the Lutheran Doctrine of Justification from Luther to the Formula of Concord (1580)* (Leiden: Brill, 2008) 35.

5. *LW* 26:168 = *WA* 40:286, 16–17.

nature of justification. When we are found in Christ it will not be a question of what we have become in him, but rather a question of the work of Christ for us and the righteousness we have received through being united with him by faith. Both texts speak of our union with Christ but whereas the Galatians text mainly addresses the life Christ empowers us to live, the Philippians text addresses mainly our continued need as sinners for Christ's righteousness.

An account of divine participation that emphasizes our sharing in Christ's attributes but also insists on a continuing distinction between this and what Chemnitz terms Christ's absolute deity, barred to us by sin, can do justice to both these aspects. The transformation and empowerment of the believer is taken seriously but so too is our continued sinfulness. It is a Lutheran account of divine participation that, as we might expect, comports with the truth that we are simultaneously justified and sinners, a slogan that, if understood correctly rather than misinterpreted, still seems to me to be a correct summation of Paul's teaching. This double-sidedness matters, for the great strength of Chemnitz's account of divine participation, and Vainio's appropriation of it, is that it focusses not on the exaltation or ascent of the believer to God nor in any way tries to evade our continued neediness before God. In Christ, we are the richest beggars in the world but we are still beggars. Rather than focusing on us, divine participation instead directs our attention to what God has done in Christ. In Christ, God loved unlovable sinners like us and gave himself for us, and divine participation is similarly unglamorous. It involves us, in gratitude for this indescribable gift, in an analogous and secondary way, loving our unlovable neighbors.

If this is an accurate description of divine participation in relation to individual believers then surely there are also entailed consequences for the nature of the church as the community of God's people. Vainio has shown us how divine participation connects together for Chemnitz the incarnation and the atonement and the union of the believer with Christ by faith. I want to end with a question that pushes Vainio to extend the chain of connections one step further. Does Chemnitz have an ecclesiology that reflects his understanding of divine participation? If so, what are its contours? If not, should he have done and, if he should, what would such an ecclesiology look like?

THE GEOGRAPHY OF PARTICIPATION: *IN CHRIST* IS LOCATION, LOCATION, LOCATION

Julie Canlis

When Ed Sanders published his first book, *Paul and Palestinian Judaism*, just a few years after Neil Armstrong walked on the moon, we might say that it was a small step for Ed but a giant step for mankind—or at least for the biblical-theological world. From this has come a time of tremendous exploration, creativity, and reclamation. Whether through the New Perspective on Paul or Radical Orthodoxy or Patristic studies, participation is being recovered as essential for understanding Paul and Christian theology as a whole. Some smell danger and charge that participation is a recent reconstruction, a continental fad, or worse—a capitulation to metaphysics. I want to point to a greater danger sensed by those who are writing from *within* the recovery of participation.

It is articulated by Richard Hays who dialogues with Sanders thirty years later, pressing in by asking what does "'participation in Christ' actually *mean*"? (Hays's helpful article is entitled with the not-so-subtle question: "What is 'Real Participation in Christ'?" [1]) That was 2008. Vanhoozer chimed in a few years later in his introductory essay in the multi-disciplinary volume "*In Christ*" *in Paul*, noting in turn of Hays, "he too is reticent when it comes to spelling out the mechanism of participation, how really do *I* participate in *his* story?"[2] Klyne Snodgrass, in his recent article entitled the "Gospel of Participation," simply makes plain our corporate fears as academics who desire that our theology serve the church. "Is such a concept of being in Christ even conceivable and understandable for modern people? . . . Is there something 'objective' about the union? . . . But what in the world does 'objective' mean in such use? What is 'real' participation in Christ?"[3] For all of our progress over the past forty years, we fear that our talk about participation is weightless.

1. In *Redefining First-Century Jewish and Christian Identities: Essays in Honor of Ed Parish Sanders*, edited by Fabian E. Udoh et. al. (Notre Dame: University of Notre Dame Press, 2008) 336–51.

2. Kevin Vanhoozer, "From 'Blessed in Christ' to 'Being in Christ': The State of Union and the Place of Participation in Paul's Discourse, New Testament Exegesis, and Systematic Theology Today," in "*In Christ*" *in Paul,* edited by Michael Thate, Kevin Vanhoozer, and Constantine Campbell (Tübingen: Mohr Siebeck, 2014) 14.

3. Klyne Snodgrass, "Gospel of Participation," in *Earliest Christianity within the Boundaries of Judaism: Essays in Honor of Bruce Chilton,* edited by Alan J. Avery-Peck, Craig A. Evans, and Jacob

But weightlessness comes with a price—both for us academics, and for the churches that we serve. We were built for gravity. New studies are being conducted upon astronauts who have lived in zero gravity for stretches of time, with the conclusion that weightlessness has major risks. Although it may sound relaxing to float, without the pressure of gravity, muscles and even bones begin to atrophy as calcium from bones secretes out through urine—a process that cannot be completely reversed upon return to earth. Not only does floating in space feel relaxing, it actually does cause several key systems of the body to relax and (quite literally) go to sleep. Astronauts report grave disruption to their proprioceptive system which helps their body keep track of its parts. Without gravity, one cannot tell where one's arm is in relation to one's leg; in fact, the sense experience can be that of a total loss of one's limbs. Worse, re-entry into gravity can cause astronauts to collapse when walking even after returning to earth, as they cannot bear the weight of physicality anymore.[4]

This was anticipated by Sanders, in his unforgettable passage on participation in Christ:

> But what does this mean? How are we to understand it? We seem to lack a category of 'reality'—real participation in Christ, real possession of the Spirit . . . I must confess that I do not have a new category of perception to propose here. This does not mean, however, that Paul did not have one . . . [5]

For French philosopher Pierre Hadot, this consciousness is a closed door. "We have here to do with two radically different kinds of relationship to the world."[6] Is it true that we no longer have the right tools to even appropriate this way of thinking? That it is "impossible" for those of us living after the scientific revolution (so Owen Barfield[7])? Or for those of us condemned to live and think after Scotus (so John Milbank[8])? Is the anemic nature of much of contemporary evangelicalism linked to the ill-effects of prolonged weightlessness? Are we collapsing under the weight of the sacraments and the demands of an embodied, localized faith—for which we have no conceptual category? Have we lost track of our arms and legs—other members in the body of Christ to whom we can no longer perceive an organic connection? Do our academic discussions only serve the general weightlessness? I too am still

---

Neusner (Leiden: Brill, 2016) 417.

4. Elizabeth Howell, "Weightlessness and Its Effect on Astronauts," in *Space.com* (30 Sept 2013) http://www.space.com/23017-weightlessness.html.

5. E. P. Sanders, *Paul and Palestinian Judaism: A Comparison of Patterns of Religion* (Minneapolis: Fortress, 1977) 506.

6. Pierre Hadot, *Philosophy as a Way of Life* (Oxford: Blackwell, 1995) 273.

7. Owen Barfield, *Saving the Appearances: A Study in Idolatry* (New York: Harcourt Brace Jovanovich, 1965).

8. John Milbank, *The Word Made Strange* (Oxford: Blackwell, 1997).

receiving emails from people asking, "what IS participation?" despite all my writing on the subject. Recently I received an email from a woman who had just read *Calvin's Ladder,* my book on Calvin and participation,[9] in which she asks "but what does my body have to do with participating in the triune relations?" I too have succumbed to weightlessness.

As Teilhard de Chardin warned nearly a century ago, "Unless it receives a new blood transfusion from matter, Christian spirituality may well lose its vigor and become lost in the clouds."[10] I have good news: Christian participation has always involved matter—which means people, places, sacraments, earth, water, wine, oil, bodies. A recovery of Christian participation will involve a recovery of gravity. It will involve matter and physicality. It might even be able to be mapped with a GPS location.

Calvin and Participation

Today, I want to explore the theology behind the assertion that participation in Christ *still involves matter*—it is not a spiritual realization, or interior experience, or mystical aeon but must involve real places that are concrete, practical, and geographical. For this assertion, we will be taking our cue from Calvin's insights on the ascension (an irony given that de Chardin is worried that we will become lost in the clouds!) Life in Christ is: *location, location, location.*

Calvin's Biblical Theology of Participation

> "When we hear the gospel preached by men, we ought to consider that it is not so much they who speak, as Christ who speaks by them. And this is a singular advantage, that Christ lovingly allures us to himself by his own voice . . . "[11]

Calvin's theology shimmers with participation. He cannot write without writing from *within* this assumption that human life has been engrafted into God's very life, specifically in the person of Christ. Similarly, Calvin's theology is saturated with metaphysics but I want to make the case that he does not *start* with metaphysics. His starting point is neither a model of how nature/grace work together, nor of human

9. Julie Canlis, *Calvin's Ladder: A Spiritual Theology of Ascent and Ascension* (Grand Rapids: Eerdmans, 2010).

10. Teilhard de Chardin, in his Peking lectures (28 December 1943) *On Love and Happiness* (Philadelphia: R. P. Pryne, 2015).

11. Calvin is here commenting on Ps 2:7. All references to Calvin's Commentaries are from the Calvin Translation Society volumes (Edinburgh: 1843–55) reprinted by Baker (Grand Rapids: Baker, 1979) and will be acknowledged in the footnotes in the conventional format: *Comm. Ps 2:7.*

capacity/incapacity, nor of divine/human nature. Nor was Calvin's starting point exegesis and the "bare text" itself.[12] Calvin's distinct opinion is that all exegesis is not to be faithful to an abstract text, but to the One who gives it life. "For how can the Law bestow life without Christ, who alone gives life to it? . . . We ought to read the Scriptures with the express design of finding Christ in them . . . For it was not in the Gospel that Christ first began to be manifested . . . "[13]

Already in Calvin's very *approach to the text* we can smell participation. Was Calvin aware of this? I do not know. Unlike John Milbank who graced the cover of *Time* magazine and declared his "theological project" to be participation,[14] Calvin does not have a "project." And yet even his methodology is participatory. His exegesis is not interpretation but a living communion, as the very grammar of the text is seen to be Christ. This is just as true of the Old Testament as the New. How did Calvin see God's presence in the garden? It was Christ. The insight of the prophets? They were speaking the words of Christ. The cloud in the desert? It was Christ.[15] This attentiveness to the person of Christ characterized Calvin's approach both to his exegesis of the text and his delivery of it. Oberman remarks that Calvin's legacy in Reformed churches is that the sermon came to be experienced as an "apocalyptic event," ushering us into the objective presence of Christ. For the Reformers, it was just as much a participation in Christ as the eucharistic event.[16]

Even in his earliest (what I consider to be his least exegetical, and most "metaphysical") Christian tract, *Psychopannychia* (on the life of the soul) Calvin is already mapping the Christian to the person of Christ, the Christian life to the history of Christ. In this early Christian tract, Calvin makes a reference to the "beginning, middle, and end" of the life of the spiritual person—tipping his hat to the three Platonic stages of purgation, illumination, and union. These were the classic stages through which one participated in higher and higher levels of divinity, being cleansed of sin, and error, (and very often, one's humanity). Twenty years later, Calvin redefines the Platonic three-fold path in a manner that sums up all of his theology: "*Christ* is the beginning, middle, and end."[17] This gives us a clue as to Calvin's "metaphysic" of

12. Calvin realized that knowing the biblical languages was not enough. Men without "sound theology, although well acquainted with the Hebrew language, yet hallucinate and fall into mistakes . . ." (*Comm. Ps* 73:26).

13. Calvin, *Comm. John* 5:39.

14. John Milbank, *Being Reconciled* (London: Routledge, 2003) ix.

15. See T. H. L. Parker, *Calvin's Old Testament Commentaries* (Edinburgh: T. & T. Clark, 1986).

16. As medieval Catholic theologians saw the eucharist as objectively the body of Christ (regardless of the moral status of the priest) so the Reformers saw the preaching event as objective, transcending the preacher himself. See Heiko Oberman, "Reformation, Preaching, and *ex opere operato*," in *Christianity Divided*, edited by Daniel Callahan (New York: Sheed & Ward, 1961) 225.

17. Calvin, *Comm. Col* 1:12.

participation as it gathered momentum over his life. It is a participation in the Son and his full narrative history.

The Son and Participation

> "The flesh of Christ is like a rich and inexhaustible fountain that pours into us the life springing forth from the Godhead into itself."[18]

Calvin's basic insight into union with Christ is, to use the wonderful words of Kevin Vanhoozer, "the grace that launched a thousand soteriological ships."[19] It was not a generic principle of participation that drove Calvin, but his reckoning with the mysterious fact that the life, death, resurrection, and ascension of Christ is somehow "applied"[20] to us by Paul. How can this be? As Ronald Wallace writes, "The basic principle in Calvin's thinking on this matter is that what has already happened to Christ the head can be regarded and legitimately spoken of as having already happened to those who are members of His body . . . "[21] As Calvin underscores, "For this is a point we must know, that nothing was given in vain to Jesus Christ. Now He does not need it for His own use. But it is for His members, in order that all of us may draw upon His fullness[22] and grace for grace."[23]

Calvin here picks up the Irenaean doctrine of recapitulation in a way little seen since the patristic fathers, as central to his project.[24] In this scheme, Calvin's Christ becomes the center—the location of all of human history, anthropology, ontology, metaphysics. He defines recapitulation this way:

> OUT of Christ, all things were disordered . . . We are alienated from God by sin, and how can we but present a broken and shattered aspect? The proper condition of creatures is to keep close to God. Such a "gathering together" (*anakephalaiōsis*) as might bring us back to regular order has been made in

---

18. Calvin, *Institutes* IV.17.9. All references to Calvin's *Institutes of the Christian Religion* are to the 1559 edition, in *Library of Christian Classics* (20–21) edited by John T. McNeil, translated by Ford Lewis Battles (Philadelphia: Westminster, 1960).

19. Kevin Vanhoozer, "From 'Blessed in Christ' to 'Being in Christ,'" 13.

20. Calvin, *Comm. Rom* 6:11.

21. Ronald Wallace, *Calvin's Doctrine of the Christian Life* (Grand Rapids: Eerdmans, 1961) 82.

22. I love the Torrance translation of "fatness" instead of fullness, for its emphasis on the human nature burgeoning with gifts for humanity. See, for example, how the Torrances' translate Calvin's *Comm. Heb.* 1:9 as "Besides, he was anointed for our sake, in order that we may all draw out of his fatness ..." in *Calvin's New Testament Commentaries—A New Translation*, edited by David and T. F. Torrance (Grand Rapids: Eerdmans, 1972).

23. Calvin, *Serm. Acts* 1:4–5, translated by Leroy Nixon, *The Deity of Christ and Other Sermons* (Old Paths Publications, 1997).

24. See "Introduction" in Julie Canlis, *Calvin's Ladder* (Grand Rapids: Eerdmans, 2010) 21.

> Christ. Formed into one body, we are united to God, and closely connected with one another. Without Christ, on the other hand, the whole world is a shapeless chaos and frightful confusion. We are brought into actual unity by Christ alone.[25]

Christ was not just doing something that would later change the world. Christ was uniting the lost world "and history itself" to himself.[26]

We owe a debt of gratitude to an enemy who forced Calvin to clarify exactly *in what* and *how* we are participating when we participate in Christ.[27] Like Calvin, Andreas Osiander (a contemporary pop-star German theologian) argued that participation in, and union with, Christ is the key to salvation. The only caveat is that it is not the historical Jesus of Nazareth with whom we are united but the divinity within him. Christ's human nature is likened to the exterior "dry wood" of a vine, housing the inner juice, able to be discarded once it has completed its function. Calvin responded with a wholesale rethinking of the humanity of Christ as the key to our participation, rather than his abstract divinity. Of salvation, Calvin writes "therefore he does this for us not according to his divine nature, but in accordance with the dispensation enjoined upon him."[28] What was this dispensation? To be fully human, dependent upon the Spirit (not a divine nature) opening up human life once more to become a place of communion with the Father. "He has achieved [salvation] for us by the whole course of his obedience."[29] Christ really was the new Adam, refusing privileged access to his divine nature, so that he could "take Adam's place in obeying the Father."[30]

Jesus' mission has accomplished what Adam failed to do: to be a loving son. His narrative history of loving trust and communion ("righteousness")[31] was thrown open to all of humanity for their participation. Calvin writes, "Both things happen to us by participation in Christ. For if we truly partake in his death . . . that corruption of original nature may no longer thrive. If we share in his resurrection, through it we are raised up into newness of life to correspond with the righteousness of God."[32]

---

25. Calvin, *Comm. Eph* 1:10.

26. Quoted by Mike Horton, *Locating Atonement* (Grand Rapids: Zondervan, 2015) 234.

27. Both Osiander and Calvin battled a common enemy: abstract, forensic righteousness. Calvin here distanced himself from "mechanical imputation" and instead argued for participation: "we put Him on and are made members of His body, and He has deemed us worthy to be united with Him" (Calvin, *Institutes* III.11.10).

28. Calvin, *Institutes* III.11.8.

29. Calvin, *Institutes* II.16.6.

30. Calvin, *Institutes* II.12.3.

31. "As if he could atone for our sins in any other way than obeying the Father!" (*Institutes* II.16.12)

32. Calvin, *Institutes* III.3.9.

The history of Jesus Christ has become our history. The "exchange" is not his divinity for our humanity (as some mistakenly read the patristic formula found in Irenaeus and Athanasius). The exchange is not of natures, but of an alienated history for a newly enacted communion history; his narrative of sonship for our narrative of desolation.[33]

The Spirit and Participation

"For they leave nothing to the secret working of the Spirit, which unites Christ himself to us."[34]

If the *what* is the humanity of Christ, the *how* is the Holy Spirit who brings humanity to participate in the *whole* Christ. Calvin's charge against Osiander is that he was so busy focusing on the natures and how they participate, rather than the Spirit—who keeps Christ (and ourselves) in relation *as persons*. "But because [Osiander] does not observe the bond of this unity, he deceives himself. Now it is easy for us to resolve all his difficulties. For we hold ourselves to be united with Christ by the power of his Spirit."[35] The Spirit enmeshes the believer with the human, crucified, ascended life of Jesus in such a way that we have a "bond so close that we can find *in our nature* that holiness of which we are in want."[36] The entire life that Christ lived ("recapitulated") for us would still remain isolated from us were it not for the Spirit. But due to the grafting of the Spirit, Christ and his narrative history becomes ours.[37]

The fact that Calvin incessantly tied our participation in Christ to "the secret agency of the Spirit"[38] changed the medieval participation game. For Calvin, the role

33. "For there he is properly speaking not of those gifts which he had in the Father's presence from the beginning but of those with which he was adorned in that very flesh wherein he appeared" (*Institutes* IV.17.9).

34. Calvin, *Institutes* IV.17.31.

35. Calvin, *Institutes* III.11.5.

36. Calvin, *Comm. Heb* 2:11. If everything we need for salvation is lodged "like a treasury" in the person and history of Jesus, then union can become just another mechanism for getting the benefits of Christ. Here Calvin's point is not that we "get holiness," but that our union with the holy Son bears fruit in our human lives.

37. This is likened to marriage, by which we become "one person" with Christ—not, says Calvin, "because he has a human nature, but because, by the power of his Spirit, he makes us part of his body, so that from him we derive our life" (Calvin, *Comm. Eph* 5:30–31).

38. He wrote to Westphal, and defended his use of the term participation: "No term could better explain the mode in which the body of Christ is given to us, than the term *communion* [koinōnia], implying that we become one with him, and being ingrafted into him, truly enjoy his life. It is clear and certain that this is not done naturally, but by the secret agency of the Spirit" (Calvin, "Last Admonition" in *Tracts and Treatises in Defense of the Reformed Faith*, edited by H. Beveridge [Grand Rapids: Eerdmans, 1958] 2.414).

of the Spirit was to keep Christ *human* so that the integrity of the created realm is maintained. Even his relationship with the Father was on human terms, "The Son of God became man in such a manner, that God was his God as well as ours."[39] Without Calvin's emphasis on the Spirit, his whole scheme of participation falls apart—and so, incidentally, does the integrity of the created realm. Furthermore, the Spirit ensured that Calvin's doctrine of participation remained *personal*—a true relationship of triune *koinōnia*, not simply interpenetration of natures.[40]

The Ascending Goal of Participation

"As God he is the destination to which we move; as man the path by which we go. Both are found in Christ alone."[41]

Participation in Christ is historically guaranteed by the ascension, where Christ ripped open a space in our history for the Spirit to descend and bear us up to him. For "Christ did not ascend to heaven in a private capacity," explains Calvin, but so that we might have heaven (and his Father!) "in common with him."[42] The ascension is the final outworking of Christ's great mission, where a disordered creation is definitively re-headed (re-*capit*-ulated) and reunited with the one who is at its center. This is not just an ascent to victory or unity, but to relationship: Christ "gathers believers into participation in the Father . . . And certainly for this reason Christ descended to us, to bear us up to the Father, and at the same time to bear us up to himself, inasmuch as he is one with the Father."[43] Adoption is Calvin's more precise term for "union with Christ," designating the end goal of that union as knowing the Father once again. [44] Adoption is both a familial reality and a location: we are now

---

39. Calvin, *Comm. Eph* 1:17.

40. Oberman comments how in Calvin we find a "shift of accent [away] from a natures-Christology," while Jenson comments that Calvin is in keeping with the Reformers' emphasis on the Holy Spirit as "person" (and away from the medieval emphasis on "power" or "grace"). Calvin self-consciously believed himself to be a truer follower of Paul here, saying, "Thus I interpret that place of St Paul, 1 Corinthians 1.9, where he says the faithful are called into the *koinōnia* of His Son: for the word "Fellowship" or "Society" does not sufficiently express his mind. In my judgment, he designates that sacred unity by which the Son of God engrafts us into His body . . ." (From Calvin's letter to Peter Martyr Vermigli, 8 August 1555; CO 15.723. An obscure English translation can be found in George C. Gorham, *Gleanings of a Few Scattered Ears, During the Period of the Reformation in England and of the Times Immediately Succeeding* [London: Bell & Daldy, 1857] 349).

41. Calvin, *Institutes* III.2.1.

42. Christ "has entered into heaven and He bears us there" (*Serm. Acts* 1:6–8).

43. Calvin, *Institutes* I.13.26.

44. Due to the Spirit, *koinōnia*-participation takes the shape of the relation of a Father with his child/Son. Calvin defines adoption as our "'participation in the Spirit,' without which no one can taste either the fatherly favor of God or the beneficence of Christ" (Calvin, *Institutes* III.1.2). Not only does

"in" the one who has poured out his Spirit upon us to draw us "up" to his Father in the communion he enjoys.[45] As usual, Calvin's pattern for our "ascent" to God's fatherhood is the history of Jesus himself: "Ascension follows resurrection: hence if we are members of Christ we must ascend into Heaven."[46]

Yet for all this talk of being drawn "upwards," Calvin's doctrine of the ascension simultaneously *grounds our human, embodied existence*. If Christ has re-created our humanity in his own body and history, then it would not do as his ultimate act to abandon it! Although Jesus' flesh was transfigured, "becoming different from what it was before,"[47] Calvin insisted on the *physical limitations* of Christ's glorified body. It is still "contained in space, [having] its own dimensions and its own shape."[48] Christ's ascent was not the diminution of his humanity (or createdness) but its fulfillment. The ascended, human, transfigured Jesus entered heaven "in our flesh, as if in our name"[49] and represents a creature fully in communion with God.

The Lord's Supper as our Model of Participation

> For although the faithful come into this Communion (*koinōnia*) on the very first day of their calling; nevertheless, inasmuch as the life of Christ increases in them, He daily offers Himself to be enjoyed by them. This is the Communion (*koinōnia*) which they receive in the Sacred Supper.[50]

Calvin's doctrine of the ascension forced him to rethink location, the Holy Spirit, and embodied existence. This is most clearly seen in his treatment of the Lord's Supper. In the Lord's Supper, the Spirit comes upon a specific piece of creation and makes it *a means to union with Christ*—lifting us "up" to him. There is no need for creation to change—that would be an "insult" to the Spirit.[51] Worse, it would be to insist, like Osiander did, that it is the divinity involved that makes the eucharist effective. No, says Calvin in speaking of bread, "we defend the reality of the human nature on

---

the Spirit "testify to us that we are children of God," (Calvin, *Comm. Rom* 8:16) but the final goal of our union with Christ is the outworking of our adoption, for "the Apostle intended shortly to show that the final end of our adoption is, that what has in order preceded in Christ, shall at length be completed in us" (Calvin, *Comm. 1 John* 2:2).

45. "Christ has, so to speak, presented us to his Father in his own person, that we may be renewed to true holiness by his Spirit" (Calvin, *Comm. John* 17:19).

46. Calvin, *Comm. Col* 3:1.

47. Calvin, *Institutes* IV.17.14.

48. Calvin, *Institutes* IV.17.29.

49. Calvin, *Institutes* II.16.14.

50. Calvin, Letter to Peter Martyr, 8 August 1555. See n40 above for details.

51. Calvin, *Institutes* IV.17.33.

which our faith is founded."[52] The bread *staying bread* is essential to Calvin's whole recapitulative scheme—for the integrity of the created realm must be maintained by the Spirit who alone allows creation *as creation* to participate. This is founded upon Christ who, with his *human* nature and narrative, returns us to the Father. This is how the Spirit fulfills within us Spirit-ual life—through Christ's human life, through bread, through our ordinary existence. It is *this* that he takes—not changes—and unites to Christ.

This, for Calvin, is not less than transubstantiation—it is more. As Calvin says, "it would be extreme madness to recognize no communion of believers with the flesh and blood of the Lord."[53] But this is a miracle of the Spirit—not an automatic blessing of the "divine nature." As Calvin says,

> It seems incredible that we should be nourished by Christ's flesh, which is at so great a distance from us. Let us bear in mind, that it is a secret and wonderful work of the Holy Spirit, which it were criminal to measure by the standard of our understanding . . . Allow [Jesus] to remain in his heavenly glory, and aspire thou thither, that he may thence communicate himself to thee.[54]

When we understand that this is the Spirit's mission—to allow creation as creation to participate in the One who is its Head—then we realize how very practical and concrete is participation. Calvin calls the Lord's Supper a "spiritual" feeding, though not because it is "spiritual" as opposed to "substance" but because (due to the ascension) Spirit is now the realm of substance. He retorts, "we are TRULY made partakers of the proper substance of the body and blood of Jesus Christ . . . which is made effectual by the secret and miraculous power of God, and that the Spirit of God is the bond of participation, this being the reason why it is called spiritual."[55] Substance is the work of the Spirit, not its opposite.

The Geography of Participation

Calvin took geography seriously, particularly the current GPS of Jesus. His best pastoral writings flow out of his strong belief that the risen, transfigured, human Jesus ascended. "Thus, since He has gone *up there*, and is in heaven for us, let us note that we need not fear to be *in this world* . . . " (we will forgive Calvin if he now digresses into his favorite pastime, which is recounting the tumult and anxieties of the sixteenth century) " . . . It is true that we are subject to so much misery that

---

52. "Last Admonition" in *Tracts and Treatises,* III.226.

53. Calvin, *Institutes* IV.17.9.

54. Calvin, *Comm. 1 Cor* 11:24.

55. Calvin, "Short Treatise" in *Tracts and Treatises,* II.197.

our condition is pitiable, but at that we need neither be astonished nor confine our attention to ourselves. Thus, we look to our Head Who is already in heaven, and say *Although I am weak, there is Jesus Christ who is powerful . . . Although I am feeble, there is Jesus Christ who is my strength . . . "*[56]

Calvin was always a wanderer, an exile, which perhaps underscored (on an emotional level) the locative emphasis of being "in Christ."[57] When Calvin thought of "living *en Christō*" I believe what came to his mind was an enfleshed human at the right hand of the Father—who is like, and not like us. And yet he did not think of Christ as literally hovering above us, for, he writes, heaven is not a "dwelling among the spheres . . . nor is it literally a place beyond the world, but we cannot speak of the kingdom of God without using ordinary language."[58] One might say that heaven is where the ascended, glorified Christ is—and we now live *in him*. This is a new geography, oriented pneumatologically on Heaven which simultaneously pushes us back onto *terra firma*, so to speak.

Steeped in the biblical drama, and the metaphysics of the church fathers, Calvin does not forge a new metaphysic but gently reminds us that all metaphysics must reckon with the ascension: Christ is at the right hand of the Father. And we are in Christ. Deissmann famously argued that it was not intelligible Greek to use the preposition *en* with a personal name,[59] for one person cannot be literally *in* another. Deissmann could only make sense of this by de-personalizing Christ into some atmospheric gas. Porter's answer was to try and describe living *en Christō* in terms of intimate friendship—but this in no way makes sense of true participation, or the Johannine "remain in me" (John 15). Nor does Ernst Best's notion of corporate personality. Calvin's Commentaries, however, emphasize the prepositional phrase "in Christ" again and again. This can be seen in his exegesis of Rom 6.11 ("consider yourselves dead to sin, but alive to God" . . .):

> But I prefer to retain the words of Paul, [alive to God] *in* Christ Jesus, rather than to translate with Erasmus, [alive to God] *through* Christ Jesus; for thus the grafting, which makes us one with Christ, is better expressed.

It also appears in his exegesis of 1 Cor 1:4:

> The phrase *in ipso* (in him) I have preferred to retain, rather than render it *per ipsum* (by him) because it has in my opinion more expressiveness and force.

56. Calvin, *Serm. Acts* 1:6–8 (emphasis mine).

57. See Julie Canlis, "John Calvin: Knowing the Self in God's Presence" in *Sources of the Christian Self: A Cultural History of Christian Identity*, edited by James M. Houston & Jens Zimmerman (Grand Rapids: Eerdmans, 2018) forthcoming.

58. Calvin, *Comm. Eph* 4:10.

59. Adolf Deissmann, *Die neutestamentliche Formel 'in Christo Jesu'* (Marburg: N.G. Elwert, 1892).

> For we are enriched in Christ, inasmuch as we are members of his body, and are engrafted into him: nay more, being made one with him, he makes us share with him in everything that he has received from the Father.

And also in his exegesis of 2 Cor 5.21:

> It is in the same manner, assuredly, that we are now *righteous in him* . . . On this account, I have preferred to retain the particle *en* ("in") rather than substitute in its place *per* ("through") for that signification corresponds better with Paul's intention.

Calvin's emphasis on "in Christ" seems to reveal a clunky locative sense, as seen in his description of the Spirit whose work is to nourish us with things "at so great a distance from us."[60] But this is only "clunky" if we misunderstand his pneumatology. Calvin uses "distance" terminology in order to highlight the fact that *Christ is ascended! Our identity is elsewhere*—not, as can be easily inferred, somewhere distant.[61] "The Holy Spirit did descend from heaven to this end; whereby we learn that the distance of place doth no whit hinder Christ from being present with those that be his at all times."[62] For Calvin, it is self-evident that we are *located* in Christ. Not just included. Not just in the atmosphere of. Not just involved with. Not just in his sphere of influence. But *in*. By the Spirit, we are geographically *en Christō*, the human one who grounds our humanity.

So it is nearly time to leave Calvin, taking our cue from him and not to "insult the Holy Spirit"[63] by letting participation be something that happens in our noetic spheres alone. As we write papers on participation, the danger is that we will figure out our theology of participation, all the while forgetting that we are human—with bodies which are given to us *for the purpose of participating*. If we participate in a person who is heading up the new creation, then we need to look at some specific locations where he has promised to be. But a summary of Calvin first:

1. *Participation is now oriented to Christ's human body.* Paul maps participation to the ascended body of Jesus: "So if you have been raised with Christ, seek the

---

60. Calvin, *Comm. 1 Cor.* 11:24.

61. See in particular his definition of union with Christ, which challenges any language or notion that we are somehow separate from Christ and needing to be joined to him. "Therefore, that joining together of Head and members, that indwelling of Christ in our hearts—in short, that mystical union—are accorded by us the highest degree of importance, so that Christ, having been made ours, makes us sharers with him in the gifts with which he has been endowed. We do not, therefore, contemplate him outside ourselves from afar in order that his righteousness may be imputed to us but because we put on Christ and are engrafted into his body—in short because he deigns to make us one with him" (Calvin, *Institutes* III.11.10).

62. Calvin, *Comm. Acts*, Argument.

63. Calvin, *Institutes* IV.17.33. See also n51.

things that are above, where Christ is, seated at the right hand of God. Set your minds on things that are above, not on things that are on earth, for you have died, and your life is hidden with Christ in God. When Christ who is your life is revealed, then you also will be revealed with him in glory" (Col 3:1–4). Jesus' body means that our future is associated with *his body*. [64] Calvin says, "For thus they leave nothing to the secret working of the Spirit, which unites Christ himself to us. To them Christ does not seem present unless he comes down to us. As though, if he should lift us to himself, we should not just as much enjoy his presence!"[65] Christ's transposed body and our bodies are real things, with real limitations. Calvin was unwilling to tamper with this. But neither did it keep him from making Christ's ascended body the center of the new cosmos. The Spirit unites us with an embodied one, who maintains the integrity of the created realm in a new way. "I willingly confess that Christ is ascended that he may [fill] all things; but I say that he is spread abroad everything by the power of his Spirit, not by the substance of his flesh."[66]

2. *Participation now happens in our human bodies.* Paul also maps participation to our *human bodies.* We are "always carrying in the body the death of Jesus, so that the life of Jesus may also be made visible in our bodies" (2 Cor 4:10). This is not a mental transformation, or a new aeon to recognize, but something happening to us that could not occur without our physical bodies. Our bodies are gifts, GPS locations where the life of Christ is happening. We have Christ's ascended body and our own bodies, and the Holy Spirit who "joins in one, things that are separated by distance of place, and far remote."[67] We are already partaking of a deep and abiding "communion" with Christ, but we are invited—indeed commanded—to partake of this communion in ways appropriate to Christ's body, and ours. The ascended Son has *self-identified* with things *of the earth*—bread, wine, the body of Christ, the prisoner, the sick, two or three gathered (which to me always means my local – sometimes boring – church). These are not sub-spiritual. They are where we meet the risen, embodied Jesus.

3. *Participation in Christ is Location, Location, Location.* So what does it mean to participate? To "remain" in Christ (John 15)? It might be more simple than we think. There is no spiritual life that is not simultaneously tethered to the physical realm. As Luther said, "The Spirit cannot be with us except in material and

---

64. "The flesh of Christ is like a rich and inexhaustible fountain that pours into us the life springing forth from the Godhead into itself" (Calvin, *Institutes* IV.17.9).

65. Calvin, *Institutes* IV.17.31.

66. Calvin, *Comm. Acts* 1:9.

67. Calvin, *Comm. 1 Cor* 11:24.

physical things such as the Word, water and Christ's body and in his saints on earth."[68] Remaining looks like my neighbor. It looks like cubes of wonderbread and small cups of grape juice. It smells like the musty halls of my one-hundred-year-old church building. It is water being sprinkled, splashed, dunked. These are GPS locations, like my body is, where this pneumatological reality of life in Christ is being lived.

I want to remind us that although we may have lost the classical conceptual framework for participation, we have not lost the church! Nor have we lost the embodied practices given to us by a church of a different consciousness. Nor have we lost Paul, who consistently maps participation to our bodies and Christ's ascended body. Could we not, perhaps, return to these practices as ways to "participate in participation"? They arise from the acknowledgement that the Holy Spirit has freely chosen specific *places* to help us remain in Christ in embodied ways. We do not have the Son in a noetic union, but in an embodied/enacted one—for as Calvin says, "For it is only through the ministry of the Church that God begets sons for Himself."[69] If salvation is to be sought in the "flesh of Christ," then Calvin directs us straight to the sacraments. "I showed, on the contrary, that salvation and life are to be sought from the flesh of Christ in which he sanctified himself, and in which he consecrates Baptism and the Supper."[70]

Perhaps we do not need better ways to communicate about participation, but we need better ways to highlight and re-narrate the practices in our church that help us embody participation in three dimensions. Take Hays's article "What is 'Real Participation in Christ'?"[71] in which he gives us four *possible ways to think about participation*. This is not a bad thing, but it is perhaps illustrative of why we are having a hard time "understanding" participation. Irenaeus goes about it a different way, when he says "But our opinion is in accordance with the Eucharist, and the Eucharist in turn establishes our opinion."[72] Here we see theological reflection arising from church practice, and vice versa. Hays's four possible conceptual frameworks overlook the concrete entry-points ("locations") that the church offers for these conceptual frameworks, that lead us into deeper participation (not deeper thinking about participation).

68. *Luther's Works* (*LW*) American Edition, ed. Pelikan and Lehmann (55 vols.; Philadelphia: Fortress Press, 1955–86) 37:95.

69. Calvin, *Comm. Gal* 4:26.

70. Calvin, "True Partaking" in *Tracts and Treatises* II.554.

71. Hays, "What is 'Real Participation in Christ'?" 339.

72. Irenaeus, *Against Heresies* in Ante-Nicene Fathers, ed. Alexander Roberts and James Donaldson, vol. 1 (1885; reprint, Grand Rapids: Eerdmans, 1996) IV.18.5.

I am going to close with an attempt to turn Hays's four conceptual categories into a few concrete church practices where these conceptual categories can be seen in action. Our focus will be upon:

- baptism
- the church calendar
- the body of Christ

These practices remind us that participation does not happen in our minds, but that God has given locations where our bodies can actively participate in his body. For this, I'm going to use what we have been doing in our small church, and how we have been attempting slowly to move our congregation in this direction. My husband and I find that as we ask our church in Wenatchee (WA) *"How do we 'remain' in Christ?"* this can be a fearful question (*am I remaining? how do I remain?*) until we help people to see that God has given us very practical ways to remain in the embodied one. For this, we have his Sonship, his Story, and his Body.

The Location of BAPTISM: Remaining in his Sonship

Scripture has provided a way to see participation in the triune relations in action: baptism. Baptism does not begin with our faith in Jesus, but with God's thunderous blessing over Jesus when he emerged from the waters: *this is my beloved Son* (Luke 3:22). Calvin says that this was not for Christ to hear, but for us to hear—and when we are *in Christ,* we suddenly are able to hear the thunderous applause of the Father.[73] Baptism is dying a death to our individualistic identities, and rising to a new set of relations that form our new-creation-selves. We are not merely in a Greco-Roman family, as part of the extended household of a *paterfamilias* (Hays).[74] We are actually *in the sonship of the Son.* Calvin summarizes salvation as "calling God Father."[75] Baptism enacts this tightly Trinitarian version of participation perfectly. Our church probably grows tired of hearing this(!) and yearly at our annual baptism service, we invite *everyone* to remember their baptism by wading into the water as well. Remembering one's baptism is remembering our primary identity—that we are included in the Triune relations, even if we can't figure out ontologically how this works.

---

73. Calvin, *Comm. Matt.* 3:17.

74. Hays, "What is 'Real Participation in Christ'?" 340.

75. Heiko Oberman, "Preaching and the Word in the Reformation," *ThTo* 18 (1961) 19.

The Location of the CHURCH CALENDAR: Remaining in his Story

Hays refers to another way to conceive of participation as "living within the Christ Story."[76] Although it is difficult to move congregants from a solely penal-substitution version of the atonement and into the importance of the vicarious humanity of Christ, I find that the church calendar does most of the work for me. As we invite congregants to not just remember different aspects of Christ's life, but to *enter into it* through the very real language and practical steps of the church calendar, something begins to change. Christ's narrative becomes their living narrative, with its sufferings, activism, alienation, self-giving, and long stretches of boredom (i.e., the joys of ordinary time!) Here the church calendar is not a new way of telling time, but it is the way that time is transfigured. In Vanhoozer's language, we re-enact the story in our own lives, as a living drama where the story of Jesus begins to become the pattern of our own year.[77] We are not just following his story, we discover that we have been inserted into it—and our small narratives take on meaning as it is both his narrative and ours. The church calendar is the Christ-story thrown open for our active participation.

The Location of the ECCLESIA: Remaining in his Body

As church begins on a Sunday morning, we often congratulate the congregation that they are not at home listening to a better sermon on a podcast! They laugh . . . weakly, knowing their narrow escape. The language Hays uses here is of "participation in a specific social group"[78] which is weak, but he is stronger when he writes that "participation in the body of Christ provided the setting in which Paul's soteriology took shape and made sense."[79] The church might be one of the last frontiers where virtual reality has no place, because it is founded upon the embodied one who gathers when our bodies are gathered. Our job as pastor (and pastor's wife!) is to narrate and re-narrate why people are at church, who they are sitting next to in their uncomfortable pew (C. S. Lewis's "There are no ordinary people . . . "[80]) and how their local, ordinary church is the context where they are working out their salvation. As Dan Berrigan SJ once said of being part of the *local* church, "Your faith is rarely where your head is at and rarely where your heart is at. Your faith is where

---

76. Hays, "What is 'Real Participation in Christ'?" 345.

77. See Kevin Vanhoozer, *The Drama of Doctrine* (Westminster John Knox Press, 2005).

78. Hays, "What is 'Real Participation in Christ'?" 344.

79. Ibid., 345.

80. C. S. Lewis, *The Weight of Glory* (Macmillan, 1966).

your ass is!"[81] Participation in Christ is contextless without the believers who are, mysteriously, part of our new creation selves. And we receive this context weekly (sometimes weakly!) when we swim against the virtual tide and find ourselves on a pew (Berrigan), listening to an apocalyptic sermon (Oberman), next to a near god or goddess (Lewis),[82] or receiving the bit of creation that puts us into the one at its Head (Irenaeus). We may not always feel the Fatherhood of God, but we can eat at his table with our siblings whether we feel his Fatherhood or not. As Tom Wright reminds us, Jesus did not leave us a written message but a *meal*.[83]

Participation is our greatest weapon against weightlessness—both the weight-lessness to which the academy is prone, as well as the weightlessness that our virtual society promises. Participation is a theological doctrine that must never be pulled apart from the locations where the church has always recognized participation to be happening. These are pilgrimage sites, not tourist sites; as Calvin reminds us in the words of Jesus, "'Abide in me,' says he; 'for I am ready to abide in you.'"[84] Despite the weightlessness that is always lurking around discussions of participation, there has been participation even in that weightless place, the moon! After exiting the spacecraft behind Neil Armstrong, Buzz Aldrin, in the least-publicized aspect of the 1969 lunar landing, pulled from his pocket little blessed plastic packages which contained Christ's body and Christ's blood. He remembers the wine slowly furling and unfurling, undulating up the sides of the cup. He quietly recited, "I am the vine, and you are the branches. Whoever remains in me, and I in him . . . "

---

81. As told by Timothy Radcliffe in his *Why Go To Church: The Drama of the Eucharist* (London: Continuum, 2008) 4.

82. Lewis, *The Weight of Glory*, 23.

83. N. T. Wright, "The Cross and its Caricatures: a Response to Robert Jenson, Jeffrey John, and a New Volume entitled Pierced for Our Transgressions, Eastertide 2007," article URL: https://www.fulcrum-anglican.org.uk/articles/the-cross-and-the-caricatures/.

84. Calvin, *Comm. John* 5:1–5.

RESPONSE TO CANLIS

Mary Patton Baker

Recently, in preparation for my response to Julie Canlis's paper, I withdrew from my bookshelf my extensively marked up copy of *Calvin's Ladder*. As I opened the volume and reread my notations, I was once again reminded how much my understanding of Calvin and participation in Christ was influenced by this work when I first read it seven years ago.[1] I am not alone in valuing the importance of Canlis's work in recovering Calvin's rich pneumatological vision of the Christian life with our participation in Christ as its ground and identity. Building upon Todd Billings's *Participation in Christ*, Canlis's *Calvin's Ladder* continued the work of rescuing Calvin from the hands of the theologians of Radical Orthodoxy with their unfair portrayal of Calvin as the great nominalist who viewed justification simply as an "external" act of God.[2] John Milbank and others failed to grasp that for Calvin imputation is also impartation and that there is an inseparable bond that exists between justification and sanctification as the double grace of salvation.[3]

Therefore, it is a privilege to be given the opportunity to respond to her thoroughly delightful and winsome paper. Her writing as usual uses apt analogies so the reader can grasp not only the concepts, but also the enthusiasm she has for her topic: Calvin's doctrine of the believer's participation in Christ. If this is what theology for the church can look like, then Canlis has much to offer. I would like to offer here what I believe to be a summary of her paper's most important contributions, as well as an appeal for some conceptual clarification in understanding them.

---

1. Julie Canlis, *Calvin's Ladder: A Spiritual Theology of Ascent and Ascension* (Grand Rapids: Eerdmans, 2010).

2. For example, see John Milbank, "Alternative Protestantism: Radical Orthodoxy and the Reformed Tradition," in *Radical Orthodoxy and the Reformed Tradition: Creation, Covenant, and Participation*, edited by James K. A. Smith and James Olthuis (Grand Rapids: Baker Academic, 2005) 25–42. These charges by Milbank and others are addressed by Todd Billings in *Calvin, Participation, and the Gift: The Activity of Believers in Union with Christ: Changing Paradigms in Historical and Systematic Theology* (New York: Oxford University Press, 2007).

3. Quoting from 1 Cor 1:30, Calvin states in the 1559 *Institutes*: "Christ is given unto us for righteousness, wisdom, sanctification, and redemption," Calvin adds, "Therefore, Christ justifies no one whom he does not at the same time sanctify. These benefits are joined together by an everlasting and indissoluble bond." *Institutes*, III.3.16. All references to Calvin's *Institutes of the Christian Religion* are to the 1559 edition, in *Library of Christian Classics* (20–21) edited by John T. McNeil, translated by Ford Lewis Battles (Philadelphia: Westminster, 1960).

I appreciate that Canlis allows us to hear Calvin in his own right—and not through any theological constructs that we might want to impose upon him. Her presentation of Calvin's understanding of participation is definitely strengthened by her citations of Calvin's commentaries, a treasure trove often overlooked. She makes the hugely important point that participation in Christ for Calvin is not a "project" as with John Milbank, but the ground of his understanding of our very existence in Christ, so even his biblical vision becomes participatory. Canlis sums this up well when she states: "His [Calvin's] exegesis is not interpretation but a living communion, as the very grammar of the text is seen to be Christ. This is just as true of the Old Testament as the New. How did Calvin see God's presence in the garden? It was Christ. The cloud in the desert? It was Christ." As Canlis well knows, it is not only through accessing the resource of patristic exegesis that we can find a christological center in our biblical interpretation, it is also all right there in Calvin's biblical commentaries.

I also laud Canlis for her robust presentation of Calvin's theology of the ascension. I can only hope she is leading the way in renewed examination of the implications of Christ's ascension, not only in issues of soteriology, but also in the doctrine of God, anthropology, and sacramental theology. Yes, Christ still has a body, and the great mystery is that in eucharistic participation, through the Holy Sprit, we are united to that body. Calvin felt strongly that both Roman transubstantiation and Luther's doctrine of consubstantiation negated the doctrine of the bodily ascension of Christ for "it is the true nature of a body to be contained in a place, to have its own dimensions and its own shape."[4] Our salvation is found in Christ assuming our flesh, a finite body that he bore up to heaven, which cannot then be on the altar or in many places all simultaneously. Importantly, these passages from Calvin about Christ's ascended body are contained in Calvin's extended arguments concerning how Christ is present in the Lord's Supper. Calvin makes clear that contra Luther or Rome, Christ's flesh "remains at a distance" and only "by the secret and wonderful work of the Holy Spirit" are "we TRULY made partakers of the proper substance of the body and blood of Jesus Christ."[5]

However, Canlis's assertions also raise many questions and could do with some further conceptual clarification especially when she points out that Calvin stressed that the believer communes with Christ's flesh and blood in the Supper, not through his divinity or in her words, not by "an automatic blessing of the divine nature." Why Christ's flesh and blood in the supper must refer to his humanity and not his divinity

---

4. Canlis here quotes Calvin from *Institutes,* IV.17.29.

5. Canlis here cites Calvin, *Comm. 1 Cor* 11:24, and "Short Treatise" in *Tracts and Treatises in Defense of the Reformed Faith,* edited by H. Beveridge (Grand Rapids: Eerdmans, 1958) II.197, 8–9.

might be more clearly understood if Canlis clarified Calvin's reliance on Chalcedon in this matter. Calvin believed that in Christ's divinity, he truly is everywhere and fills all of creation, but unlike Luther, Calvin did not believe that Christ's body must share the attribute of the omnipresence of his divinity.[6] Calvin was careful to protect the distinctness of the two natures so that our union with Christ according to his human nature does not in any way compromise his being one with the Father in his divinity.[7] I think this distinction adds clarification when speaking not only of Calvin's belief in the miracle of the Spirit in the Supper, but also can serve as a key to understanding all Canlis's allusions to the "geographic location" of our participation in Christ.[8]

The last section of Canlis's paper is perhaps her most important contribution here as she speaks of the practical ways the church can realize their participation in Christ: through church practices such as baptism and celebrating the church calendar, and even as local church assemblies gather as one body on the Sabbath. Her plea is that "we need better ways to highlight and re-narrate the practices in our church that help us embody participation in three dimensions."

I was particularly struck by the title that begins this section: "Participation in Christ is location, location, location." Canlis also brought up the location analogy in the earlier section on the ascension, where she states: "Adoption is Calvin's more precise term for 'union with Christ,' . . . Adoption is both a familial reality and a location: we are now "in" the one who has poured out his Spirit upon us to draw us up to his Father in the communion." I would agree with Canlis that in Calvin's soteriology our location in Christ means we are the recipients of a grace that transfers us from the location of being alienated from God to a new location/status as forgiven adopted children in Christ. For Calvin understands that the juridical act of God in justification is the act of the adoption of each believer by the Father to

---

6. Calvin says, in what is most likely a direct reference to Luther: "Unless the body of Christ can be everywhere at once, without limitation of place, it will not be credible that he lies hidden under the bread in the Supper. To meet this necessity they have introduced the monstrous notion of ubiquity." *Institutes*, IV.17.30.

7. Calvin, consistent with Chalcedonian Christology, upheld the principle of the *communicatio idiomatum*, that what is true of Christ's divinity may also be true of his humanity, but believed that this interchange of attributes takes place in the person of Christ, not between his divine and human natures, without *mixing* them, and yet importantly, not separating them. See Richard A. Muller, *Dictionary of Latin and Greek Theological Terms* (Grand Rapids: Baker Academic, 1985) 72. Mueller adds that the Lutherans moved "beyond the dichotomy between Antioch and Alexandria . . . to formulate a doctrine of the communication of divine attributes to the human nature, not against, but as part of, the *communicatio idiomatum in concreto*" (73).

8. For instance, Canlis asserts the significance of location by pointing to Calvin's interpretation of Paul's vocabulary of being in Christ: "Not just in his sphere of influence. But *in*. By the Spirit, we are geographically *en Christō*, the human one who grounds our humanity."

become brothers and sisters of Christ: "The Holy Spirit "is called the 'Spirit of adoption' because he is the witness to us of the free benevolence of God with which God the Father has embraced us in his beloved only-begotten Son to become a Father to us."[9] For while the origin and certainty of our righteousness is Christ outside of us, *extra nos*, salvation is not understood by Calvin to consist purely of a transactional declaration by God, but the believer's true incorporation into Christ by receiving her new location as a righteous child of God in an indissoluble union with Christ.

Yes, our adoption in Christ is the reason we find ourselves located in Christ. But would Calvin also categorize participation as *location* as Canlis states? Preceding the section where she offers suggestions for embodied participation, Canlis asks these questions: "So what does it mean to participate? To 'remain' in Christ?" But her questions only raise others for me: if we are located in Christ in an indissoluble union, why do we need to speak of remaining in Christ? Can the believer be relocated? What I would like Canlis to consider is the suggestion that our union with Christ in our adoption is our location and that participation means *actively residing in that location.*

What would be helpful here is to draw on Calvin's soteriological understanding of the two graces of salvation that I mentioned above, to better understand the distinction Calvin makes between adoption and participation. Calvin understands that our salvation consists of the double grace of our union with Christ, which leads to our justification/adoption, and our sanctification, or the regenerating life of the Spirit.[10] Concerning the interrelationship between justification and sanctification, Calvin emphasizes "when this topic is rightly understood it will better appear how man is justified by faith alone, and simple pardon; nevertheless actual holiness of life, so to speak, is not separated from free imputation of righteousness."[11] Calvin maintains that the legal pronouncement that we are righteous *ex nobis*, the result of justification, is not made any less true by also affirming that in the first moment of sanctification or regeneration, Christ becomes *in nobis* through the Holy Spirit. Similarly, regeneration for Calvin does not signify only the regeneration that occurs in salvation, but the ongoing renewing of our souls by the Spirit, which he often called "the vivification of the Spirit."[12] For Calvin believed the initial act of relocation or incorporation into Christ's body (justification) was just the beginning of the pilgrimage of sanctification to becoming more like Christ. The source of this transformation is found in the deepening of our union with Christ through our 'spiritual

9. *Institutes*, III.1.1.
10. See n3 above.
11. *Institutes*, III.3.1.
12. See *Institutes*, III.3.5.

communion' with him, through our *participation* in the Spirit. Thus, Calvin makes a distinction between the initial act of relocation (justification) and the deepening of that union in sanctification through our participation in the Spirit.

Perhaps the place in Calvin's writing where he best distinguishes between union and *communio/participatio* is in a response to a letter from Peter Martyr Vermigli wherein he asks Calvin for clarification on his doctrine of union with Christ. Calvin responds by first describing our mystical union in Christ as the point when we are brought into communion with God "by the sacrifice of His death in no other way than as He is ours and we are one with Him."[13] But here Calvin also identifies another communion "which is the fruit and effect of the former." Calvin continues: "in this second communion, by which Christ dwelling in us not ineffectually, brings forth the influence of his Spirit in his manifest gifts." By it, the believer is enabled to be "strong in hope and patience," and to continue "earnestly in prayer, that meditation on the life to come which draws us upward."[14]

In the beginning of Canlis's paper, she cites Klyne Snodgrass who asks, "Is there something 'objective' about the union? ... But what in the world does 'objective' mean in such use? What is 'real' participation in Christ?"[15] She does not however in this paper directly answer Snodgrass's question. She does elsewhere: in *Calvin's Ladder* Canlis defines participation as "a present-tense activity in which humans, by the Spirit, are drawn into the life of the Son of God."[16] But here as Canlis launches into her presentation she begins to use "union with Christ" and the term "participation" interchangeably in her analogy to location, while as I have argued here, I do not believe Calvin does.

I believe this distinction continues to be important because I want to hear Canlis say yes to Snodgrass's question about whether union is objective. According to Calvin, it is objective because our union has been freely given to us in justification, based on Christ's righteousness, not our own. Our adoption is our eternal hope for as Calvin states: "believers should be convinced that their only ground of hope for

---

13. Calvin to Vermigli, *CO* 15.723. The English translation is from George Cornelius Gorham, *Gleanings of a Few Scattered Ears, During the Period of the Reformation in England and of the Times Immediately Succeeding.* (London: Bell and Daldy, 1857) 349. This correspondence is also referenced in Canlis's paper as she draws on Calvin's definition of union from Calvin's response to Vermigli (137 n40).

14. Calvin to Vermigli, *CO* 15.723: "*Iam venio ad secundam communicationem, quae illius prioris mihi fructus est ac effectus.*"

15. Klyne Snodgrass, "Gospel of Participation," in *Earliest Christianity within the Boundaries of Judaism: Essays in Honor of Bruce Chilton,* edited by Alan J. Avery-Peck, Craig A. Evans, and Jacob Neusner (Leiden: Brill, 2016) 417.

16. Canlis, *Calvin's Ladder,* 14.

the inheritance of a Heavenly Kingdom lies in the fact that being engrafted into the body of Christ, they are freely accounted righteous."[17]

Why am I asking for this clarification? Because I believe that Canlis is right to encourage the church to engage in participatory acts such as prayer, feeding on his body and blood, and dipping our toes into the waters of baptism, for by doing so we proclaim and participate in our union with Christ through the grace of the Spirit. We need to be reminded that our lives are inside the history of his, but we also need to affirm that our location does not change when we fail to participate—when we try to turn our hearts against that very Sprit who joins us to Christ. Our location in Christ is not based on our best efforts, but on the unfailing mercy of the God who has placed us in Christ. This is a grace-filled place to live.

Conclusion

As Canlis states so well: "Calvin's theology shimmers with participation." And so also does her work shimmer with the wisdom of Calvin. Canlis has given us the Calvin who understands that the complete renovation of the heart is hastened through daily spiritual participation in the Spirit of Christ. The believer is not to be passive in the pursuit of his relationship with God but must be active and present to the Spirit's work in his life as the Spirit forms us into the image of Christ. I hope the church will pay attention to Canlis when she suggests that the church's practices further the Spirit's mission. This is the kind of preaching we need in the church—along with the exhortation that these practices allow us to appreciate and deepen our understanding of our location in Christ, our eternal union in him through his glorious salvation.

17. *Institutes*, III.13.5.

JEWS AND GENTILES TOGETHER IN CHRIST? THE JERUSALEM COUNCIL ON RACIAL RECONCILIATION

Ashish Varma

In his recent big screen adaptation of Shûsaku Endô's *Silence*, Martin Scorsese draws to the fore a timely theme about the intersection of Christian missions, the growth of the church, and life in Christ. In the film, two priests head to Japan in search of their mentor Cristóvão Ferreira, a Jesuit missionary and priest who was rumored to have renounced his faith amid heavy persecutions instigated by the Japanese government. When the two priests Sebastião Rodrigues and Francisco Garupe reach Japan, local Christians quickly whisk them away into hiding. For the locals, the priests' arrival is a blessing, yet they know that the government officials are showing zero toleration towards any agent of Christianity. Leaders in the community themselves had been leading secret local church services, but, due to the restrictions of church hierarchy, they were not free to perform the full mass. Nevertheless, to the degree that they could and that some church officiant was needed, they followed the liturgy that they held so dear. The arrival of our two priests meant full participation in the mass. The movie vividly displays the joy of villagers throughout the region as the priests secretly travel from town to town to perform the mass, evading the Japanese officials for a time.

Yet another stark image also quickly surfaces. The performance of the mass, as befitting of the seventeenth century setting, was entirely in Latin. What is more, it quickly becomes evident that the villagers do not know Latin. For the Christians' part, this does not appear to bother them, for they only care that the priests perform the mass by which grace passes to them, which for them is a matter of urgency after such a long drought due to persecution. The local leaders, at least, seem to demonstrate genuine love of Christ, but their church services themselves apparently function only as formal ceremony for the dispensing of grace. The villagers are not entering into the mass. Their participation is not one of active worship, bringing their particularity to the body and blood of Christ that lie at the center of the mass. There is nothing discernibly Japanese about their worship, much less their performance of the church service. The local Christians partake in the body of Christ, yes, but they do so through Latin—linguistically, ceremonially, culturally. The implication is one of purity: Europeans may directly approach the *Latin* body of Christ while the Japanese partake through the mediation of the Latin body. Latin identity subsumes the *Jewishness* of Christ and Japanese particularity. Rather than proclaiming the equidistant nature of all peoples from the body of Christ, European peoples become the mediators. This implication becomes central later in the movie when Rodrigues stands face-to-face with the Japanese Grand Councilor Inoue Masashige. Inoue informs Rodrigues that Japan is a swamp that will never be capable of sustaining Christianity. When Rodrigues replies that many Japanese had already converted and that it was persecution at the hands of Inoue and his agents that began to stomp out the faith, Inoue gets to the point. The missionaries had not converted people to Christianity. Rather they had made the locals Portuguese. He may have overstated the nature of the situation, for many of the converts seemed genuinely to love Christ. Nevertheless, reality lay somewhere between Rodrigues and Inoue: the local Japanese Christians had converted to *Portuguese* Christianity.

The theme of the Jerusalem Council in Acts 15 is precisely this sort of presumption of mediation where the body of Christ no longer sits as the mediator. Instead Christ's body itself requires mediation. In the case of Acts 15, the question before the Council is whether the Jewish Jesus Christ comes to the Gentiles through the mediation of the Jewish covenant in the law of Moses. In other words, must participation in Christ first be participation in the law? While the Gentiles certainly owed at least a debt of gratitude to their Jewish brothers and sisters in Christ for their own theological and ethnic heritage that prepared the way for Jesus Christ, the question before the apostles was one of ongoing Jew-Gentile dynamics in the church: does the Gentile debt of gratitude toward Jewish Christians translate into cultural and liturgical conformity to Jewish expression of the faith? The question illuminates the one with which Christians in North America contend amid the racially charged legacy of the American church side-by-side with the perpetuation of a European form of the faith. The reality is only more starkly brought into parallel with the early church when one considers the Euro-American legacy of tying what theologians and sociologists call "whiteness" to the assumption of reconstituted Jewish identity in the Euro-American theological and racial identification.[1] Willie James

1. J. Kameron Carter describes the birth of the "theological problem of whiteness" in two stages: first, the creation of "race," especially in order to distinguish the "white" people of the European "Occident" from the Jewish race of the "Orient" in their midst, and second, the declaration of hierarchy such that the Jewish race was "deemed inferior to Christians of the Occident or the West." The first stage pertains to racialization and the second to racism. J. Kameron Carter, *Race: A Theological Account* (New York: Oxford University Press, 2008) 4. Later, Carter clarifies that "white," "black," and "race" refer "perhaps only secondarily to color. Rather, they signify a political economy, an *ordo* or a social arrangement" (8).

Jennings astutely defines "whiteness" as "an inverted, distorted vision of creation that reduced theological anthropology to commodified bodies. In this inversion, whiteness replaced the earth as the signifier of identities."[2] That is, rather than see all peoples as joined by the dust of the ground—the earth from which all come and to which all return—and tied to their particular land, whiteness "presented itself as the only real option given the aggressive desacralization of the world."[3] This distortion of creation feeds the distortion of redemption by tying the person of Jesus Christ to whiteness and, thus, requiring participation in Christ to pass through peoples' becoming "white."

In what follows, I do not claim to be an expert on race relations, though I navigate academic and social waters as an Indian-American in a white evangelical academic landscape. My goal, then, is not to claim subtle knowledge either of white Christian self-understanding or, as the majority minorities in the US, of the black Christian psyche. Instead, I rely heavily upon Jennings and Brian Bantum to relay the racialized Western condition. From my own experience, their descriptions ring true, and perhaps more importantly, their descriptions help illuminate core theological issues regarding historic Western "Christian imagination" and hybridity that pave the way to looking at the church's identity in Christ in racialized space. My method, then, is to examine the account of the Jerusalem Council in Acts 15 through the lens of Jennings and Bantum in order to propose a virtuous ecclesial way forward for the body of Christ. Specifically, Jennings helps diagnose the problem and bring the present into close narrative proximity to the theological and cultural struggle before the apostles. Bantum, on the other hand, helps me think about the lead actor, Jesus Christ, in a way that brings the contemporary racialized stage into close proximity to the early church. My method of theological interpretation in this instance may be described as narratival and paradigmatic: I assume the narrative character of Scripture as one that envelops our reality and provides paradigms for wise reappraisal of our contemporary space. The result is a move tied to Paul Ricoeur's claim about the power of Scripture to create imaginative worlds of possibility. He writes, "Above and beyond emotions, disposition, belief, or nonbelief, is the proposition of a world which in the biblical language is called a new world, a new covenant, the kingdom of God, a new birth."[4] This new world, like fiction and poetry, conveys itself "through the modality of possibility"—that is, opening up the imagination to new kingdom

---

2. Willie James Jennings, *The Christian Imagination: Theology and the Origins of Race* (New Haven: Yale University Press, 2010) 58.

3. Ibid., 58.

4. Paul Ricoeur, "Philosophy and Religious Language," *JR* 54 (1974) 81.

based possibilities for living in the world.[5] In the current essay, I use Jennings and Bantum to describe the racialized world in which the church exists and participates and to offer a correction, namely return to reflection upon life in Christ. The turn to Acts 15 opens up rich possibilities for imagining the racialized dynamic in theological terms and offering theological solutions of excellence in communal participation in Christ.

This emphasis on "excellence" (from the Greek *aretē*, which is often also translated "virtue") pertains to the present drawing together of biblical and racialized spheres insofar as it fits with the call to *be* in Christ. That is, to *be* is not a statement of static ontology whereby we may reflect on status (e.g., "in Christ") independent of the ways that belong to being. Rather, to *be* is inherently joined to the task of *being*, performing our life in Christ, and *becoming*, as a performative development in process.[6] In the words of Paul, an equivalent gloss would be to have the mind of Christ (Phil 2:5) or to think on things above (Col 3:2). In each instance, the presumption of who we are (in Christ) weighs upon the life patterned after Christ (participation in him). James calls for a similar conjunction when proclaiming that faith without works is dead (see Jas 2:14–26). The connection that I am making to virtue is fairly straightforward, though assumed here: the call to life in Christ is the call to excellence according to the purposes of God in Christ by the Spirit. Beyond human flourishing in a natural sense—though it is not discounted—life in Christ is the call toward excellent fellowship with God and, by connection, with the fellow creatures of God. This call is the call to virtue, being in Christ who the Spirit would have us be. As it pertains to this essay, the particular call is to be agents of reconciliation as the church in a racialized sphere of existence and to be so virtuously. I take up this call through theological appropriation of the Acts account of the Jerusalem Council, specifically drawing upon the virtues of courage and humility.

The Jerusalem Council: Acts 15:5–21

Through much of Scripture prior to Acts, the drama of redemption foreshadows the coming of the kingdom of God beyond the borders of the people of Israel. For instance, Exod 12:43–48 relays God's command concerning the Passover feast, wherein foreigners were welcome to partake provided they committed themselves

---

5. Ricoeur, "Philosophy and Religious Language," 80.

6. See the recent trend toward drama in Christian theology. For example, see Kevin J. Vanhoozer, *The Drama of Doctrine: A Canonical-Linguistic Approach to Christian Theology* (Louisville: Westminster John Knox, 2005); *Faith Speaking Understanding: Performing the Drama of Doctrine* (Louisville: Westminster John Knox, 2014); Wesley Vander Lugt, *Living Theodrama: Reimagining Theological Ethics* (Burlington, VT: Ashgate, 2014).

to the narrative of God's working in and through Israel. In other words, in order to enter into God's story of redemption, people—whether Jew or Gentile—had to bear the mark of one who belonged to God's story. That mark was no trifle, for it required nothing less—of males, anyway—than circumcision. In other words, short of an ethnic designation per se, the mark of the Jew, the people of the promise unto redemption of the world, was the mark of the covenant in the flesh. Even by the time we encounter the ministry of Jesus in the New Testament, this covenantal marker remains significant and central to participation in God's economy and to reception of the subsequent benefits. Most notably, one may turn to Jesus' own encounter with the Canaanite woman in Matt 15:21–28, where Jesus initially refuses to heal her on account of her non-participation in the people of Israel. The centrality of Israel—of surprise neither to those in the narrative nor to anyone who has read the text—in the mission of redemption persists even through the life, death, and resurrection of Jesus Christ.

Yet with the dawn of Acts, we quickly move to what Paul in Ephesians refers to as the "mystery" of God, "which he purposed in Christ—namely the joining of Jews and Gentiles together in Christ (Eph 1:9; see also 2:11–18). The progression of Acts is fairly swift, moving out from the core group after Christ's ascension to touch Jews across the world, then Samaritans, and finally Gentiles. From the present vantage point nearly 2000 years later, the joy is palpable, for the Spirit is mightily at work confirming this stretching of the story into new spaces through acts of the Spirit consistent with those performed among the Jews. The message of Acts is hopeful, moving towards the inclusion of every tribe and tongue and nation. Considering that the core disciples were themselves Jews and that the apostles sent forth were an expanded set of Jews (including such people as Paul's companion Barnabas) the transition from a story tied to covenant markers belonging to a single ethnic group to a story opened to all of the children of Adam was rather peaceful through Acts 14.[7] Of course, Peter himself needed some visionary coaxing to begin the movement toward the Gentiles, but his initial resistance seems to be relatively slight even if his hesitance and surprise emanate from the account in Acts 10. Besides, given OT law and even Jesus' words in Matt 15, Peter's hesitancy may be understandable.[8]

---

7. I am assuming biblical scholars are correct in tying Luke and Acts into one narrative unit. Given that Acts narrates the movement of the gospel (and, thus, the growth of the church) out from Jerusalem and Jewish identity to the "ends of the earth" unto Gentile inclusion in the hope of Christ (cf. 1:8), it should not be surprising that Luke chose to extend his genealogical account from Jesus back to Adam—the patriarch of all humanity, Jews and Gentiles—rather than only to Abraham, the chief patriarch of Israel.

8. One may object here that I have moved too loosely between covenant identity and ethnic identity. The examples of Exod 12 and Lev 17–18 surely resist the equation of covenant to ethnic group. Agreed. Nevertheless, it is difficult to ignore that by the time of the New Testament, the two

As in any good story, though, we should expect disturbance to arise on account of traditional imaginaries. After all, transformation in Christ does not usually entail the sort of radical, immediate conversion of imaginaries as it appears Saul/Paul underwent in Acts 9. Even the disciples were hesitant to believe Saul/Paul had changed so drastically until they witnessed the change themselves and saw the anger of the "Hellenistic Jews" against Paul during his visit to Jerusalem (Acts 9:26–29). So, when we arrive at Acts 15:5, we can breathe a sigh of relief: we modern skeptics are not as different from the early Christian as we thought. Indeed, what had already taken place in the church at Antioch in Syria in 15:1 proves to be true even in Jerusalem in v. 5: the Pharisees converted to Christ came forth and contended that the new way was not actually so different from the old way, for while Gentiles are welcome, they must keep the law of Moses, especially circumcision. Imagining their vantage point, this may not have been so snooty as we might be inclined to think it today. After all, Gentiles were already invited into the story of God provided they were circumcised and kept the law. What is more, the early Christians were not only Jews, but we can imagine that they were also Jews who firmly believed that they were the true faithful Jews continuing the story of Israel in the way it was to go—namely, in Christ. Why should continuity not reign, then? In the same manner as the foreigner among the Israelites prior to the incarnation, as far as these Pharisaic Christians were concerned, Gentiles were welcome to become one of them on the condition that they became *just* like them. This latter appeal already alludes to the paradigmatic parallel to the early modern and modern racialization of the church and Western culture.

As the obviously abridged narrative of the Council goes, Paul and Barnabas arrive in Jerusalem to take up precisely this matter with the apostles and elders of the church. Based upon Paul's own account of the happenings in Antioch in Gal 2, it appears that Peter needed some coaxing to take the courageous stand that he eventually would, but, in any case, at the Council itself, Peter stands to give a rousing speech, hitting three significant points. First, Peter recalls what has been a deliberate appeal throughout Acts in narrating the movement of the church out from its epicenter in Jerusalem: the same Spirit of Pentecost has descended upon Jewish and Gentile Christians, indicating no ethnically-determined tiers of purity in faith. Second, even

---

appear to become inflated within the Jewish social imaginary, hence the strong Jewish aversion to the mixed Samaritans and Paul's need to chastise a view that conflated Jewish theological identity with physical descent from Abraham (Gal 4:21–31). On the other hand, the conflation is understandable to a degree, for the covenant to which Israel belongs in the OT is made with a particular group of physical descendants of Abraham (those through Isaac). Even if some branches were chopped from the tree from time to time, genealogical lineage remains down to Christ. Aliens grafted in entered through the covenant signs given to this people group, and the Messiah belonged to this *physical* lineage too. So, while covenant/theological identity is not identical to Jewish ethnicity in the OT, the two were not separate either.

the Jews have had a hard time keeping the law, indicating general Jewish impurity if law-keeping is an expectation. That is, regardless of the dynamics of continuity between the covenants, membership in the covenant, even when generational, is not synonymous with purity defined by law observance. Third, the grace by which Jews and Gentiles may be saved is the same grace, and it is the grace of "our Lord Jesus," not that of the law (Acts 15:7–11). Peter's passionate appeal goes out of the way to level the playing field for Jews and Gentiles, making no distinction on the basis of ethnic identity or in the means of communication of grace. Both are saved by the "grace of our Lord Jesus" (15:11), irrespective of the law (15:10), and no distinction in purity persists (15:9) since the same Spirit works actively in the same ways among Jewish and Gentile Christians (15:8). Rendering the text theologically according to the broader message of the New Testament, both Jewish and Gentile Christians are who they are because they are *in Christ*. This beginning point of spiritual equality becomes the basis for James's turn to Amos 9:11–12 to affirm that this had been the intent all along in the old economy. God had always planned to make his covenant with Israel as the story by which the Gentiles would see the Lord and come to him (Acts 15:16–18).

Yet the end of what is recorded in James's speech seems to rub against the grain of the equality established by Peter. Following Peter's tenor and declaring his intent to "not make it difficult for the Gentiles who are turning to God" (15:19), James seems to take back this desire and push against the grain of Peter's passionate remarks, urging that the Gentile Christians continue a few Jewish practices—namely, "to abstain from food polluted by idols, from sexual immorality, from the meat of strangled animals and from blood" (v. 20). While these suggestions were certainly less invasive and central to Jewish identity than circumcision, James's rationale remains the status quo of Jewish identity: Jews are living all over the world, so—presumably—the Gentile Christians need not scandalize them unnecessarily. In the end, the Council—which includes the same Peter who delivered the passionate remarks dispelling claims to Christian purity through old covenant Jewish practice—affirms James, making the very requests of the Gentile Christians that James advocates (v. 29). Does this, then, nullify Peter's case for equality in Christ and establish a cultural hierarchy for Christian identity and practice?

What Has Antioch to Do with Jerusalem?

A few considerations yet remain: the pragmatic, the canonical, and the narratival. The strongest affirmation of cultural hierarchy no doubt would have included the expectation of circumcision of all male Gentile Christians, yet this Pharisaic

imposition was clearly rejected by the Council. One could take a pragmatic approach and argue that Jewish Christians simply would not ever know whether or
not the Gentile Christians complied with a commendation of circumcision, thus
leading the Council ultimately to side with the Pharisees but to do so through the
commendation of more publicly visible signs of continuity between old covenant
Jewish identity and Christian identity. Such is certainly possible, but this pragmatic
approach fails to account persuasively for Peter's passionate speech. What purpose
does its inclusion in the narrative of Acts serve if it is dispensable to the development
of Christianity beyond the walls of Jerusalem. To borrow from Tertullian, what has
the inclusion of Antioch to do with Jerusalem? On this sort of pragmatic reading,
nothing. Additionally, this pragmatic reading would miss the connection of Peter's
words to the narrative in the preceding chapters of the growth of the church beyond
Jerusalem. Peter's words are interpretive of this narrative, and fairly uncontrovert-
ibly so, given the way the narrative unequivocally ties the coming of the Spirit to the
Gentiles to the event of Pentecost. I will revisit this below.

Further, we must consider what a pragmatic declaration would even entail. After all, pragmatism requires a goal. Perhaps the goal could have been the imposition
of Jewish custom in order to elevate Jewish Christianity as normative. Such a goal
would mean the sweeping to the side of Peter's impassioned speech, in which case
the narrative would certainly note an ultimate rejection of his theology. In this form,
pragmatism does not seem to fit. Alternatively, Richard Bauckham wonders about
a pragmatism aimed at compromise in order to establish shared "table fellowship
between Jews and Gentiles." He rightly recognizes that this reading is unconvincing
on account of the thrust of the passage, which seems to offer deep theological consideration of the ongoing relevance of the law of Moses to Christian practice and of
the relationship of this law to Gentiles.[9] Such a pragmatic aim makes no sense of the
care the passage demonstrates for theological rationale. Even Peter's remarks are not
dismissive of the law itself. Rather, he is careful to point to impurity before the law
and to the need of both Jews and Gentiles for the grace found in the body of Christ.[10]

9. Richard Bauckham, "James and the Jerusalem Church," in *The Book of Acts in Its Palestinian
Setting*, edited by Richard Bauckham, 415–80, vol. 4 of *The Book of Acts in Its First Century Setting*,
edited by Bruce W. Winter (Grand Rapids: Eerdmans, 1995) 463–64. I am grateful to Hauna Ondrey
for drawing my attention to Bauckham's careful exegetical work on Acts 15, thereby enabling me to
strengthen my argument through interaction with his insights.

10. Nevertheless, it seems to me that Bauckham illegitimately rejects the possibility that the goal of
table fellowship could be in play by tying it only to a pragmatic rationale. After all, shared eucharistic
fellowship, insofar as it is an institution of communal partaking of the body and blood of Christ, *is*
a goal of life together in Christ, for—per Peter's rationale—both Jews and Gentiles require the same
grace of Christ by the same Spirit of Christ from the same position of impurity. Acts 2:46 arguably
refers to this goal of life together partaking of Christ's body. To the degree that Acts narrates the Spirit's
growth of the church out from Jerusalem unto the equal inclusion of Gentiles in Christ, a parallel

Canonically, we may look at the specific practices that were commended. Apparently not all were commended everywhere in the early church, for Paul himself nuances the request for abstaining from food offered to idols. In 1 Cor 8, Paul addresses the same issue, calling for charity to rule in a given moment. Offering food to idols does nothing to the food itself since the gods (or "demons" in 1 Cor 10:20) to whom the idols belong have no power over the food. The real issue is the mutual uplifting of the church: all things being equal, feel free to eat such food; however, if eating it causes another to sin, then do not do it. But does Paul undermine himself two chapters later by declaring participation with false gods (again, "demons") through eating food offered to idols to be mutually exclusive to eucharistic communion with Christ (1 Cor 10:20–22)? Despite initial appearances, evidently he does not, for he reasserts the matter of conscience (1 Cor 8:7–12; 10:25–30). Specifically, the goal is protection of the other in order to edify her unto faithful participation in Christ (see 1 Cor 10:23–24, 31–33).

Similarly, in 1 Cor 6, Paul addresses "sexual immorality" with regard to the other. On the creaturely level, failure here defiles the bond of marriage, making mockery of the "one flesh" that joins and binds husband and wife. All the more, beyond the purely creaturely domain, sexual immorality mocks and defiles the spiritual bond (effected by the Holy Spirit) by which the church is united with Christ. As in 1 Cor 8, the issue here again is a matter of relational charity. Surely failure in this area harms the perpetrating person, but it is equally significant (at least) that sexual immorality does injustice to the other, both on the creaturely plane and in union with Christ.

As for the final commendation, not to partake of meat from strangled animals or of blood, there is no NT parallel. However, with the other two commendations, we can recognize that all three belong to Jewish custom through old covenant law, as v. 21 affirms. It would be reasonable in this latter case to take the same approach of relational charity. Just as concern for the good of the body of Christ corporately and individually reigns over the other two commendations elsewhere in the NT, we can assume here too for canonical reasons that the Council's decision to ask Gentiles to abstain from blood and from the meat of strangled animals was a commendation to charity. The reading could go something like this: while the Pharisaic Christians are wrong to expect Gentiles to adopt Jewish law, subscribing to these other Jewish practices would go a long way to establishing unity in the expanded vision of Christ

theological purpose of the conciliar decision in Acts 15 could be the inclusion of Christian Jews and Gentiles together at the eucharistic table of Christ. Acts could be seen as theologically narrating the extension of the Jewish Christian table fellowship in Acts 2:46 to Gentile inclusion. That is to say that following Bauckham in rejecting *pragmatism* in the conciliar narrative is not necessarily rejection of the same goal of table fellowship on theological grounds.

beyond the bounds of Jew-Gentile distinctions without destroying the particular expressions of the way of Christ commensurate to both groups. For the sake of the other, both sides must be willing to recognize the life of Christ in the ways of the respective foreigners. On this reading, the Council's adoption of James's suggestion befits the spirit of Peter's three-fold declaration without destroying cultural difference. Nevertheless, by rejecting the stronger proposal to require circumcision, Jewish expression of life in Christ was not granted unmitigated approval to demand cultural assimilation to its ways.[11]

Still, though, I think we can go deeper by drawing out the narratival logic of the apostles' and elders' decision. Most significantly, the conciliar commendations seem to be ethically driven, fleshing out corporate concern for shared life in Christ across cultural spheres within the church. In other words, the cultural concern that is evident in the canonical consideration appears to be also an ethical concern when read within the narrative of Acts. Arguably, there may also be an apologetic endeavor in the request, knowing that the Jewish Christian leaders of the council presented a message that they intended to affirm as the true continuation of old covenant promises. In this case, the commendation may not be pointing to Jewish Christians around the world but rather Jewish non-Christians, to whom the message of Christ might be more compelling if it more obviously picked up where the old covenant left off in tangible and visible ways.

However, narratively, there is less reason to affirm apologetics as the primary purpose of the conciliar decision *in the text*. Instead, given the movement of the book of Acts out from a beginning point in Jerusalem, and given the deliberate moves toward untethering the way of Christ from the ongoing practice of Jewish cultic ritual (for example, see Acts 10 where the Lord directs Peter to go among the Gentiles and eat like them), the narrative reads more easily as a conciliar desire to incarnate the way of Christ in new, culturally significant ways without running over the culturally particular expressions of Christian identity embodied in the practices

---

11. Bauckham believes that the four-fold expectation was binding in all places for Gentiles, regardless of whether or not Jewish Christians were present: "James and the Jerusalem Church," 464. For Bauckham, James's pulling of the list of requirements from Leviticus 17–18 and joining them to the quotation of Amos 9:11–12 forms the basis for why just these requirements were laid upon the Gentile Christians (458–62). While Bauckham convincingly shows the deliberate posture taken by the council to require these points of obedience to the law of Moses, he does not compellingly explain why these commandments were binding upon all Gentiles everywhere on account of the continued activity of the law of Moses. Rather than reflect on the significance of the conciliar decision in this particular situation, he universalizes the conciliar judgment to an abstracted principle. Why could the conciliar decision not have been an affirmation of mutual and equal indwelling in the body of Christ that destroys claims of purity, as I am suggesting? After all, Peter's remarks already dismissed the thought of Jewish purity and the need for Jewish legal priority in Christian identity and practice. In other words, why is the conciliar decision a matter of reinforcing law rather than wisely enacting love?

of fellow Christians. Furthermore, the narrative even commends the transgression of one's own boundaries in order to take the good news of Christ both to and into another culture. To borrow this time from the title of Dietrich Bonhoeffer's book, the emphasis seems to be "life together" without cultural railroading. As in the case of Peter with Cornelius in Acts 10, the conciliar decision seems to encourage the transgression of the boundaries of the established community in order to make known the riches of Christ in a local community. This narratival logic does not stop there, for if it did, between Peter's experience in Acts 10 and Peter's speech in Acts 15, the account would be complete: transgress boundaries so that the church may fully take the form of the receiving culture. The narrative thrust of James's contribution steps in just here, though, to drive home the ethical mutuality. Yes, transgress boundaries rather than replicate Jewish identity. However, to the Gentiles in Antioch, the message is "you, too, transgress boundaries in order to honor the church in adjacent cultures, not least the culture that brought life in Christ to you."

In other words, both cultures engage in a cultural transgression that does not do violence to the other but also does not leave their own culture unchanged. The three-fold articulation of life in Christ by Peter circumscribes this shared identity by refusing distinctions of purity, provided the grace received belongs to life in Christ. Indeed, the identity of Christ himself calls for this new mixed identity in him. The former grounds the latter since Jesus Christ in his very person perfectly draws together two disparate realities—divine and human—without confusing the two yet also without leaving the human unchanged.

The Mulatto Christ and Mulatto/a in Christ

In his rich work *Redeeming Mulatto*, Brian Bantum draws upon the theological resources of the incarnation of Jesus Christ to anchor endeavors into racial reconciliation that respect cultural difference without allowing this difference to undermine the life of the church as first and foremost *in Christ*—not in the dominant or subjugated cultures. Among the many contrasts he presents, he perhaps most helpfully situates his work between the extremes of James Cone and John Milbank. The former, Bantum contends, reacts to the colonial so strongly as to render "decolonial" theology that relocates the person and work of Christ from the oppressor to the oppressed. The result is that "Cone's theological vision has also served to enclose the image of God within the lives of the oppressed," thereby restricting God's work to and among the oppressed.[12]

---

12. Brian Bantum, *Redeeming Mulatto: A Theology of Race and Christian Hybridity* (Waco, TX: Baylor University Press, 2016) 3–4.

Conversely, Milbank's "colonial" theology effectively doubles down upon tradition, solidifying the tendencies that have contributed to the "disembodiment of ideas and idealization of a body."[13] To be clear, Bantum's concern does not appear to be with Milbank's reverence for tradition but rather for the attempt to enliven it through confession without considering the practices that interpret it. Milbank certainly argues for the animation of confession such that right confession bears forth corresponding acts, but the problem, says Bantum, is that the codifying of the confessions reinforces the traditional forms as well. So, Bantum acknowledges that one might partake of the Eucharist and rightly consider the implications of "giving to the poor or the needy," but rarely does the very stage of the performance change. He argues, "Confession thus fences imagination of what constitutes salvation around thoughts *about* worship, rather than rendering their very bodies as worship." Thus, Milbank's Radical Orthodoxy "concretizes the positions of those who seemingly confess properly *within their pews*" (emphasis added) maintaining cultural, ecclesial, and dogmatic separation from the "Spanish-speaking congregation that rents their sanctuary at seven o'clock every Sunday evening."[14]

The narrative of Acts helps frame Bantum's concerns with Cone and Milbank. Per Bantum's articulation, Cone's solution would be akin to the Gentile church in Antioch not only resisting the Pharisaic demands for circumcision, but also extracting Jesus from the confession of the Jewish Christians in order to localize him purely within the Gentile community of Antioch. The case might take the form of denying continuity between the old covenant narrative that paves the way for Jesus and the early church consisting of Jewish Christians. In this setting, the movement of the church *outward from* Jerusalem would be a movement *away from* those who still inhabit Jerusalem and misappropriate the old covenant Jewishness for themselves. To be Gentile, the outcast, is actually to be at the center of the story of redemption.

On the other hand, the Milbank way would be a reaffirmation of the old covenant cultic system and a doubling down on the works of the law. However, if the Jerusalem Council had decided in favor of this option, it need not have constituted a rejection of Gentiles: to the contrary, it would be a continuation of the old covenant stipulations of Gentile inclusion but with more vocalized, open invitation for Gentiles to join the covenant by embracing the works of the law, especially circumcision. The goal would be reformation of practice by returning to the source, doubling down on the old covenant's invitation to Gentiles by attempting to strip away the layers of cultural hostility wherein Gentile conversion may have become discouraged, either explicitly or implicitly through the prevailing attitudes of Jewish believers.

13. Ibid., 2–3.

14. Ibid., 6.

To rephrase Bantum's remarks concerning the "Spanish-speaking congregation," this approach opens its doors to the latter without accounting for the hermeneutical change that the new people group could and should elicit upon the existing community by the mere inclusion of the former. In other words, taking each setting in order, moving from Acts to the world of this essay, (1) the church would be a continuous operation of OT Jewish practice into which the Gentiles of Antioch would be welcome, (2) the Spanish-speaking congregation would be welcome to join the pure orthodoxy of the Augustinian tradition of Milbank's vision of the Catholic church, and (3) the minority church is welcome to fellowship with the white church as the latter continues its liturgical styles, dogmatic construals, and culturally prophetic sermons pertaining to the questions, concerns, and life of the majority community.

In contrast to these two extremes, Bantum presents a third way that "complicates identities rather than confirms them." He asks, "Does Jesus' presence among us as God, as a Jew, as oppressed, but also divine and human, born of Spirit *and* flesh, make possible not only a wider set of allegiances, but require it of our lives as disciples?"[15] Bantum's explication of Jesus Christ as the "redeeming mulatto" is a move of just this sort to challenge presumptions of "purities" and to encourage life in Christ that engenders the "transgression" of the perceived purities. Just as the mulatto/a challenges the purity of "whiteness" and its antithesis of "blackness," Jesus transgressed the relatively uncomplicated divide of Creator-created by embarking on his mission as the Son of God who hypostatically took upon himself the identity of a creaturely man without confusing the two: Jesus remained (and remains) fully God and fully human.[16] Yet in the person of Christ, the pure perception of God's necessary transcendence that could only be polluted by embracing communion with the creaturely is itself transgressed in the hypostatic union. Similarly, the pure perception of humanity is challenged and transformed through Jesus Christ, the second Adam who gives new life and heightened potential to the life of the first Adam.[17] Bantum writes, "In the incarnation notions of personhood become conflated and reimagined in their relation with one another." This divine transgression in Christ the mulatto enables us "to interpret humanity christologically."[18]

Bantum emphasizes the language of "mixture," usually a characteristic description of the mulatto. In interracial marriage, the mixed child—so the narrative usually goes—is neither what the one parent is nor what the other parent is. To use my own children as an example, they would generally be considered half Canadian, half

15. Ibid., 5.
16. Ibid., 91–92.
17. Ibid., 90.
18. Ibid., 89.

Indian (or, perhaps, my wife's mixed European heritage might be cited to declare more precise percentages of the mixture present in her and then halved to identify the percentages for our children). Adding the composite percentages together, each of my children would then be 100 percent human but impure as to each component ethnic or racial part. Bantum wishes to challenge this math by appealing to the incarnation to christologically transgress and transform our racial calculus in which to be "mixed" is to exist somewhere between the poles of purity. If we were to apply this sort of mixture-method to Christ, the result would be the Christology of Apollinaris, where the joining of divine and human natures in the person of Christ leaves us with some kind of person other than God or human.[19] Instead, following Chalcedon, Bantum argues that the logic of the ecumenical, conciliar decision was its confession of the "neither/nor—but," wherein Jesus is *neither* God apart from being human *nor* human apart from God *but* God bound to human and human bound to God while remaining 100 percent God and 100 percent human. This operation does not follow the usually presumed math, for 100 percent God joined to 100 percent human does not give us the Nestorian two persons (or 200 percent being) but rather one person both fully God and fully human without confusion. Yet, herein, it would not be appropriate to speak of poles of purity transgressed to create a mixture somewhere between the two. Instead, in the person of Christ, we have a mixture who just is God for humanity and humanity for God. In Christ, our imagination expands, transforming our conception of God as wholly transcendent other and our view of humanity as being defined by racial and ethnic purities. Returning to my children, this reimaging of humanity christologically would lead me to view each of my children as 100 percent Canadian and 100 percent Indian. They are "mixtures," but not of the Apollinarian kind. Instead, as Bantum puts it, "the mulatto/a life, while rendered visible through the negation of possibilities, in fact inhabits all possibilities within the mulatto/a performance of life."[20] In the case of my children, as fully Canadian and fully Indian, they contain in their mixed personhoods rich resources to live imaginatively into being Canadian *and* being Indian in a manner that transforms both ways of being through improvisational being into each. They are not less Canadian and Indian; rather they are uniquely Canadian and Indian and can transform both. Put another way, "the assertion of purity is the actual illusion."[21]

However, if Bantum were to leave his trajectory at this point, he would not have gone far enough for our purposes of reimagining the ecclesial dynamic of being in Christ in Acts 15 according to the climate of racialization. Indeed, Bantum brings

19. Ibid., 105–6.
20. Ibid., 119.
21. Ibid., 125.

the concept of christological mixture home to life in Christ. After all, "the mission of Christ was not merely to make a way for creation to know God and recognize God, but to share in God's life, to recreate humanity as a 'holy mixture.'"[22] The church is this recreated humanity and, as such, is defined by this new life of participation in Christ. Drawing upon Jesus's challenging of the notion of "family" in the kingdom of God, Bantum points to the discontinuity that this posits in relation to the biological and social. Far from rejecting particular ethnicities and cultures—which would be to fall to the extreme of Milbank—life in Christ nevertheless transgresses the purity of these identifiers, transforming us first into creatures in Christ. This inherently means differentiation from the supposedly pure marks of ethnicities and cultures, whether black or white, Jew or Gentile. Bantum refers to the alienation from such purities in terms of the "weight of exclusion." Conversely, life in Christ is participation in "truthful existence" that challenges and transforms the ethnic, cultural, racial, and familial.[23]

Returning to Acts 15, this new theological posture of participation in Christ encroaches upon both Jew and Gentile. It's worth noting that in Acts, even the Jewish Christian dynamic devoid of Gentile inclusion was not so straightforward as to invoke a notion of purity. After all, the early portions of Acts portray much persecution of Christ's disciples, and this not from Gentiles. As in the crucifixion of Jesus, the early persecution is spearheaded by non-Christian Jews. This is to say that the Jewish Christians' own status of "purity" would have been debatable. They already existed as a displaced mixture, defined by something, or more properly someone, other than purely Jewish—even if that someone else was Jewish. Recognition of the challenges presented by life in Christ to their prior life did not negate their Jewish identity, but it did undermine any presumption of pure Jewish identity and force them to confront a new way of being Jewish. Thus, when Peter passionately denounces the thought that pure Christianity is necessarily Jewish, he also rejects the illusion of a prior Jewish purity: "why do you try to test God by putting on the necks of Gentiles a yoke that neither we nor our ancestors have been able to bear?" (15:10). So, not only is Jewish Christianity not the pure form of Christianity or the pure form of being Jewish, as it turns out, even pre-Christian Judaism failed the purity test.

The same can be said about the Gentiles, though, understandably, a commensurate argument does not seem to be needed in the Acts narrative. On account of leaving behind whatever forms of non-Jewish identity the Antiochene Christians did, it is clear that they are migrating toward the Jewish Jesus and away from the forms of Gentile existence to which they belonged. That is, they, too, have "transgressed" their

22. Ibid., 118.
23. Ibid., 129.

particular boundaries and, like the Jewish Christians, their identity lies in Christ. Peter confirms their shared and equal identity on account of their shared participation in the grace of Christ (15:11). Bantum's reflections on the mulatto Christ making muluttos/as of all who are in Christ befits the situation of Acts 15: "Christ's work serves to break open identities that were once enclosed, but now are marked by a rhythm of redemption that reiterates an identity of love and procreation through the transgression of incorporation." As if directly glossing the decision of the Jerusalem Council, he continues, "To participate in Christ's life is to welcome the many and the transformation of practices, lives, and culture that such mutual incorporation requires." Indeed, "this process of incorporation [into Christ's body] is not a loss of identity but its reorganization, identity's rearticulation."[24]

Therefore, the expansion of the church is an expansion from a group of mixed people to the inclusion of another group of mixed people. Peter and the Council understood this. It is not a stretch, then, to affirm with Bantum that the "patterns and culture [of the church] must shift to welcome that new life into its walls."[25] The Jewish Christians of Acts 15 did this by sacrificing their rich, even divinely bestowed cultural expectations in welcoming the Gentile Christians into equal fellowship. And presuming the Gentile Christians heeded the verdict of the Council, they also sacrificed their freedom in Christ (e.g., eating food offered to idols) by following Jewish custom in the prescribed ways (15:20–21). Both groups were able to maintain their cultural identities in large part while humbly sacrificing their normal patterns to "welcome that new life into its walls."

Jew-Gentile or Gentile-Gentile?
Recalibrating Ecclesial Dynamics in Light of Race

In Acts 15, as already repeatedly rehearsed, the setting clearly pertains to Jewish expectations concerning Gentiles. The Jewish Christians, in line with Mosaic law, expected the alien to become Jewish ritually. Yet the crux of Peter's retort hinges on an implicit shift of economies, wherein the old covenant does not, strictly speaking, take priority. The parallel with the contemporary racial predicament should be evident, particularly if one sees the status quo of the Euro-American church as the relative equivalent of the Jewish church of the Jerusalem Council.[26] In this framing,

24. Ibid., 119.

25. Ibid., 144.

26. Apart from the majority-minority element, there may be parallel here in the self-perception of certain minority communities, who see a need for deliberate counter-cultural articulation of identity in order to preserve their distinctiveness. In order to step out of the culturally imposing and assimilating shadow of the majority culture, minority cultures sometimes deliberately develop patterns of

the colonizing work on which Bantum sees Milbank doubling down is on display, establishing the cultural, conceptual, and linguistic construals of dogmatic and liturgical encounter with Christ.

It is precisely this scenario that is the subject of Willie James Jennings's instant classic *The Christian Imagination*. Over the course of the first two hundred pages, Jennings masterfully combs accounts of European exploration and colonization during the Renaissance and early modern period of Western thought. His argument is too expansive to summarize here, but the gist is this: European expansion through exploration was intimately tied to the program of exportation of European Christendom. The logic and methods of colonization were deeply tied to Christian theology and belief in missions. This program quickly took on the burgeoning character of the developing racial imagination, which was tied to the logic of Christendom. Jennings's argument, then, is that the birth of the modern conception of race is tied to a defective Christian theology, particularly in the areas of the European self-perception of their superseding the Jews as the people of the divine promise and a distorted view of creation that abstracts humanity from the land of creation. A new racial imagination overlays these theological dysfunctions and creates a racial matrix that equates "white" with refined civilization, intelligence, and capacity to understand Christianity. Meanwhile, "black" lay at the other end of the spectrum, denoting lack in each of the same ways and even a lesser form of human existence (if human at all). All encountered people were plotted between these extremes and judged accordingly. The solution was the expansion of Christendom: civilization, Christianity, and racial matrix in one, neat package.

Again, rehearsing Jennings's argument in detail is not possible in the present space, but the import for Acts 15 should be evident. Unlike the decision at the Jerusalem Council, the racialized motive was to export European civilization—itself seen as the new Jewish civilization—in order to take Christianity to the countless lower civilizations throughout the world. As the new Jewish people, their decision was to require circumcision (albeit, metaphorically) of the new Gentile—i.e., non-European, non-white—Christians. Jennings's quotation of the Spanish priest José de Acosta illustrates this well:

> So then we need to teach the Indians [= First Nation's], and all other unfaithful people, about the mystery of Christ. To exclude any human lineage from this general principle is a grave error, not to say open heresy . . . But then you well may ask—What about a person who is incapable, ignorant, stupid, old and decrepit, or some Ethiopian black, thick as two short planks, a bison that is

---

life (e.g., diction, dialect, and dress) in opposition to the force of assimilation. See Jennifer A. Herdt, "Christian Humility, Courtly Civility, and the Code of the Streets," *Modern Theology* 25 (2009) 541–61.

hardly different from the wild beast? Are you to oblige them and others like them to learn about the mystery of the Trinity, which is difficult even for the greatest and sharpest of minds? Are you going to require something that goes beyond the capacity of human reason from a person of such stolidity? Well, I say that I am not obliging people to understand the mystery of Christ . . . but I am obliging them all to believe it . . .[27]

This attitude serves as a reversal specifically of Peter's remarks at the Jerusalem Council in all three of the ways outlined above. First, it affirms a pure version of the faith, specifically one articulated through the cultural-linguistic development of Christendom. Even if the same Spirit is at work among the new Gentiles, it works through the mediation of the new Jews. Second, rather than follow Peter's example in reminding his fellow leaders of the church that they and their ancestors were equally unable to fulfill faithfulness to the law and are thus on the same plane as the Gentiles, Acosta touts his superior intellect and understanding and that of his fellow European Christians, implying a greater level of faithfulness. Third, unlike Peter's equalizing declaration of the same grace of Christ saving both Jew and Gentile, Acosta's move sees his people as the mediators of Christ to the new Gentiles. Far from what Bantum referred to as an openness to welcome "new life into its walls," Acosta's approach seeks to make the new Gentile in the image of the new Jew, even if an inferior instantiation thereof through the mediation of the pure new Jew.[28]

Of the theological problems that Jennings identifies, the one that results in the short circuiting of Acts 15 as I have described it is the move of a Gentile entity—in this case, the European church(es) of Christendom—to reduce biblical Israel to an ethnic group and replace it with a new theological referent: themselves. The particularity of Israel as the place of "divine disclosure" is lost.[29] Subsequently, so too is the particularity of Jesus as the one who brings Jew and Gentile together, as the one who "entered fully into the kinship structure [of Israel] not to destroy it but to reorder it—around himself."[30] Peter grasped this new reality in Christ when he recognized

27. Quoted in Jennings, *Christian Imagination*, 111–12. Although the example I have chosen is that of a Catholic Jesuit, neither Jennings's nor my account wish to convey that the problem of racialization belongs merely to Roman Catholicism. Jennings's account visits the narratives of both early modern Roman Catholicism and Protestantism. The problem belongs to the western church and its complicity in the creation of "whiteness." Given the deeply Protestant roots of the United States, not surprisingly, Protestants—including evangelicals—are the main culprit in the USA. See Peter Goodwin Heltzel, *Jesus and Justice: Evangelicals, Race, and American Politics* (New Haven: Yale University Press, 2009).

28. Jennings, *Christian Imagination*, 239 describes the same sort of dynamic between slave owner and slave in the antebellum south: "Whereas for the slaveholder (and even for those whites opposed to slavery) the authority of the Bible stood as the unmediated foundation of Christian life and doctrine, for the slave the Bible was offered only in conjunction with the interpreting word of the slave master."

29. Ibid., 254.

30. Ibid., 263.

that it was the shared grace of Christ that overcame the distance between Jew and Gentile and, indeed, trivialized the difference by relating both to himself by the same Spirit. The modern racialized landscape in which the church currently exists suffers from racial distance because of the ongoing and structural effects of Christendom's distorted reckoning of biblical Israel, wherein those who were Gentiles "claim[ed] for themselves what was true only for Israel."[31] That is, the Gentile church set itself up as Israel rather than turn to Jesus first like Peter did.[32] The result, per Jennings, has been the mediation of Christ by the self-perceived "new Israel" to the new racially-other "Gentile" church—rather than the Jewish Jesus, we now have the ubiquitous image of a Germanic Jesus, "validating" a reconstituted identity for Israel along racialized lines. Recalling Bantum, distance remains on account of a Milbank-like doubling down on traditional Euro-American forms rather than openness to new shared forms. This is not simply an abstract mediation. Christ's body, the place of redemption where humanity from the dust of the ground joins with God, itself becomes white, for it is in whiteness that the hope of humanity lies. So, while Jewish in birth, Jesus comes to be seen as transcending his Jewishness, throwing it off, and becoming white.[33] The white body (visually in art, intellectually in the universalizing of reason, culturally in the development of free civilization) comes to mediate the person and work of Christ. He was Jewish, but only theologically, not ethnically.

Assuming Jennings is right, which I do, does this make Acts 15 irrelevant to the race situation moving forward? I don't think so. Though the passage explicitly talks about the Jew-Gentile church dynamics of the early church, it implicates Gentile-Gentile dynamics moving forward, which are all the starker when read in the contemporary climate that often functionally presumes the Jew-Gentile dynamic.[34]

31. Ibid., 257.

32. See ibid., 259: "There is, of course, an intrinsic applicability of his [= Jesus's] life, an important connection for all humanity. But the way to that connection requires that we turn our attention back to his relationship with Israel. In so doing we must resist the temptation to read Jesus as though we are his disciples before we are Gentiles."

33. See J. Kameron Carter's analysis of Immanuel Kant's development of this racialized portrait of Jesus, re-creating the Jewish Jesus in the image of the "white" European body and, most particularly, the "white" German body. *Race*, 79–121.

34. This presumption is at the core of my use of the Acts 15 passage to advocate the mode of racial reconciliation in grabbing a hold of the *Jewish* body of Christ. The supersessionist logic of the Western church has (wrongly) presumed a Jew-Gentile dynamic in its relation to the non-white world and, therein, has categorized culture, tradition, and—most heinously—Christian expression according to a racial logic of purity. Yet even amid this false presumption, what Acts 15 helps us regain is that even the original, biblically warranted Jew-Gentile divide did not provide sufficient theological grounds for declarations of purity, whether cultural, traditional, or religious. Thus, if Jewish people cannot claim purity in Christ, the varieties of Gentile identities in Christ most certainly cannot. The Jewish Christ alone can claim purity, and even he does so through the modality of mixture. My purpose has not been to reaffirm supersessionist logic but rather to expose it on two grounds: (1) its insufficiency as

If the distance between Jewish Christians and Gentile Christians is closed by the mediating presence of Christ, any distance between differing Gentile Christians is most certainly relativized. If Acts 15 can commend mutually transgressed boundaries of purity between Jew and Gentile, there is no excuse in perpetuating false lines of purity among varieties of Gentile Christians.

A Concluding Admonition to Life in Christ: Courage and Humility

The transgressed boundaries of Jew and Gentile in Acts 15 commend a similar step forward for Christians in a racially charged world. To take a similar step forward, though, like the Christians in and around Acts 15, virtuous postures and actions will have to take center stage. To conclude this essay, I would like to consider briefly the virtues of courage and humility that emanate from the account of the Jerusalem Council. First, I turn to courage.

While courage did not always come easily to Peter, the Jerusalem Council may be the defining moment of his new resolve in Christ coalescing with his zeal. Of course, Peter certainly demonstrated hints of courage in the past. After all, Luke 22 and John 18 both allude to Peter's bold swipe at the ear of an agent who had come to arrest Jesus in Gethsemane. Yet, Jesus's reaction indicates that Peter's zeal, while approaching courage, was something less, even if slightly. After all, Jesus disavowed and even undid Peter's act. Perhaps telling of the events still to come, Jesus's rejection of Peter's wielding of the sword indicates Peter's wrongheaded understanding even this late in the ministry of Jesus for, not long after, Peter outright denies Jesus, showing cowardice when his own life is on the line. However, the story does not end for Peter, who in Acts 10 again shows hints of courage, this time when told in a vision to go against his dietary and social training in the law; he was to go to the Gentiles and eat with and as them. Again, though, his apparent courage turned to cowardice when confronted by other Jewish Christians in Antioch over the same actions for which he had just stepped out boldly (see Gal 2:11–14).

So, considering the close proximity (apparently) of Paul's chastising of Peter for introducing distance from Gentile Christians on the basis of a conception of purity, one could not be blamed for being surprised that Peter did take a stand in Acts 15. Nevertheless, a stand he took, and a courageous one at that. In the face of the same detractors that he faced in Antioch, at the Council Peter passionately engages not only the issue at hand—whether Gentiles Christians should be circumcised—but also the theological rationale for the Pharisees' claims. Peter boldly goes where faithful old covenant Jews would never dare go before: he dismisses the claim of purity

---

grounds for purity and (2) its false appropriation.

of himself and fellow Jews, both past and present, on account of failed faithfulness. In its place, he posits the same grace of Christ and the same Spirit of Christ for Jews and Gentiles alike. Though being in the form of a Jew, Peter thought his identity nothing to be grasped. Instead he took the form of *the* servant, courageously stepping into the shoes of the Gentiles, refusing to consider himself anything on account of ethnic status. In this action, he embodies the life of Christ, who courageously suffered separation from the Father despite his own innocence, the same Christ who resisted the sword and undid its action in Gethsemane. Peter's courage was itself active participation in the courage of Christ.

In the same fell swoop, he demonstrates the humility of Christ, risking rejection by his own people through identifying with Gentiles. Not considering his status as a Jew in a Council consisting of apostles and elders who were Jews a thing to be grasped, Peter took the form of *the* servant, humbly stepping into the shoes of the Gentiles. He even denounced his status as something insignificant to his position in Christ. His courageous rejection of purity joined with his humble identification with those who were considered other. In this way, Peter demonstrated formation in the life of Christ—and participation therein—beyond anything he had done before, at least as recorded in the narrative.

In the way of racial reconciliation, this commendation of courage and humility in the person of Peter stands as witness to the courage and humility of Christ and as model for imitation (see Phil 2). The western world is not alone in its racial struggles, but the church in the USA stands at another crossroads, increasingly similar in intensity to that faced by the church in the 1960s. Fifty years after the Civil Rights Movement, the American church still stands largely in a position of functional segregation. The prospects for overcoming this require church leaders to be courageous in instituting new life in liturgical and even confessional form through an openness to ethnic, cultural, and linguistic mixture. This kind of courage requires a boldness to say that tradition is valuable but must also be living and capable of reinterpretation. There must be an interest in listening to articulations of past damage done through construals of purity. Courage dictates willingness to be told that one's imagination is stilted and, therefore, artificially limits the possibilities of life in Christ according to monolithic cultural-linguistic forms. This same courage requires the humility to acknowledge continued recalibration to life in Christ *together* and the humility to admit the riches of another church's traditions, especially those of foreign ethnicities. In this way, life in Christ will be active and healing, even as is the life of Christ in all times and places.

If, as Oliver O'Donovan suggests, the prophetic ministry of the church internally is to turn—in turn—to prophetic participation in the "redemption of the world,"[35] it must be attentive to the call to the "mulatto/a" within its walls. Segregation within the church has, not surprisingly, mirrored an inability to respond prophetically and theologically—especially from the pulpits of majority culture churches—to racial turmoil outside the church, instead functionally (if not explicitly, in some settings) reinforcing the church's role in the historic development of and continued commitment to "whiteness" as a move of power and control rather than servanthood and as a project that seeks the perfection of creation in the image of European identity. As in *Silence*, the body of Christ continues to be mediated. Until the majority church ceases to be the majority church (either through thoroughgoing fellowship with other traditions or through the entropy of time) the theological moorings of whiteness will remain intact.[36] The virtues of life in the Jewish Christ formed by and performed into Christ through the power of the Spirit of Christ have the sacrificial power to lead the church more fully into the mixed life of Christ *together*, as demonstrated by the courage and humility of the Peter of Acts 15, the Peter who finally internalized the beauty of mixture in Christ.[37]

35. See Oliver O'Donovan, *The Desire of the Nations: Rediscovering the Roots of Political Theology* (New York: Cambridge University Press, 1999) 188–89.

36. It is important to note that integration is not merely the inclusion of variety in the visual spectrum of pigment. After all, the structure of whiteness can and has sought to assimilate all, regardless of pigmentation. This is the polarity of Milbank above, wherein the structures remain according to "tradition" without the openness to new possibilities through openness of oneself or one's group to penetration and change at the hands of the other. Whiteness can assimilate all into its structure such that the change of pigmentation in demographics may change over time but the project of whiteness may remain behind. Conversely, structural change requires courage and humility that surpass the mere integration of new parts into the existing reality. To use the table metaphor, inviting others to the table but maintaining the head seats at the table or even the rules of table fellowship only reinforce the structure represented by the table. The nature of table fellowship must be fair game for change, so long as table fellowship always entails at its core participation in the Jewish body of Jesus Christ.

37. I am grateful to the organizers, attendees, and fellow presenters/responders at the North Park Symposium for a rich conversation and for feedback on the draft presentation of this essay. Both were invaluable. Thanks especially to Hauna Ondrey, my respondent who raised many good questions with which I had to wrestle. Thank you, also, to David Finkbeiner at Moody Bible Institute, who encouraged me to write this essay and to David Rim and Michael McDuffee, who not only read an earlier draft but also have been on a journey with me on the matters reflected in this essay. Years of conversing hopefully bear fruit here. Finally, thank you to Thomas Breimaier, James Spencer, Marcus Johnson, John Clark, and Craig Hendrickson, all of whom offered insight on an earlier draft. Any shortcomings in this essay belong to me while this wonderful chorus deserves the praise for helping me where this essay succeeds.

RESPONSE TO VARMA

Hauna Ondrey

In his paper, "Jews and Gentiles Together in Christ? The Jerusalem Council on Racial Reconciliation," Ashish Varma focuses on corporate identity in Christ, specifically as the church in Christ exists in the present racialized context of the United States. Acknowledging the ways race and racism have deformed the church, belying its unity and mutuality in Christ, Varma seeks to "reimagin[e] an ecclesial dynamic of being in Christ" that calls the church to courageous, humble, and mutual transgression of cultural boundaries.

Varma finds an exemplar for this mutual transgression in the Jerusalem Council of Acts 15, as Jewish Christians decided not to impose the entire Mosaic law on Gentile Christians, and, in turn, Gentile Christians submitted to several legal obligations. Varma's final conclusion is that, if Jewish Christians and Gentile Christians could be made one in Christ through mutual cultural accommodation rather than Gentile assimilation, contemporary Gentile-Gentile ethnic groups should certainly be able to do the same. Today's church should be marked by mutual accommodation between cultures rather than a dominant Euro-American church imposing its culturally-particular form of Christianity on other ethnic groups. The "particular call" of his paper "is to be agents of reconciliation as the church in a racialized sphere of existence and to be so virtuously." The virtues he highlights are courage and humility for mutuality: "In other words, both cultures engage in a cultural transgression that does not do violence to the other but also does not leave their own culture unchanged."

First and foremost, I want to thank Varma for asking what union with Christ means *corporately* and pressing its specific meaning for the American church in its current racialized context. I want to affirm Varma's contemporary argument, which I read as the primary point of his work: that virtuous corporate being-in-Christ—in *this* time and *this* place—requires that the white church recognize and confess its complicity in the racial sins of the United States and the more and less subtle ways white supremacy continues to set the norms within the church. Certainly, diversity in the American church must be more than either unilateral imposition of a dominant culture on marginalized cultures or permission to enter into a fully-established cultural form of Christianity. Rather, it requires adaptation, mutuality, and a re-thinking of which aspects of Christian thought and practice are culturally rather than biblically determined.

At the end of his paper, Varma emphasizes the importance of listening—of healing and expanding the imagination through hearing the full body of Christ and being changed in this encounter. For this reason, I'm conscious of some irony in moving from the above points of affirmation into critique. In many contexts, I should stop here and simply listen. Given the dialogical purpose of our exchange, however, I offer a few questions toward, I hope, strengthening Varma's final, contem-porary aim, which is critically needed for the church's obedience and witness today.

My primary question is whether the Jerusalem Council does in fact serve the contemporary aim to which Varma puts it. Certainly, it does in the most basic sense, insofar as Acts 15 affirms the trans-ethnicity of communal identity in Christ, providing conciliar deliberation and declaration of what we find elsewhere in New Testament texts: that in Christ there is no longer Jew or Greek (Gal 3:28); that Christ has broken down the dividing wall between Jew and Gentile to create a new, single humanity (Eph 2:14–16); and that God in Christ has given us the ministry of rec-onciliation (2 Cor 5:18). In this way, Acts 15 supports Varma's point that there is no ethnic or cultural hierarchy in Christ, and any circumscription of Christianity within a single ethnic group violates this foundational apostolic decision and so is a less-than-virtuous ecclesial expression of being in Christ.

Yet I wonder whether pressing the Jerusalem Council as an exemplar beyond this basic, albeit significant, point may actually work against the conclusion Varma wishes to reach. Varma's contemporary application depends upon an interpretation of the council's decision as affirming a mutual transgression of boundaries: on the one hand, that of the established Jewish Christian community in relativizing the Mosaic law in reference to the Gentile believers—what Varma calls Peter's "coura-geous rejection of purity"; and on the other, of the Gentile believers who "sacri-ficed their freedom in Christ (e.g., eating food offered to idols) by following Jewish custom"[1] as an expression of reciprocal compromise. But is this the most adequate reading of the council?

What, when considered in closer detail, was the nature of the conciliar decision in Acts 15? What, in Jacob Neusner's striking phrase, was the "final solution to the

---

1. Varma portrays such reciprocal compromise as standing in contrast to two alternative typologies that he draws from the work of Brian Bantum: James Cone's relocation of Christ to the oppressed (which, in Varma's application, would shift the presence of Christ from Jewish to Gentile Christians) and John Milbank's version of Radical Orthodoxy, characterized by Bantum as "colonial" (which, in Varma's application, would require Gentiles to become Jews in order to be Christian).

Gentile problem"?[2] Richard Bauckham argues for a reading of James's speech in Acts 15:13–21, and consequent prohibitions extended in Acts 15:28–29, not as *transgression* of boundaries for Jewish Christians but as the *imposition* of Mosaic moral boundaries on Gentile believers, consistent with obligations imposed on resident aliens in Lev 17 and 18 (Lev 17:8, 10/12, 13; 18:26).[3] James's exegesis of the prophetic texts furnishes his conclusion that Gentiles *qua* Gentiles would enter the eschatological people of God; his qualification of this claim with requisite prohibitions is not motivated by concern for Jew-Gentile table fellowship but his reading of Torah:

> The four prohibitions of the decree are not simply a pragmatic compromise, dealing with the problem of table fellowship in a context where it is not debatable that Gentile Christians do not have to keep the Law. In the thinking of those who formulated them, the same exegetical case which demonstrates conclusively that Gentile Christians do not have to keep the Law also shows that they do have to observe these four principles.[4]

The concern here is not cultic or ethnic impurity but ethical impurity,[5] namely, idolatry, sexual immorality, and taking innocent life, "concrete practices which were indeed widespread in non-Jewish societies and regarded by Jews not as minor deviations but as major offences rendering Gentile society as a whole iniquitous and abhorrent to God."[6] So the prohibitions of Acts 15:28–19 (cf. 15:19–20) correspond to these points of Gentile immorality—and obedience to these points of the Mosaic law constitutes the very purification Peter declares (Acts 15:9).[7]

2. Jacob Neusner, "What, Exactly, Is Israel's Gentile Problem? Rabbinic Perspectives on Galatians 2," in *The Missions of James, Peter, and Paul: Tensions in Early Christianity*, edited by Bruce Chilton and Craig Evans, NovTSup 115 (Boston: Brill, 2005) 276.

3. Richard Bauckham, "James and the Jerusalem Church," in *The Book of Acts in Its Palestinian Setting*, edited by Richard Bauckham, 415–80, vol. 4 of *The Book of Acts in Its First Century Setting*, edited by Bruce W. Winter (Grand Rapids: Eerdmans, 1995) see esp. 452–67.

4. Ibid., 462. See also Cornelis Bennema, "The Ethnic Conflict in Early Christianity: An Appraisal of Bauckham's Proposal on the Antioch Crisis and the Jerusalem Council," *JETS* 56.4 (2013) 753–63.

5. Varma's equivocal use of "purity" could benefit from clarification. He begins speaking of purity in terms of cultic purity, then shifts to ethnic purity when bringing in Bantum's argument, then seems to reference ethical purity in Peter's admission that "even pre-Christian Judaism failed the purity test" through the inability to obey the entire law. How these three—ritual/cultic purity, ethical purity, and ethnic purity—relate, and which he has in mind at key points in his argument makes a difference and could be helpfully clarified. When Varma commends Peter's "courageous rejection of purity," which purity is in view? My assumption is that ritual purity is intended rather than ethical purity. Clearly ethnic purity is bound up in ritual purity, but Varma does not clearly specify how.

6. Richard Bauckham, "James, Peter, and the Gentiles," in *The Missions of James, Peter, and Paul: Tensions in Early Christianity*, edited by Bruce Chilton and Craig Evans, NovTSup 115 (Boston: Brill, 2005) 97.

7. Ibid., 120: "If God has indeed, as Peter claims, 'purified their [the Gentiles'] hearts by faith,' these are the impurities—the typical Gentile sins—from which they are henceforth to be pure."

Therefore, while the Gentiles were admitted to the Christian church as Gentiles and not as Jews, they were nevertheless admitted on the terms of God's revelation to Israel, as the righteous Gentiles of the Mosaic law. The apostolic decree in Acts 15 "deals with the question of Gentile Christians in a way which by no means sets aside the authority of the law of Moses, but fully upholds it, by requiring of Gentile Christians obedience to the four commandments which the Law itself imposes on them."[8] If the council's decision in Acts 15 is not mutual transgression of boundaries, as Varma reads it, but rather extension of ethical boundaries on Gentile believers in accordance with the Law of Moses, does it still provide an exemplar for today's racialized church in the way he wishes, or does it rather underscore the danger of casting a dominant culture as parallel to Israel?

Though after surveying Willie Jennings' account of the misappropriation of Old Testament Israelite identity by, in the example he offers, Iberian colonizers, Varma clarifies that it is not his goal to perpetuate the misappropriation; instead he then shifts to an argument from greater to lesser: if Jew-Gentile, then certainly Gentile-Gentile. But the majority of his paper and the core of his argument seem rather to assume this very analogy. He speaks, for example of the "paradigmatic parallel to the early modern and modern racialization of the church and Western culture" and names "the status quo of the Euro-American church as the relative equivalent of the Jewish church of the Jerusalem Council," among other examples.[9]

I have no special knowledge of the complex interpretive issues involved in Acts 15—the particularities of Second Temple Judaism or contemporary debates around reconstructing the chronology between Acts and Galatians. But I do know something of the effective history of misappropriations of Israel's identity as God's chosen people—whether by crusaders, conquistadors, or Puritans—as well as denials of Jewish ethnic particularity, and I want to be appropriately cautious about both. Bauckham's reading, whereby Mosaic ethics are extended to Gentiles, reminds us that the apostolic church did not set aside the particularity of God's revelation to Old Testament Israel. Rather, this revelation retained normativity, setting the terms not

8. Bauckham, "James and the Jerusalem Church," 463.

9. For example: "That is, did the Gentile debt of gratitude toward Jewish Christians translate into cultural and liturgical conformity to Jewish expression of the faith? The question illuminates the one with which Christians in North America contend amid the racially charged legacy of the American church side-by-side with the perpetuation of a European form of the faith." Also, "In other words, taking each setting in order moving from Acts to the world of this essay, (1) the church would be a continuous operation of OT Jewish practice into which the Gentiles of Antioch would be welcome, (2) the Spanish-speaking congregation would be welcome to join the pure orthodoxy of the Augustinian tradition of Milbank's vision of the Catholic church, and (3) the minority church is welcome to fellowship with the white church as the latter continues its liturgical styles, dogmatic construals, and culturally prophetic sermons pertaining to the questions, concerns, and life of the majority community."

only for Jews but also Gentiles. Varma seems to overlook this when he speaks of a Jewish "expression of the faith" that Gentile Christians may or may not conform to:

> While the Gentiles certainly owed at least a debt of gratitude to their Jewish brothers and sisters in Christ for their own theological and ethnic heritage that prepared the way for Jesus Christ, the question before the apostles was one of ongoing Jew-Gentile dynamics in the church. That is, did the Gentile debt of gratitude toward Jewish Christians translate into cultural and liturgical conformity to Jewish expression of the faith?

There is a danger here of implying that there is a fixed, accessible body of the faith that existed prior to its Jewish expression, such that both Jewish and Gentile expressions of the faith represent parallel second party appropriations of it. But this is simply not the case. Jewish expression of the faith is neither historically nor theologically speaking a second party appropriation. It is, on the basis of election, the primary location of divine revelation such that all subsequent expressions of the faith involve the joining of others to an inherently Jewish story. God's revelation of himself to Israel is not merely an interim preparation but a relationship of ongoing dependence. As Paul says to the Gentile Christians in Rome, "But if some of the branches were broken off, and you, a wild olive shoot, were grafted in their place to share the rich root of the olive tree, do not boast over the branches. If you do boast, remember that it is not you that support the root, but the root that supports you" (Rom 11:17–18). God's revelation to Old Testament Israel is unavoidably particular and therefore inevitably culturally-bound. This presents contemporary Christians with work to do, but it does not negate its foundational significance.

And this brings me to my final question: Just so, are parts of a historically mediated, and therefore likewise unavoidably culturally-bound, catholic tradition normative even within today's trans-ethnic church? Just as God chose to work in the particularities of Israel's history, God has chosen to reveal himself in the particularities of the Christian church, however dissatisfying this may be at times. What, if anything, belongs to a common Christian tradition? Are, for instance, any privileged interpretations of Scripture worked out within the patristic church, even if, necessarily, in the thought-forms of the patristic mind?

I would like to see Varma develop more fully his constructive proposal. He speaks generally regarding the need to renegotiate "the cultural, conceptual, and linguistic construals of dogmatic and liturgical encounter with Christ"; calling for "instituting new life in liturgical and even confessional form through an openness to ethnic, cultural, and linguistic mixture." It would be helpful for him to populate this general proposal with concrete examples, addressing as well the means by which one may gain access to apostolic content apart from the tradition that has mediated it across particular times and spaces, with all the moral complexity this entails.

I hope some of these questions can help facilitate Varma's desired end: the church as virtuous agents of reconciliation in Christ.

LETTING THE MUSIC PLAY (MATTHEW 22:34–40)

Cynthia Peters Anderson

One of my favorite seminary theology professors liked to tell a story about teaching a required undergraduate religion class in which an exasperated freshman broke into the conversation, rolled his eyes and asked, "So how is all this stuff going to help me sell more tacos?"[1] In a utilitarian culture, it is the question that gets asked a thousand ways—with the implication that any knowledge or activity is valuable or relevant only if it is perceived to be useful. And those of us in the church can bristle in the face of such a utilitarian question. So, let me say, I am not here to talk about how the idea of participation in the life of God can help us sell tacos—though I love tacos and I am genuinely glad they are widely available. But I do come before you as someone who every Sunday stands in front of a congregation filled with people who are asking—how does all this stuff we are talking about impact my life? We have wondered in our discussions about how to translate this into the life of the church so that the idea of participating in the life of God is, as Julie Canlis said in one of our symposium sessions, not some boneless chicken but rather takes on form and flesh in the lives of people.

I am aware that every Sunday as I look out on the faces in the church, people are asking themselves: How does this talk about God matter when I will wake up tomorrow to a chorus of people who tell me I am never enough no matter what I do? Or when I turn on the news and I feel absolutely helpless to do anything about it? Or how does it matter, when I wake up to another day of dealing with disappointments, overwork, chronic illness? How does this talk about God impact my life at 3:00 a.m. when I feel so alone I ask myself if any of it really matters? Those are the questions rumbling not far beneath the surface. We have spent our symposium discussions immersed in this idea of participation and its implications—and I believe passionately that it provides a way of seeing God and our lives that infuses us with meaning, purpose, and power to engage in God's mission in the world. But every day I ask: how do I talk to people who do not spend their days immersed in study about this

---

1. My thanks to Dr. D. Stephen Long for sharing this story in a systematic theology class while I was in seminary.

and help them catch a glimpse of what it might mean to see God, themselves, and the world differently?

And where I have learned to start is where they start—their deepest fears, their most desperate needs and longings and questions. Questions about whether they are seen, loved, valued—about if or how their lives matter. They live in a world that tells them alternately that they are entitled to everything, but they deserve nothing—that they are only as good as their purchasing power and their last performance review—that there is always someone chasing them, trying to get ahead of them or take what matters most. So, I am going to start at that point of need because I think it is where Jesus starts.

As I was thinking about what scriptural text we might reflect on, the verses that came to me contain a conversation between Jesus and a Pharisee, who, trying to trap Jesus, asks for the greatest of all the laws. Jesus responds that what really sums it all up is this: wholeheartedly love God and love your neighbors as yourself. And the good news throughout the gospels is that Jesus repeatedly tells us, look, I will actually make it possible for you to be free and enabled for wholehearted love of God, yourselves, and your neighbors—because that is God's intended purpose for you. But over and over, Jesus walks into all these distorted images of who God is—and with them distorted images of who humans are—that keep people in captivity. And we still have them. Friends, as I work with people every day, I am still surprised at how many operate out of an image of God as a stern, removed taskmaster whose primary interest in us is judgment and getting us to toe some line or getting us on the right side of some ledger in the sky. For others, God has been watered down to a benevolent, generalized "spirit" whose only interest is in making us feel good about ourselves without making us uncomfortable. The first god is transcendent without loving, immanent involvement and the second god is locked in our immanence with no transcendent power to transform anything—and can easily be manipulated to bless anything in our self-interest.

That is complicated enough, but I think there is something even more deeply distorted in our image of God that impairs our ability to love God wholeheartedly: it is our disbelief that God loves us wholeheartedly and with that our inability to see ourselves rightly as those who are in the position of receiving that love—of allowing it to simply wash over us and flow through us, recognizing that there is nothing we can do that will make God love us less or love us more. This idea of a God who loves wholeheartedly in extravagant self-giving as a gift—and this idea of ourselves as primarily recipients of that love—radically challenges us and our culture. We live in a society that pushes performance, individualism, self-making, and self-control. The idea that we are simply and profoundly recipients of God's wholehearted love in Jesus Christ and that our response is to receive it—is deeply foreign and even offensive to more of us than we want to acknowledge. It really is. It undoes everything we ordinarily build our lives around.

One of my favorite quotes is from Cyril of Alexandria, who said that "the mystery of Christ runs the risk of being disbelieved precisely because it is so incredibly wonderful."[2] That is still true. We have somehow shrunken the gospel down to an intellectual assent to doctrine, or a formula for getting from here to heaven, rather than helping people step into a relationship with a living Person who invites them into a whole new way of being human—from now through to eternity. I have become convinced that the problem for most people is not that we think too highly of ourselves—but that we do not see the beauty and fullness and goodness of own humanity in Christ. So, we live disconnected from God, ourselves, and other people. We easily fall prey to the messages that we must earn, perform, and consume our way into value and that we are in competition for scarce goods. It is not a recipe for wholeheartedly loving our neighbors.

Here is where I think that this conception of participation can be so life-giving. It opens us up to see the sweep—Ben Blackwell called it the arc—of God's story in a different way. It helps us see this astonishingly beautiful, good, gracious, self-giving God who just persistently, extravagantly loves us. God loves us in creating us to be in relationship with God and one another. God loves us when we refuse this relationship. God loves us so extravagantly that God comes fully into our humanness in order to draw us into the life of God by destroying sin and death and anything else that could separate us from the life of God. And God loves us in breathing into us the gift of the Holy Spirit to dwell in us and to move through us—to make our lives gifts to the world. This idea that we are created and redeemed and restored to participate in the life of God is astonishingly good news and some of our people in the church have never really heard it. That understanding has the ability to shift not only our ideas about who God is, but also to reorient our ideas about who we are and who are neighbors are, to see our lives and the world within a framework in which our human partnership with God really matters. We so want the church to have impact, to be missional, to stand in countercultural ways against the oppressive and toxic structures that harm so many. But we often lose sight of the reality that our ability to be a force for change is directly an outflow of our ability first to be wholeheartedly loved by God and to see our lives as a response to that love.

Theologians and poets have long used music as an analogy for God's movement in our lives. For me, this idea of participation is like music. Many Sundays we listen

---

2. Cyril of Alexandria, *On the Unity of Christ*, translated by John McGuckin (Crestwood, NY: St. Vladimir's Seminary Press, 1995) 61

to and sing a variety of music, and, much of the time, I look out across the congregation and we are barely moving our mouths. We are singing the notes—but we have not really entered the music. We are moving through the technique, but something is missing. But then there are these moments when something happens and somehow the music moves through the room and enters people and we find ourselves swept up in something larger than ourselves. The music is playing not outside of us—but in us and through us and we become connected in ways that are so grace-filled and powerful—we even find ourselves moving in new ways. Participation is like that—God invites us to be drawn into the music of God's life. If we truly want to live in more wholehearted love of God, ourselves, and our neighbors—then we have to let the wholehearted love of God play us—play in us and through us.

The idea of participation in the life of God helps us to see more clearly that God in Jesus Christ comes down so that we can hear and become part of the music of God's loving, redeeming grace that is transforming the world. We cannot just learn about it. We must be caught up in it. Through the power of the Holy Spirit, we have to be caught up in the rhythms of that grace, moved by the melody of that love, swept up in joyfully sharing it with others. Are we allowing Jesus' invitation to participate in the fullness of God's life play us—to permeate every part of our hearts and minds and spirits and actions? That is what it means wholeheartedly to love God, and in loving God to love ourselves and our neighbors into God's transformation of the world through Jesus Christ.

ANNOTATED BIBLIOGRAPHY
ON PARTICIPATION IN AND WITH CHRIST

Anderson, Cynthia Peters. *Reclaiming Participation: Christ as God's Life for All*. Minneapolis: Fortress, 2014. Anderson seeks to reclaim participation in Christ as the heart of the gospel and the focus of the transformation of human life. She does so by exploring and brining into dialog the theologies of Cyril of Alexandria, Karl Barth, and Hans Urs von Balthasar.

Athanasius, *On the Incarnation*. In this classic text of Christian theology, the incarnation is the essential action of God in breaking the bondage of humanity to sin and death. This is conceived more broadly than simply atonement, with Christ the creating Word understood as the one able to re-create humankind through union with himself. Multiple editions are available, some online.

Baker, Mary Patton. *Participation in Christ and Eucharistic Formation: John Calvin and the Theodrama of the Lord's Supper*. Milton Keynes: Paternoster, 2015. Baker argues that the Lord's Supper is an embodied dramatic realization of union with Christ. She brings together Calvin's theology of the Supper with Vanhoozer's proposal that Christian doctrine is direction for the church's participation in the drama of redemption, suggesting that rightly approached the Supper is a powerful means of spiritual formation.

Bantum, Brian. *Redeeming Mulatto: A Theology of Race and Christian Hybridity*. Waco, TX: Baylor University Press, 2016. Bantum traces the dynamics of "mixed" Christology, in which, as the one who is both human and divine, Jesus occupies an in-between existence. His Mulatto identity refuses existing racial polarities and hierarchies, giving us the gift of seeing ourselves as richly transformed people living in him between "purities," regardless of socially conceived racial boundaries.

Billings, J. Todd. *Calvin, Participation and the Gift: The Activity of Believers in Union with Christ*. Oxford: Oxford University Press, 2009. This is a careful scholarly work, focused on the place of union with Christ in Calvin's soteriology. The criticisms made of Calvin in Radical Orthodoxy and much recent Gift theology are refuted, with an account offered of the positive role performed for Calvin by human reciprocity in response to divine gift.

———. *Union with Christ: Reframing Theology and Ministry for the Church*. Grand Rapids: Baker Academic, 2011. As the title suggests, this volume contains various essays explicating the significance of union with Christ for the life of the church. Billings begins with adoption, a theme often neglected when considering the benefits that flow from union with Christ and conceptualizing appropriate patterns of life in Christ. The subsequent essays deal with sin, communion with God in Christ, justice, and ministry.

Blackwell, Ben C. *Christosis: Engaging Paul's Soteriology with his Patristic Interpreters*. Grand Rapids: Eerdmans, 2016. Writing in the context of recent renewed interest in theosis, Blackwell goes to the exegetical roots of the doctrine by exploring Irenaeus and Cyril of Alexandria's interpretations of Paul's soteriology. As well as offering careful historical analysis, Blackwell also assesses their relevance for contemporary Pauline interpretation. This volume is a revised edition of an earlier (2011) Mohr Siebeck publication.

Boakye, Andrew, "Inhabiting the 'Resurrectiform' God: Death and Life as Theological Headline in Paul." *Expository Times* 128.2 (2016) 53–62. This article explores death and resurrection in Paul, specifically in 2 Corinthians, suggesting that both must be held in tandem with neither regarded as less important than the other. Participation in Christ should be viewed not only in terms of participation in his death but also in new life through his resurrection, new life which is consummated at the eschaton.

Bonhoeffer, Dietrich. *Discipleship*. Vol. 4 of *Dietrich Bonhoeffer Works*. Translated by Barbara Green and Reinhard Krauss. Minneapolis: Augsburg Fortress, 2001. Bonhoeffer's classic *Nachfolge*, previously translated as *The Cost of Discipleship*, attacks cheap grace and expounds the meaning of discipleship in terms of costly participation in Christ.

Braaten, Carl and Robert Jenson eds. *"Union with Christ" The New Finnish Interpretation of Luther*. Grand Rapids: Eerdmans, 1998. This important work is one of the main statements in English of the controversial Finnish perspective on Luther. Its seven essays correct anachronistic readings of Luther and portray justification not only in forensic terms, but also as involving the transformation of the believer through union with Christ.

Burger, Hans. *Being in Christ: A Biblical and Systematic Investigation in a Reformed Perspective*. Eugene, OR: Wipf & Stock, 2009. This is the most thorough contemporary, constructive account of union with Christ. Rather than treating the biblical and theological dimensions of the topic as two completely different steps, Burger moves between the two. He also explores some of the most important reflections on union with Christ in the history of the Reformed tradition in order to employ them as resources for his own analysis of "Being in Christ."

Campbell, Constantine R. *Paul and Union with Christ: An Exegetical and Theological Study*. Grand Rapids: Zondervan, 2012. Campbell makes careful study of each deployment of the expression "in Christ" in Paul and of the other prepositional expressions that link salvation to some kind of union with him. This careful and important work of detailed grammatical exegesis is oriented towards constructive theological goals.

Canlis, Julie. *Calvin's Ladder: A Spiritual Theology of Ascent and Ascension*. Grand Rapids: Eerdmans, 2010. In an act of theological retrieval, Canlis offers rich analysis of union with Christ in Calvin's theology. The centrality of the theme in early Christian spirituality is explored, especially in Irenaeus, as the backdrop to Calvin's re-working of it as vital to his own theological vision. Particular emphasis is placed on union with Christ as the mode by which believers are drawn towards triune participation.

———. *A Theology of the Ordinary*. Wenatchee, WA: Godspeed, 2017. Writing at a popular level, Canlis seeks to provide a pastoral counter balance to popular Christian emphasis on the extraordinary and the radical. Canlis uses three stories modeled on the Trinity to demonstrate how Christian participation in the Trinity should bring attention to the holiness of everyday, ordinary life.

Chester, Stephen J. *Reading Paul with the Reformers: Reconciling Old and New Perspectives*. Grand Rapids: Eerdmans, 2017. Chester seeks to challenge widespread misconceptions about the Reformers' interpretation of Paul. In the process he asserts the centrality of union with Christ to the doctrines of justification developed by both Luther and Calvin and explores the continuing relevance of this for contemporary Pauline interpretation.

Despotis, Athanasios, ed. *Participation, Justification and Conversion: Eastern Orthodox Interpretation of Paul and the Debate between Old and New Perspectives on Paul.* WUNT 2.442. Tübingen: Mohr Siebeck, 2017. This important collection of scholarly essays explores the similarities and differences between various Orthodox and various New Perspective approaches to Paul, with special attention paid to participation in Christ.

Eastman, Susan Grove. *Paul and the Person: Reframing Paul's Anthropology.* Grand Rapids: Eerdmans, 2017. An exploration of Paul's understanding of the human person/self, that brings his thought into dialog with the Stoic philosopher Epictetus and with contemporary scientific theories of human development. Eastman argues that the self is intersubjective, so that relationality presupposes individuality and not vice versa. Participation is therefore a central dimension of what it means to be human.

Fairbairn, Don. *Life in the Trinity.* Downers Grove, IL: IVP Academic, 2009. This introductory work seeks to understand the relationship between God the Father and God the Son in the context of the life and theology of the early church. It then seeks to expound upon how Christians enter through participation in Christ into this relationship between the Father and the Son.

Fesko, J. V. *Beyond Calvin: Union with Christ and Justification in Early Modern Reformed Theology (1517–1700).* Göttingen: Vandenhoeck & Ruprecht, 2012. This study looks specifically at the development of union with Christ in the Reformed tradition after Calvin, specifically Reformed Orthodoxy. It examines various views of the order of salvation to demonstrate that a strong emphasis on it and a strong emphasis on union with Christ coexist within Reformed Orthodoxy.

Finlan, Stephen. "Can We Speak of Theosis in Paul?" In *Partakers of the Divine Nature: The History and Development of Deification in the Christian Traditions*, edited by Michael J. Christensen and Jeffery A. Wittung, 68–80. Grand Rapids: Baker Academic, 2007. Finlan argues that there is a theology of theosis in Paul, which is best understood in light of Paul's emphasis on the spiritual and glorious resurrection body. Recognizing potential challenges raised by exegetes like Tom Wright, Finlan interprets several Pauline passages as supporting theosis of the spiritual body.

Finlan, Stephen, and Vladimir Kharlamov, eds. *Theosis: Deification in Christian Theology: Volume 1.* Princeton Theological Monograph Series 52. Eugene, OR: Pickwick, 2006. This first of two volumes of essays (see under Kharlamov for the second volume) provides a broad overview of the concept of theosis. Most of the articles focus on deification within the theology of early Christian thinkers, but some also give attention to theosis as a concept within scripture itself and its pre-Christian roots.

Flogaus, Reinhard. *Theosis bei Palamas und Luther: Ein Beitrag zum ökumenischen Gespräch.* Göttingen: Vandenhoeck & Ruprecht, 1997. A study by the most thorough German critic of the Finnish perspective that compares Luther's position on theosis with that of Gregory Palamas, a key figure from the Orthodox tradition. Palamas famously distinguished between God's essence and God's energies, considering participation in Christ to unite believers with the latter. Flogaus is critical of the Finns' view of Luther's ontology and the part played in their perspective by the concept of substance.

Garcia, Mark A. *Life in Christ: Union with Christ and Twofold Grace in Calvin's Theology.* Paternoster: Studies in Christian History and Thought. Eugene, OR: Wipf & Stock, 2008. Garcia argues that union with Christ is essential in Calvin's soteriology to both justification and sanctification. He also demonstrates the crucial role played in Calvin's understanding of union with Christ by the Holy Spirit and offers an account of Calvin's engagement in the Osiander controversy.

Ghiselli, Anja, Kari Kopperi and Rainer Vinke, eds. *Luther und Ontologie: Das Sein Christi im Glauben als strukturierendes Prinzip der Theologie Luthers.* Helsinki and Erlangen: Schriften der Luther-Agricola-Gesellschaft, 1993. The third of three collections of essays in German that offer evaluations by European scholars of the Finnish perspective on Luther, especially of the work of Mannermaa. This volume focuses on issues of ontology.

Gorman, Michael J. *Cruciformity: Paul's Narrative Spirituality of the Cross.* Grand Rapids: Eerdmans, 2001. An exploration of Paul's spirituality of cross-shaped participation in Christ, focusing on the central Pauline themes of faith, hope, love, and power, and on their significance for Pauline communities and for the church today.

———. *Inhabiting the Cruciform God: Kenosis, Justification, and Theosis in Paul's Narrative Soteriology.* Grand Rapids: Eerdmans, 2009. A study of Paul's understanding of salvation as justification by co-crucifixion with Christ, which is inherently participatory and transformative and which can be properly described as theosis, or deification.

———. *The Death of the Messiah and the Birth of the New Covenant: A (not so) New Model of the Atonement.* Eugene, OR: Cascade, 2014. Gorman suggests that not enough attention has been given to understanding the atonement as inaugurating a new covenant people living in obedience to God. Focusing on what the atonement does rather than how the atonement works, Gorman argues for the participation in Christ of a new covenant people as the goal towards which atonement is directed.

———. *Becoming the Gospel: Paul, Participation, and Mission.* Grand Rapids: Eerdmans, 2015. A detailed exegetical study of participation in Christ in Paul's letters in light of missional hermeneutics. Gorman calls on Christians not simply to believe the gospel but to become the gospel and so participate in the life and mission of God.

Hastings, Ross. *Missional God, Missional Church: Hope for Re-evangelizing the West.* Downers Grove, IL: IVP Academic, 2012. A study of the church's participation (which is termed theosis) in the life and mission of God. This involves both discovering and disseminating shalom, a key concept understood through the lens of the Gospel of John.

Hays, Richard B. *The Moral Vision of the New Testament: Community, Cross, New Creation; A Contemporary Introduction to New Testament Ethics.* San Francisco: HarperCollins, 1996. This landmark study includes a brief but classic treatment (chap. 1, pp. 16–59) of Paul's cross-shaped "ethic."

———. "What is Real Participation?" In *Redefining First-Century Jewish and Christian Identities: Essays in Honor of Ed Parish Sanders,* edited by Fabian E. Udoh et al. 336–51. University of Notre Dame Press, 2008. Using E.P. Sanders' *Paul and Palestinian Judaism* as a starting point, Hays moves beyond Sanders' basic argument that Paul's theology is centered on participation rather than justification, into an actual definition of participation. He proposes four models for understanding participation in Paul: as family, as political or military solidarity, in the *ekklesia,* and living within the story of Christ.

Heath, Jane M.F. *Paul's Visual Piety: The Metamorphosis of the Beholder.* Oxford: Oxford University Press, 2013. Heath argues that Pauline studies has a disciplinary blind spot, understanding faith too exclusively in relation to an interior vision of the glorious 'face' of God. Focusing on 2 Cor 3:18, she asserts that, for Paul, the transformation of the believer is in fact strongly connected to a this-worldly visual piety that builds up faith.

Hooker, Morna D. *From Adam to Christ: Essays on Paul.* Cambridge: Cambridge University Press, 1990. This volume includes significant essays exploring texts in Paul that contain the motif of "interchange" (Christ identifies with the human condition that we might be identified with his). Hooker's exegetical re-working of this patristic motif leads to the assertion of a central place for participation in Paul's soteriology.

Horton, Michael. "Atonement and Ascension." In *Locating Atonement: Explorations in Constructive Dogmatics*, edited by Oliver D. Crisp and Fred Sanders, 226–50. Grand Rapids: Zondervan, 2015. Horton seeks to correct theologies that view the Ascension as separate event from the Atonement. He uses the contrasting theologies of Irenaeus and Origen, viewed from the perspective of the Reformers, as resources for the development of a Protestant account of Ascension as a form of deification.

Jenson, Robert W. *Systematic Theology: Volume 1: The Triune God.* Oxford: Oxford University Press, 1997. Using a method and outline that differs slightly from traditional systematic approaches, Jenson seeks to construct a theology that avoids the pitfalls of confessionalism. The final section of this work focuses on the human being's part in God. It examines participation in the Triune God through the lens of theological epistemology—the knowability of God and the relation that holds to our participation in God.

Johnson, Marcus. "Luther and Calvin on Union with Christ." *Fides et Historia* 39 (2007) 59–77. This concise article does an excellent job of demonstrating the significance of union with Christ for the two greatest theologians of the Protestant Reformation. Johnson explores some of the metaphors that Luther and Calvin use and shows how they function in each Reformer's theology. He reaches the conclusion that for both union with Christ is the core soteriological truth from which all the blessings of salvation flow.

———. *One with Christ: An Evangelical Theology of Salvation.* Wheaton: Crossway, 2013. In this work, Johnson seeks to fill a perceived gap in Evangelical scholarship and articulation of the gospel. His goal is to demonstrate that the crucial role of union with Christ in salvation has been neglected in Evangelical theology and to restore it to its proper place.

Kärkkäinen, Veli-Matti. *One with God: Salvation as Deification and Justification.* Collegeville, MN: Liturgical, 2004. This important work seeks to put both western theologies of justification and eastern theologies of deification into the framework of a larger conversation about the nature of salvation itself. A higher degree of compatibility between west and east is demonstrated than is often thought and the dangers of a limited soteriology that does not include deification are highlighted.

Kharlamov, Vladimir, ed. *Theosis: Deification in Christian Theology: Volume Two.* Princeton Theological Monograph Series 156. Eugene, OR: Pickwick, 2011. This second of two volumes of essays (see under Finlan for the first volume) responds to the recent trend in theological scholarship to give more attention to theosis. Seeking to enrich the conversation, the essays included provide nuanced and varied perspectives on deification as a theological concept.

Laird, Martin. *Gregory of Nyssa and the Grasp of Faith: Union, Knowledge, and Divine Presence.* Oxford: Oxford University Press, 2004. For Gregory, faith played a central role in his understanding of union with the divine. This study explores that role, arguing that through apophatic ascent the believer is united with God the Word who then speaks in the deeds and words of the believer.

Lehmkühler, Karsten. *Inhabitatio: Die Einwohnung Gottes im Menschen. Forschungen zur systematischen und ökumenischen Theologie 104.* Göttingen: Vandenhoeck & Ruprecht, 2004. This study investigates in great detail the theme of divine inhabitation of human lives. It is shown to have been important not only in Roman Catholic and Orthodox doctrine but also in the history of Lutheranism.

Letham, Robert. *Union with Christ: In Scripture, History, and Theology.* Phillipsburg, NJ: Presbyterian and Reformed, 2011. This useful and accessible volume provides a good entry point into the Reformed doctrine of union with Christ and its various textual sources in Scripture and tradition.

Macaskill, Grant. *Union with Christ in the New Testament.* Oxford: Oxford University Press, 2013. Macaskill affirms the doctrine of union with Christ in its Reformed articulations, demonstrating their continuity with Patristic accounts, before reading across the New Testament texts to identify the biblical basis of the doctrine. This book is the broadest and most important recent study of union with Christ in the biblical material itself. A paperback edition will be published in 2018.

Mannermaa, Tuomo. *Christ Present in Faith: Luther's View of Justification.* Minneapolis: Fortress, 2005. In this English translation of one of the foundational works of the Finnish perspective on Luther, Mannermaa articulates a view of Luther's theology that regards union with Christ through faith as essential to justification. The believer participates in Christ in a very real way in justification and is transformed by this participation.

———. *Two Kinds of Love: Martin Luther's Religious World.* Minneapolis: Fortress, 2010. In this second of his significant works translated into English, Mannermaa further develops his emphasis on the effective dimension of Luther's account of justification. Mannermaa argues that Luther must be understood not only as a theologian of faith but also as one of love and that the Heidelberg Disputation must be accorded a significant place in our understanding of Luther's theology.

Mannermaa, Tuomo, Anja Ghiselli, Simo Peura, eds. *Thesaurus Lutheri: Auf der Suche nach neuen Paradigmen der Luther-Forschung: Referate des Luther-Symposiums in Finnland, 11.-12. November 1986.* Helsinki: Finnische Theologische Literaturgesellschaft, 1987. The first and most general of three collections of essays in German that offer evaluations by European scholars of the Finnish perspective on Luther, especially the work of Mannermaa.

Marshall, Bruce. "Justification as Declaration and Deification." *International Journal of Systematic Theology* 4.1 (2002) 1–17. Marshall proposes a functional model for understanding how justification might include not simply a forensic declaration but also include deification – a transformative justification. Marshall uses Luther himself as an example of how these two views, though often seen as contradictory, may coexist.

Nikkanen, Markus. "Participation in Christ: Paul and Pre-Pauline Eucharistic Tradition." PhD Diss., University of Aberdeen, 2018. Within recent scholarship the significance for Paul of the believer's participation in Christ's death and resurrection is widely recognized, yet there is no consensus regarding the origin of Paul's understanding. This study argues that it lies in pre-Pauline Christian beliefs reflected in and shaped by the practice of the Eucharist, itself understood against the background of Passover and the concept of covenant.

Owens, L. Roger. *The Shape of Participation: A Theology of Church Practices.* Eugene, OR: Cascade, 2010. A work of theology and practical theology that understands the church in terms of embodiment and understands church practices, such as the eucharist and preaching, as participation in the life of the Triune God.

Peura, Simo. *Mehr als ein Mensch? Die Vergöttlichung als Thema der Theologie Martin Luthers von 1513 bis 1519*. Philipp von Zabern: Mainz, 1994. This is one of the most important studies in the development of the Finnish perspective on Luther beyond the initial work of Mannermaa. Peura traces the theme of divinization in the early theology of Luther, emphasizing the effective element in his understanding of justification.

Peura, Simo, and Antti Raunio, eds. *Luther und Theosis: Vergöttlichung als Thema der abendländischen Theologie*. Helsinki and Erlangen: Schriften der Luther-Agricola-Gesellschaft, 1990. The second of three collections of essays in German that offer evaluations by European scholars of the Finnish perspective on Luther, especially of the work of Mannermaa. This volume focuses on theosis as a theological theme.

Powers, Daniel G. *Salvation through Participation: An Examination of the Notion of the Believers' Corporate Unity with Christ in Early Christian Soteriology: Contributions to Biblical Exegesis and Theology 29*. Leuven: Peeters, 2001. A study of various aspects of Paul's theology and the experiences of the communities he founded that shows how he and they understood salvation fundamentally as participation in Christ's death and resurrection.

Repo, Matti, and Rainer Vinke, eds. *Unio: Gott und Mensch in der nachreformatorischen Theologie: Referate des Symposiums Finnischen Theologischen Literaturgesellschaft in Helsinki*. Helsinki and Erlangen: Schriften der Luther-Agricola-Gesellschaft, 1996. This volume of essays in German explores the theme of union with Christ in Post-reformation theology.

Russell, Norman. *The Doctrine of Deification in the Greek Patristic Tradition*. Oxford: Oxford University Press, 2006. This volume is widely considered to be the definitive study of its subject and crucial to the dispelling of earlier caricatures of theosis. Russell traces the story of deification as a theme in the eastern theological tradition down to the seventh century. He also asserts its distinctively Christian nature.

Schnelle, Udo. *Apostle Paul: His Life and Theology*. Translated by M. Eugene Boring. Grand Rapids: Baker Academic, 2005. A massive, important study of Pauline themes and Paul's letters, with significant emphasis on participation in Christ.

Snodgrass, Klyne R. *Who God Says You Are: A Christian Understanding of Identity*. Grand Rapids: Eerdmans, 2018. This broad exploration of nine key factors in biblical teaching about identity places strong emphasis on participation in Christ as an essential aspect of the gospel.

Tan, Rachael. "Conformity to Christ: An Exegetical and Theological Analysis of Paul's Perspective on Humiliation and Exaltation in Philippians 2:5–11." PhD Diss., Southern Theological Seminary, 2017. Tan works to correct dichotomous views of Philippians 2:5–11 as either kerygmatic or ethical. She accomplishes this by putting the Christ hymn in conversation with Philippians 3:7–11 after first thoroughly examining both passages independently. Tan argues that Philippians 3:7–11 involves an ethical living out of the participation in Christ instructed in 2:5–11.

Tanner, Kathryn. *Christ the Key*. Cambridge: Cambridge University Press, 2010. In this brief and accessible work, Tanner offers a theological model for understanding human nature that views unity with God through participation in Christ as the key for understanding humanity. Patristic theologies are used to argue that human nature only makes sense when viewed in light of the Trinity and of divine grace. In Christ, God gives us the gift of God's own life.

Tappenden, Frederick S. *Resurrection in Paul: Cognition, Metaphor, and Transformation: Early Christianity and its Literature 19*. Atlanta: SBL, 2016. A technical but significant work using cognitive linguistics to argue that Paul sees the life of Christ-devotees as a single process of transformative participation in Christ's resurrection, from baptism to the eschaton. This process is experienced in the body by means of the divine Spirit as ongoing outer death and inner life.

Thate, Michael J., Kevin J. Vanhoozer, and Constantine R. Campbell, eds. *"In Christ" in Paul: Explorations in Paul's Theology of Union and Participation*. Grand Rapids: Eerdmans, 2018. An important volume of in-depth scholarly essays on various aspects of participation in Christ according to Paul. Essays on the history of reception and contemporary theological approaches are included alongside more directly exegetical studies. There is an excellent introductory essay by Vanhoozer that moves beyond overview into advocacy of the significance of union with Christ in scripture and for the proclamation of the gospel by the church. This volume was earlier published by Mohr Siebeck (2014).

Vainio, Olli-Pekka. *Justification and Participation in Christ: Studies in Medieval and Reformation Traditions 130*. Brill: Leiden 2008. Writing as a committed advocate of the Finnish perspective on Luther, Vainio seeks to fill a crucial gap in scholarship surrounding Lutheran discussions of justification. His study examines the part played by union with Christ in theologies of justification within the Lutheran tradition from the death of Luther to the *Formula of Concord*.

———. "Luther and Theosis: A Response to the Critics of Finnish Luther Research." *Pro Ecclesia: A Journal of Catholic and Evangelical Theology* (2015) 459–474. In this brief but helpful article, Vainio gives an apology for the Finnish perspective on Luther. He not only provides a defense to some common criticisms but in the process offers one of the most helpful short summaries available of Finnish Luther research and the relevance of theosis for understanding Luther.

———, ed. *Engaging Luther: A (New) Theological Assessment*. Eugene, OR: Cascade. 2010. This volume is a helpful collection of essays that examine several different aspects of Luther's theology from the new Finnish perspective. Each essay is reflective of the Finnish bent towards emphasizing the presence of Christ as a reality in the life of the believer. The opening essay by Risto Saarinen provides an important retrospective on the development of the Finnish perspective.

Vanhoozer, Kevin J. "Putting on Christ: Spiritual Formation and the Drama of Discipleship." *Journal of Spiritual Formation and Soul Care* 8 (2015) 147–71. The modern period saw unfortunate divisions arise and solidify between theological disciplines. In the last few decades many have advocated reunification between biblical studies and theology, or between biblical studies, theology, and missions. Vanhoozer here seeks the reunification of spiritual formation and theology, arguing that the former itself involves the *doing* of theology. Participation in Christ is the location where the two converge.

Varma, Ashish. "Fitting Participation: From the Holy Trinity to Christian Virtue." In *"In Christ" in Paul: Explorations in Paul's Theology of Union and Participation*, edited by Michael J. Thate, Kevin J. Vanhoozer, and Constantine R. Campbell. 477–501. Grand Rapids: Eerdmans, 2018. The articulation and defense of virtue has not been a high priority within the Reformed and Lutheran traditions. Those who have valued the historic category of "virtue" have usually been Roman Catholics, who typically depend upon Aquinas's baptism of Aristotle's philosophy, or postliberals, who look almost exclusively to ecclesially driven narrative readings of Scripture. Varma instead contends that union with Christ provides a distinctly Christian grounding for direction in virtue and an avenue for Lutheran and Reformed Christians to reengage with the virtue tradition.

NORTH PARK THEOLOGICAL SEMINARY SYMPOSIUM ON THE THEOLOGICAL INTERPRETATION OF SCRIPTURE

SEPTEMBER 28–30, 2017

Participation in and with Christ

PRESENTERS

Cynthia Peters Anderson
> *Senior Pastor, Batavia United Methodist Church, Illinois*

Ben C. Blackwell
> *Assistant Professor of Theology, Houston Baptist University*

Julie Canlis
> *Adjunct Faculty in Theology, Whitworth University*

Michael J. Gorman
> *Raymond E. Brown Professor of Biblical Studies and Theology, St. Mary's Seminary and University*

Grant Macaskill
> *Kirby Laing Chair of New Testament Exegesis, King's College, University of Aberdeen*

Brent Strawn
> *Professor of Old Testament, Candler School of Theology, Emory University*

Olli-Pekka Vainio
> *University Lecturer of Systematic Theology, University of Helsinki*

Ashish Varma
> *Assistant Professor of Theology, Moody Bible Institute*

RESPONDENTS

Cynthia Peters Anderson
Senior Pastor, Batavia United Methodist Church, Illinois

Mary Patton Baker
Lecturer in Biblical and Theological Studies, North Park University

Constantine R. Campbell
Professor of New Testament, Trinity Evangelical Divinity School

J. Nathan Clayton
Teaching Fellow in Old Testament, North Park Theological Seminary

Stephen J. Chester
Professor of New Testament, North Park Theological Seminary

Markus Nikkanen
Director of Studies, Theological Seminary of the Evangelical Free Church of Finland

Hauna Ondrey
Assistant Professor of Church History, North Park Theological Seminary

www.ingramcontent.com/pod-product-compliance
Lightning Source LLC
Chambersburg PA
CBHW080925100426

42812CB00007B/2369